Lecture Notes in Computer Science　　9762

Commenced Publication in 1973
Founding and Former Series Editors:
Gerhard Goos, Juris Hartmanis, and Jan van Leeuwen

Bernhard K. Aichernig · Carlo A. Furia (Eds.)

Tests and Proofs

10th International Conference, TAP 2016
Held as Part of STAF 2016
Vienna, Austria, July 5–7, 2016
Proceedings

Springer

Editors
Bernhard K. Aichernig
Graz University of Technology
Graz
Austria

Carlo A. Furia
Chalmers University of Technology
Göteborg
Sweden

ISSN 0302-9743   ISSN 1611-3349   (electronic)
Lecture Notes in Computer Science
ISBN 978-3-319-41134-7   ISBN 978-3-319-41135-4   (eBook)
DOI 10.1007/978-3-319-41135-4

Library of Congress Control Number: 2016942015

LNCS Sublibrary: SL2 – Programming and Software Engineering

Printed on acid-free paper

This Springer imprint is published by Springer Nature
The registered company is Springer International Publishing AG Switzerland

Foreword

Software Technologies: Applications and Foundations (STAF) is a federation of leading conferences on software technologies. It provides a loose umbrella organization with a Steering Committee that ensures continuity. The STAF federated event takes place annually. The participating conferences may vary from year to year, but all focus on foundational and practical advances in software technology. The conferences address all aspects of software technology, from object-oriented design, testing, mathematical approaches to modeling and verification, transformation, model-driven engineering, aspect-oriented techniques, and tools.

STAF 2016 took place at TU Wien, Austria, during July 4–8, 2016, and hosted the five conferences ECMFA 2016, ICGT 2016, ICMT 2016, SEFM 2016, and TAP 2016, the transformation tool contest TTC 2016, eight workshops, a doctoral symposium, and a projects showcase event. STAF 2016 featured eight internationally renowned keynote speakers, and welcomed participants from around the world.

The STAF 2016 Organizing Committee thanks (a) all participants for submitting to and attending the event, (b) the program chairs and Steering Committee members of the individual conferences and satellite events for their hard work, (c) the keynote speakers for their thoughtful, insightful, and inspiring talks, and (d) TU Wien, the city of Vienna, and all sponsors for their support. A special thank you goes to the members of the Business Informatics Group, coping with all the foreseen and unforeseen work (as usual ☺)!

July 2016   Gerti Kappel

Preface

The TAP conference promotes research in verification and formal methods that targets the interplay of proofs and testing: the advancement of techniques of each kind and their combination, with the ultimate goal of improving software and system dependability. This volume contains the proceedings of TAP 2016, which marks a decade of TAP conferences since the first edition in 2007. As in the three previous editions, TAP 2016 was part of STAF (Software Technologies: Applications and Foundations), a federation of leading conferences in software technology.

TAP 2016 took place in Vienna during July 5–7, 2016. The Program Committee (PC) received 19 paper submissions, each reviewed by three PC members. After two weeks of lively discussion and careful deliberation, we selected 11 contributions (eight regular papers, one tool demonstration paper, and two short papers) for inclusion in this proceedings volume and presentation at the conference. The combination of topics highlights how testing and proving are increasingly seen as complementary rather than mutually exclusive techniques, and confirms TAP's commitment to bringing together researchers and practitioners from both areas of verification.

The program of TAP was nicely completed by a keynote talk by Kim G. Larsen (Aalborg University, Denmark) and an industrial keynote talk by Klaus Reichl (Thales, Austria), whose content is also documented in this volume. We would like to thank both invited speakers for contributing exciting presentations from the different perspective of academic research and industrial practice.

We also thank the PC members and the additional reviewers for their timely and thorough reviewing work, and for contributing to an animated and informed discussion. Their names are listed on the following pages. The EasyChair system provided flawless technical support to the process.

The organization of STAF made for a successful and enjoyable conference in a wonderful location. We thank all the organizers, and in particular the general chair, Gerti Kappel, and the organization chair, Tanja Mayerhofer, for their hard work, and TU Wien for hosting us. Thanks also to Richard Schumi from TU Graz for managing TAP's website.

July 2016

Bernhard K. Aichernig
Carlo A. Furia

Organization

Program Committee

Bernhard K. Aichernig	TU Graz, Austria
Jasmin C. Blanchette	Inria Nancy and LORIA, France
Achim D. Brucker	University of Sheffield, UK
Catherine Dubois	ENSIEE-CEDRIC, France
Gordon Fraser	University of Sheffield, UK
Carlo A. Furia	Chalmers University of Technology, Sweden
Juan Pablo Galeotti	University of Buenos Aires, Argentina
Angelo Gargantini	University of Bergamo, Italy
Alain Giorgetti	LIFC, University of Franche-Comte, France
Christoph Gladisch	BOSCH, Germany
Martin Gogolla	University of Bremen, Germany
Arnaud Gotlieb	SIMULA Research Laboratory, Norway
Ashutosh Gupta	TIFR, India
Marieke Huisman	University of Twente, The Netherlands
Reiner Hähnle	Technical University of Darmstadt, Germany
Bart Jacobs	Katholieke Universiteit Leuven, Belgium
Nikolai Kosmatov	CEA LIST, France
Laura Kovacs	Chalmers University of Technology, Sweden
Shaoying Liu	Hosei University, Japan
Panagiotis Manolios	Northeastern University, USA
Karl Meinke	Royal Institute of Technology (KTH), Sweden
Brian Nielsen	Aalborg University, Denmark
Nadia Polikarpova	MIT CSAIL, USA
Andrew Reynolds	University of Iowa, USA
Augusto Sampaio	Federal University of Pernambuco, Brazil
Martina Seidl	Johannes Kepler University Linz, Austria
Jun Sun	Singapore University of Technology and Design, Singapore
Nikolai Tillmann	Microsoft Research, USA
T.H. Tse	The University of Hong Kong, SAR China
Margus Veanes	Microsoft Research, USA
Burkhart Wolff	University of Paris-Sud, France

Additional Reviewers

Bubel, Richard	Hübner, Felix
Christakis, Maria	Kumar, Ramana
Fleury, Mathias	Scheurer, Dominic
Hoelscher, Karsten	

Abstracts of Invited Contributions

From Testing and Verification to Performance Analysis and Synthesis of Cyber-Physical Systems

Kim G. Larsen

Department of Computer Science
Aalborg University, Aalborg, Denmark
kgl@cs.aau.dk

Abstract. Timed automata and games, priced timed automata and energy automata have emerged as useful formalisms for modeling real-time and energy-aware systems as found in several embedded and cyber-physical systems. In this talk we will survey how the various components of the UPPAAL tool-suite over a 20 year period have been developed to support various types of analysis of these formalisms.

This includes the classical usage of UPPAAL as an efficient model checker of hard real time constraints of timed automata models, but also the branch UPPAAL TRON which has been extensively used to perform on-and off-line conformance testing of real-time systems with respect to timed automata specifications.

More ambitiously, UPPAAL TIGA allow for automatic synthesis of strategies – and subsequent executable control programs – for safety and reachability objectives. Most recently the branch UPPAAL SMC offers a highly scalable statistical model checking engine supporting performance analysis of stochastic hybrid automata, and the branch UPPAAL-STRATEGO supports synthesis (using machine learning) and evaluation of near-optimal strategies for stochastic priced timed games. The keynote will review the various branches of UPPAAL and indicate their concerted applications to a range of real-time and cyber-physical examples.

Using Formal Methods for Verification and Validation in Railway

Klaus Reichl, Tomas Fischer, and Peter Tummeltshammer

Thales Austria GmbH, Handelskai 92, 1200 Vienna, Austria
{klaus.reichl,tomas.fischer,
peter.tummeltshammer}@thalesgroup.com

Abstract. A very promising and efficient method of showing the correctness of a complex system is using formal methods on a model of that system. To this end there exist plentiful methods and tools for easing the mathematically burdensome process of refinement and proofs, as well as the computationally complex task of model checking.

While in todays industrial applications formal methods are mostly used for verification (i.e. for showing that the system model fulfills properties such as completeness and consistency) we propose to use these methods for validation as well (i.e. correspondence of the model with the customer needs).

In this paper we show the applicability as well as the limitations of this approach for feature driven development towards continuous verification and validation. As an example we present a model of a railway interlocking system written in Event-B.

The model can be instantiated and animated, which in combination with model checking and formal proofs demonstrates the usefulness of the approach.

The resulting model can be used again to automatically generate test cases which are suitable to show the correspondence of the implementation and the model, given that the model supports a sufficient level of detail.

Contents

Invited Contribution

Using Formal Methods for Verification and Validation in Railway   3
   Klaus Reichl, Tomas Fischer, and Peter Tummeltshammer

Regular Contributions

Monadic Sequence Testing and Explicit Test-Refinements   17
   Achim D. Brucker and Burkhart Wolff

Advances in Property-Based Testing for αProlog.   37
   James Cheney, Alberto Momigliano, and Matteo Pessina

Tests and Proofs for Enumerative Combinatorics.   57
   Catherine Dubois, Alain Giorgetti, and Richard Genestier

Classifying Test Suite Effectiveness via Model Inference and ROBBDs.   76
   Hermann Felbinger, Ingo Pill, and Franz Wotawa

Lightweight Symbolic Verification of Graph Transformation Systems
with Off-the-Shelf Hardware Model Checkers.   94
   Sebastian Gabmeyer and Martina Seidl

Testing-Based Formal Verification for Theorems and Its Application
in Software Specification Verification 112
   Shaoying Liu

Your Proof Fails? Testing Helps to Find the Reason 130
   Guillaume Petiot, Nikolai Kosmatov, Bernard Botella, Alain Giorgetti,
   and Jacques Julliand

Classifying Bugs with Interpolants 151
   Andreas Podelski, Martin Schäf, and Thomas Wies

Tool Demonstration

Debugging Meets Testing in Erlang. 171
   Salvador Tamarit, Adrián Riesco, Enrique Martin-Martin,
   and Rafael Caballero

Short Contributions

Combining Dynamic and Static Analysis to Help Develop Correct Graph
Transformations   183
  *Amani Makhlouf, Hanh Nhi Tran, Christian Percebois,
  and Martin Strecker*

Automatic Predicate Testing in Formal Certification: You've only Proven
What You've Said, Not What You Meant!   191
  Franck Slama

Author Index   199

Invited Contribution

Using Formal Methods for Verification and Validation in Railway

Klaus Reichl, Tomas Fischer, and Peter Tummeltshammer[✉]

Thales Austria GmbH, Handelskai 92, 1200 Vienna, Austria
{klaus.reichl,tomas.fischer,peter.tummeltshammer}@thalesgroup.com

Abstract. A very promising and efficient method of showing the correctness of a complex system is using formal methods on a model of that system. To this end there exist plentiful methods and tools for easing the mathematically burdensome process of refinement and proofs, as well as the computationally complex task of model checking.

While in todays industrial applications formal methods are mostly used for verification (i.e. for showing that the system model fulfills properties such as completeness and consistency) we propose to use these methods for validation as well (i.e. correspondence of the model with the customer needs).

In this paper we show the applicability as well as the limitations of this approach for feature driven development towards continuous verification and validation. As an example we present a model of a railway interlocking system written in Event-B.

The model can be instantiated and animated, which in combination with model checking and formal proofs demonstrates the usefulness of the approach.

The resulting model can be used again to automatically generate test cases which are suitable to show the correspondence of the implementation and the model, given that the model supports a sufficient level of detail.

Keywords: Formal methods · Event-B · Verification · Validation

1 Introduction

The railway domain is characterized by high safety as well as reliability and availability requirements which demand thorough verification and validation. The long lifespan (25+ years) of railway systems induces need for changes caused by feature enhancements or subsystem renewal. No modification may compromise the required safety properties. This implies the necessity to reason about the system (and thus about the model) not only in the development phase, but during the whole product lifespan. The ambition to keep the cost of change minimal demands incremental verification and validation instead of full verification and validation of the whole system.

© Springer International Publishing Switzerland 2016
B.K. Aichernig and C.A. Furia (Eds.): TAP 2016, LNCS 9762, pp. 3–13, 2016.
DOI: 10.1007/978-3-319-41135-4_1

However, today's systems are too complex to be reasoned about by experts only. It is difficult to comprehend all implications of a modification, some unintended side effects can be overlooked very easily and may have fatal consequences.

The CENELEC standards [5–7] which apply to certification of safety critical railway applications qualify the use of formal methods as highly recommended. This is one of the main drivers for the use of formal methods in the railway domain.

In this paper we show how Event-B can be used to support the verification and validation in the safety critical railway domain and demonstrate this on a simple railway model. Section 2 presents the aforementioned railway model used for demonstration purposes, Sect. 3 explains some principles of formal modeling applied to the demonstration model and Sect. 4 discusses aspects of verification and validation of presented model facets as well as perceived limitations. Finally, Sect. 5 concludes the paper and outlines possible future work.

2   Railway Model

The model presented in this paper is that of a simplified interlocking system consisting of the following basic elements:

Rail Element is a unit which provides a physical running path for the trains. Rail elements are e.g. tracks, points or crossings. A rail element consist of one or more rail segments, e.g. representing different legs of points or crossings.

Rail Connector is a port of a rail element defining the element's connectivity.

Track is a simple rail element which connects to other rail elements on two ends (or only on one end in case of a station boundary).

Point is a movable rail element, which connects three rail elements in two different ways (tip–to–left or tip–to–right).

Crossing is an intersection of two tracks.

Signal is a device capable of passing indication whether a route may be entered by the train. A signal may be opened (green light meaning proceed) or closed (red light meaning stop).

Route is a safe running path for the train. A route consists of a directed series of connected rail elements and is protected by a signal, which allows the train to enter the route only if the route is correctly set up. Setting up the route means to bring all points into the correct position and ensure that the route does not interfere with any other route (interlocking functionality). Only after all prerequisites are fulfilled, the protecting signal may be opened and the train is allowed to enter the route.

Track Vacancy Detection determines if a particular track section is vacant (free) or occupied. A track vacancy detection section is a scope of one track vacancy detector, which may span multiple rail segments. As soon as the train enters the route, the protecting signal is closed and all track elements being first occupied and then freed again may be released to be used by another route.

The demonstrated model is reduced to the essential, yet is complex enough to showcase modeling techniques in the domain. The goal of this model is to exhibit important principles without going into the details rather than to provide a complete working application.

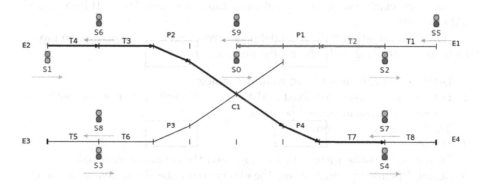

Fig. 1. Model animation of Event-B railway domain model (Color figure online)

Figure 1 shows the model using model animation on a small example. It shows a route being set (the bold line from signal S1 to signal S4 via the elements T4, T3, P2, C1, P4 and T7) and the entry signal being already opened (green light at signal S1). This route prevents the setting of any conflicting route (e.g. for the train waiting in front of signal S9 on the occupied tracks T2 and P1 shown in red).

The interlocking rules (e.g. setting and releasing the route, signaling, etc.) are the same for all stations operated by a single operator. On the other hand there is a huge variety among the railway stations – they differ in the layout and topology, but also in the specific behavior of particular elements. Therefore, it is beneficial to differentiate between the generic application describing the interlocking behavior on one side and specific applications built on top of the generic application adding the particular station data on other side.

The generic application is formulated as a railway model making assumptions about the station data (data model), but verified in a generic way, i.e. independent of any particular station data. The specific application must then assure that the provided station data meet the assumptions, i.e. are compliant to the data model. If so, then the verification of the generic application applies for all specific applications as well without having to be done again.

3   Formal Modeling

The B-Method [1] is a tool-supported formal method based on an abstract machine notation and was originally developed by Jean-Raymond Abrial. It has already been used in industrial applications such as the Paris Métro Line

14 [4,10]. Event-B [2] is a method for system-level analysis and modeling based
on B, and has been utilized in several case studies and industrial applications as
well [8,11].

Event-B is based on set theory and first order logic and is implemented in the
Rodin tool chain. In addition to the Rodin core we use ProB and BMotion Studio
for model checking, visualization and animation, as well as Atelier B Provers and
SMT Solvers.

The demonstration railway model presented in Sect. 2 is structured in layers,
each layer extending and refining the previous ones:

1. Definition of rail entities and railway topology.
2. Distinction between the fixed and the movable rail elements and notion of
   rail element movement and position.
3. Track vacancy detection.
4. Signals.
5. Definition of paths within the topology and the topology traversal.
6. Signal dependency constraining the ability to set the signal depending on the
   status of path following this signal.
7. Description of path life cycle, i.e. the sequence of steps necessary to construct
   a valid path and also dissolve is properly when not needed any more.

   ...

* Demo Station, which supplements data for a particular station.

The layers numbered 1–7 (additional layers can be introduced for additional
model functionality) define the generic application, the last refinement layer represents the specific application and is used for the visualization and animation.

The presented model defines 75 axioms and 17 invariants, which lead to 126
proof obligations, most of which are proven automatically (3 proven manually).
Note that the number of proof obligations is independent of the station's size,
but is determined solely by the model complexity.

3.1 Data Model

The data model defines the assumptions about the station data as axioms and
leaves the constants representing the data of the particular station abstract. The
last refinement representing the specific station binds the constants to specific
values conforming to the axioms. Such a formal description of the station data
is stronger (compared to e.g. an XML scheme) due to the expressiveness of the
first order logic and also to the behavioral specification found in the same model.

The example axiom below states that two overlapping sections are not possible:

TVD_SECT_SGMT·disjunct:

$\forall sect1, sect2 \cdot sect1 \in TVD\_SECT$
$\land sect2 \in TVD\_SECT$
$\land sect1 \neq sect2$
$\Rightarrow TVD\_SECT\_SGMT(sect1) \cap TVD\_SECT\_SGMT(sect2) = \varnothing$

The constant TVD_SECT represents the track vacancy detection sections in the particular station and the constant TVD_SECT_SGMT is the assignment of rail segments to the respective track vacancy detection sections.

3.2 Functional and Safety Properties

The functional properties are described as state machines, where variables represent the current state of the railway station and events represent the state change, i.e. define the system behavior. Invariants impose restrictions of the valid state due to the domain model as well as safety constraints. Below we provide an example on how functional and safety analyses led to certain refinements of the model.

During the functional analysis a feature was identified requiring the route release functionality:

Event $rem\_PATH\_CURR \ \hat{=}$
any
    $path$
where
    path·valid:
       $path \in PATH\_CURR$
then
    PATH_CURR·value:
       $PATH\_CURR := PATH\_CURR \setminus \{path\}$
    RAIL_ELEM_PATH_CURR·value:
       $RAIL\_ELEM\_PATH\_CURR := RAIL\_ELEM\_PATH\_CURR \rhd \{path\}$
end

This event removes a path from the set of current paths and also releases all used railway elements occupied by this path. This event requires only that the path to be removed is set.

The variable PATH_CURR contains the set of current paths and the variable $RAIL\_ELEM\_PATH\_CURR$ identifies the path a particular rail element belongs to. For each defined path the constant $PATH\_CTOR\_BEG$ determines the connector at which the path begins. The symbol $\rhd$ denotes the range subtraction operator. It returns a subset of the left side term (being a relation), excluding mappings to elements of the right side term.

During the hazard analysis a safety property was identified requiring that a signal may be opened only if there is a correctly set up path behind this signal.

path·depend:
  $\forall sig \cdot sig \in SIGNAL$
  $\wedge \, SIGNAL\_ASPECT\_CURR(sig) \neq SIGNAL\_ASPECT\_DEFAULT \Rightarrow$
  $($
      $\exists path \cdot path \in PATH\_CURR$
      $\wedge \, SIGNAL\_CTOR(sig) = PATH\_CTOR\_BEG(path)$
  $)$

This invariant states that for all open signals, there must be a path beginning at this signal (at the connector this signal is associated to).

The constant $SIGNAL$ represents the signals in the particular station and the constant $SIGNAL\_CTOR$ the association of the signals to the respective rail connectors. The variable $SIGNAL\_ASPECT\_CURR$ contains the current signal aspect with the default value being $SIGNAL\_ASPECT\_DEFAULT$ representing default safe state being closed.

In order to fulfill the above invariant an additional constraint to the event rem_PATH_CURR becomes necessary. This is introduced by the following refinement:

Event $rem\_PATH\_CURR \mathrel{\widehat=}$
where
   path·depend:
$$\forall sig \cdot sig \in SIGNAL$$
$$\wedge SIGNAL\_ASPECT\_CURR(sig) \neq SIGNAL\_ASPECT\_DEFAULT$$
$$\Rightarrow SIGNAL\_CTOR(sig) \neq PATH\_CTOR\_BEG(path)$$

The new guard disallows the path removal if the signal at the path beginning is open. After adding this guard to the event the signal-related invariant is valid again.

3.3   Liveness Properties

An interlocking system is an inherently parallel system, therefore, it is meaningful to reason about its liveness properties and include a subset thereof into the formal model. There are some properties (e.g. guaranteed time bounds) which are architecture dependent and hence not modeled. Other properties can be expressed in terms of model elements and can thus be included into a formal model. The most important properties are:

Convergence stating that several events refining one abstract event converge (no oscillation occurs). This property can be expressed in Event-B by marking the events as *convergent* and by defining suitable variants. The corresponding proof obligations are then automatically generated and may be proven.

Deadlock freedom assuring that for every execution path progress is possible. This property must not only hold globally, but also for a group of events handling one external stimulus and requires that at least one event of that group is enabled. It can be expressed as a predicate stating that the disjunction of guards of all events in that group is ⊤ (tautology). Such a proof obligation cannot be generated automatically, but it can still be expressed with Event-B means.

Predictability assuring that the execution path is predictable. This property must not only hold globally, but also for a group of events handling one external stimulus and requires that at most one event of that group is enabled. It can be expressed as a predicate stating that the pairwise conjunction of guards of all events in that group is ⊥ (contradiction). Such proof obligation cannot be generated automatically, but can still be expressed with the Event-B means.

Causality adding the ability to reason about a time line. This property can be expressed using temporal logic. However, currently Event-B cannot express temporal properties.

Progress ensuring that the modeled functionality is eventually fulfilling its service obligations. This property can be formulated using suitable (weak or strong) temporal logic fairness assumption.

4   Verification and Validation

The general steps of verification and validation as we intend to use them on formal models are depicted in Fig. 2.

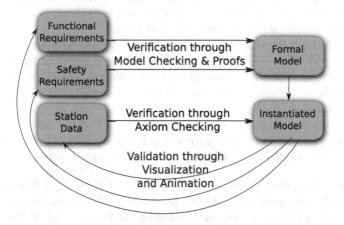

Fig. 2. Verification and validation

4.1   Verification

The verification process shall ensure that the model is unambiguous and complete. Formal models allow automatic reasoning, e.g. model finding (search for counterexamples), model checking, and model proof.

The functional and safety properties are verified semi-automatically through formal proof with Event-B. Structuring the model into independent modules reduces the scope of changes to single component only (provided the interfaces remain stable), and also the prove obligation generator invalidates only those proofs that are affected by the model modification, subsequently reducing the overall verification efforts.

In addition, the separation of the station data from the application behavior means that the verification of generic application has to be performed only once and is applicable for all stations (provided the data meet the assumptions). Hence only the verification of the specific application (data compliance) has to be done for each station.

The verification of particular station data as a specific instance of the data model representing the respective station is achieved with the automatic compliance check of the provided data against the formulated axioms.

The verification of liveness properties in our model is still subject to research. Some of these are expressible as additional invariants and can be verified as such (by model proof with Event-B); others need the expressiveness of LTL (Linear Time Logic) properties and consequently have to be verified by model checking.

4.2   Validation

The validation process shall ensure that the model is compliant to the customer requirements. It means that the functional properties express the required behavior, the safety properties express constraints derived from the hazard analysis and the data model is neither too general nor too restrictive, i.e. all particular stations can be expressed as instances of that model.

Despite the high degree of automation a complete "push-button" verification and especially validation is not feasible. Therefore it is essential to support the domain experts so that they can perform their tasks effectively. In this process, domain specific modeling, model visualization and animation (see Fig. 1) are of major assistance.

Using a precisely formulated formal model with exactly defined semantics of all artifacts for the validation purposes aids the domain experts. Additional benefits could be gained by addressing the following limitations:

- A high level language can be built on top of Event-B allowing domain experts to formulate the problem in "their" language (DSL – Domain Specific Language), still utilizing the strong mathematical background of the Event-B method.
- Object oriented constructs can help to bridge the gap between the domain model and the "technical" model eliminating the need of mental mapping between them, thus reducing the modeling and validation effort, as well as increasing the overall confidence in the model's correctness.
- Impact analysis of modifications allows performing delta verification and validation. Continuous verification and validation is beneficial in case of a feature driven development approach, especially when building a whole product family (product line) based on a common core.
- Traceability between the various artifacts (such as elements of a formal model) including (but not limited to) the requirements, test cases, design and implementation items is a prerequisite to the successful assessment.
- Report generators should allow incorporating proof obligations, proofs, as well as model checker results and found counterexamples into the verification and validation reports. This would save manual efforts and costs and would improve the traceability.

– For the broad utilization several other factors must be considered – interoperability and integration with other tools, modularization and namespaces, scalability, teamwork ability and industrial usability in general.

We have analyzed the iUML-B plugin for Rodin, which provides diagrammatic editors for Event-B. It allows to define data entities and their relationships as well as to model the behavior as a collection of hierarchical state machines. Some extra modeling features are also provided, like lifting of behavior to a set of instances in an object-oriented way or sequencing of events. Diagrams and the state machine animator help to visualize models and the translator generates Event-B code automatically.

Our next step is to evaluate, if the (deliberate) restriction in the iUML-B expressiveness (in comparison with the pure Event-B) poses significant limitations and how the results of subsequent steps (like proofs, model checking and animation) can be mapped back into the iUML-B notation.

4.3   Implementation and Testing

The general principles of formal model implementation and model based testing are illustrated in Fig. 3.

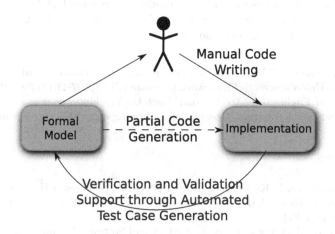

Fig. 3. Implementation and automatic test case generation

The final stage of the system development is the implementation stage. This activity involves the creation of executable components, definition of the concrete data structures, and the implementation of auxiliary functions which may have been assumed in the design and were not modeled explicitly.

Manual code writing can be supported by partial code generation, which translates the formal model into function blocks providing the implementation of the modeled aspects.

Automated test case generation helps to assure that the final implementation is compliant to the model, thus assists in both implementation verification as well as validation. There exist promising approaches to this topic, such as the MoMuT tool [3] which is currently under adaptation to support Event-B as an input language. However, care must be taken to ensure that the generated test cases deliver expressive results in order to carry the trust we gained in the model through formal methods to the implementation.

5   Conclusion

In this paper we showed how formal modeling, and in particular Event-B, can be used to assist verification and validation in the safety critical railway domain and demonstrated this with a simple railway model.

We believe that set theory together with first order logic is suitable to describe interlocking systems. The Event-B method and its implementation in the Rodin tool chain look promising, yet there is still some work to be done on the way towards an industry-ready set of tools available for the commercial usage. Moreover, there are some alternatives based on the same theoretical foundation like TLA+ (see [9]), which should also be evaluated and compared with Event-B considering not only technical, but also economical criteria.

The railway station demonstration model as presented in this publication has been released under the Eclipse Public License - v 1.0 and can be found at: https://github.com/klar42/railground.

Acknowledgements. The research leading to these results has received funding from the European Union's Seventh Framework Program (FP7/2007–2013) for CRYSTAL – Critical System Engineering Acceleration Joint Undertaking under grant agreement no. 332830 and by the Austrian Research Promotion Agency (FFG) project no. 838497.

References

1. Abrial, J.R., Lee, M.K., Neilson, D., Scharbach, P., Sørensen, I.H.: The B-method. In: Prehn, S., Toetenel, H. (eds.) VDM 1991. LNCS, vol. 552, pp. 398–405. Springer, Heidelberg (1991)
2. Abrial, J.R.: Modeling in Event-B: System and Software Engineering. Cambridge University Press, New York (2010)
3. Aichernig, B., Brandl, H., Jobstl, E., Krenn, W., Schlick, R., Tiran, S.: Momut::UML model-based mutation testing for UML. In: 2015 IEEE 8th International Conference on Software Testing, Verification and Validation (ICST), pp. 1–8. IEEE (2015)
4. Behm, P., Benoit, P., Faivre, A., Meynadier, J.-M.: Météor: a successful application of B in a large project. In: Wing, J.M., Woodcock, J. (eds.) FM 1999. LNCS, vol. 1708, pp. 369–387. Springer, Heidelberg (1999)
5. Cenelec European Standard: 50126-railway applications: the specification and demonstration of reliability, availability, maintainability and safety (RAMS). European Committee for Electrotechnical Standardization (1999)

6. Cenelec European Standard: 50129-railway applications: communication, signalling and processing systems - safety related electronic systems for signalling. European Committee for Electrotechnical Standardization (2003)
7. Cenelec European Standard: 50128-railway applications: software for railway control and protection systems. European Committee for Electrotechnical Standardization (2011)
8. Khuu, M.T.: Modeling a safe interlocking using the event-B theory Plug-in. Advance Project (2014)
9. Lamport, L.: Specifying Systems: The TLA+ Language and Tools for Hardware and Software Engineers. Addison-Wesley Longman Publishing Co. Inc., Boston (2002)
10. Lecomte, T., Servat, T., Pouzancre, G., et al.: Formal methods in safety-critical railway systems. In: 10th Brasilian Symposium on Formal Methods, pp. 29–31 (2007)
11. Singh, N.K.: Using Event-B for Critical Device Software Systems. Springer, London (2013)

Regular Contributions

Monadic Sequence Testing and Explicit Test-Refinements

Achim D. Brucker[1]([✉]) and Burkhart Wolff[2]

[1] Department of Computer Science, The University of Sheffield, Sheffield, UK
a.brucker@sheffield.ac.uk
[2] LRI, Univ Paris Sud, CNRS, Centrale Suplélec, Université Saclay, Orsay, France
wolff@lri.fr

Abstract. We present an abstract framework for sequence testing that is implemented in Isabelle/HOL-TestGen. Our framework is based on the theory of state-exception monads, explicitly modelled in HOL, and can cope with typed input and output, interleaving executions including abort, and synchronisation.

The framework is particularly geared towards symbolic execution and has proven effective in several large case-studies involving system models based on large (or infinite) state.

On this basis, we rephrase the concept of test-refinements for inclusion, deadlock and IOCO-like tests, together with a formal theory of its relation to traditional, IO-automata based notions.

Keywords: Monadic sequence testing framework · HOL-TestGen

1 Introduction

Automata-based theoretical foundations for test and model-checking techniques are omnipresent; it can be safely stated that a huge body of literature [7,16, 19,20,22] uses them as a framework for conceptual argument, comparison, and scientific communication. Usually based on naïve set-theory (in the sense of Halmos [14]) and paper and pencil notations, they proved as a very intuitive and flexible framework. In our view, this omnipresence overshadows the fact that automata theory is a kind of mould into which not everything fits. This is to a lesser extent a burden on the purely theoretical side: naïve set theory is known to be inconsistent, and the sheer number of variants of automata notions makes comparisons more delicate as one might think.

Modelling communication via an automata-product is simple and tempting, but is the resulting CSP-style, synchronous communication paradigm really what we want? The automata-paradigm becomes a problem when it comes to formal, machine-checked presentations and automated reasoning over them. In settings for the latter, underlying set-theories need either to be typed or axiomatised in a system like ZFC [11]. Applications based on *automated reasoning* over these formalisations turn out to be so difficult that successful tool implementations

© Springer International Publishing Switzerland 2016
B.K. Aichernig and C.A. Furia (Eds.): TAP 2016, LNCS 9762, pp. 17–36, 2016.
DOI: 10.1007/978-3-319-41135-4_2

exist only for particular special-cases such as symbolic regular expression representations [17,27]. In our view, it is not a coincidence that implementations of *symbolic* versions of test-systems like TGV (e.g., STG [16]) or SIOCO [12] remained in a prototypical stage.

In this paper, we present an alternative to the automata-paradigm, as far as their application in the field of testing of behavioural models are concerned. Motivated by several projects aiming at the synthesis of test-algorithms for behavioural models with very large and usually infinite state-spaces, we developed a *Monadic Sequence Testing Framework* (MST). It is formalised in Isabelle/HOL and has been used in several major case-studies [2,4,5]. While the framework is *tuned* for mechanised deduction, in particular symbolic execution based on derived rules, it provides a number of theoretic properties which are interesting in its own. MST combines 1. generalised forms of non-deterministic automata with input and output, 2. generalises the concept of Mealy-Machines, 3. generalises the concept of extended finite state machines [13], and 4. generalises some special form of IO Automata, IO LTS's, etc. [19]. Overall, MST shares with [26] the vision of a unified framework for generalising and analysing formalism for symbolic test case generation. Due to shallow representations of programs and pre-post-condition-based program specifications, the MST approach is intrinsic symbolic; no complicated "lifting" of IO Automata or IO LTS's to symbolic versions thereof like IOSTS's is necessary.

We will introduce paper-and-pencil notions for basic automata constructions (Sect. 2), the general concept of test theories (Sect. 3). In Sect. 4, we introduce higher-order logic (HOL) Sect. 4 and sketch our formalization of Sect. 2 in HOL. Finally we introduce our monadic framework, which is demonstrated in Sect. 4.4 on a small example based on an extended infinite automata. In Sect. 5, we generalise the key-concepts of the MST one step further to a formal definition of test-refinements; it is shown that this definition is powerful enough to capture a family of widely known, but up to now unrelated concepts of (sequence) test conformance. We will show that this is of pragmatic interest for proven correct test-optimisations as well as theoretic interest due to its link to IO-automata.

2   A Guided Tour on Automata Notions for Testing

In this section, we provide a brief overview of behavioural automata models, focusing on on symbolic versions of automata concepts.

The Mealy-Machine. A *Mealy Machine (MM)* [20] is a 6-tuple $(S, S_0, \Sigma_{in}, \Sigma_{out}, T, G)$ consisting of the following: – a finite set of states S – a start state (initial state) S_0 which is an element of S – a finite set of, the input alphabet Σ_{in} – a finite set of symbols, the output alphabet Σ_{out} – a transition function T : $S \times \Sigma_{in} \to S$ mapping pairs of a state and an input symbol to the corresponding next state. – an output function G : $S \times \Sigma_{in} \to \Sigma_{out}$ mapping pairs of a state and an input symbol to the corresponding output symbol. In some formulations, the transition and output functions are coalesced into a single function T : $S \times \Sigma_{in}, \to$

$S \times \Sigma_{out}$. In the literature, also non-deterministic versions are discussed, where the coalesced T has the form $T : S \times \Sigma_{in}, \rightarrow \mathcal{P}(S \times \Sigma_{out})$. Mealy machines are related to Moore machines [21] which are equivalent. If the finiteness constraints are removed, one speaks of a Generalised Mealy Machine (GMM).

The Deterministic Automata. The *deterministic finite automaton* (DFA) M is a 5-tuple, (S, S_0, Σ, T, F), consisting of – a finite set of states S, – an initial or start state $S_0 \in S$, – a finite set of symbols, the alphabet Σ, – a transition function $T : S \times \Sigma \rightarrow S$, and – a set of accept states $F \subseteq S$. If the finiteness-constraints are lifted, we speak of a *deterministic automaton* (DA). If T is generalised to a relation $\mathcal{P}(S \times \Sigma \rightarrow S)$, one speaks of a non-deterministic finite automaton (NDFA) or a non-deterministic automaton (NDA) respectively. If the alphabet Σ is structured as a set of pairs $\Sigma_{in} \times \Sigma_{out}$ of input-and output labels, we speak of *input-output-tagging* of the automata versions. The astute reader will notice that input-output-tagged NDFA's and NDA's can be mapped to generalised Mealy machines GMM and vice versa.

The interest into symbolic versions of these automata notions was raised surprisingly recently: Veanes et al. presented Finite Symbolic Automata as a tool (REX [27]) and investigated their theoretic properties [9].

The Input/Output Automata. Input-output labelled transition systems are going back to the notions of Lynch and Tuttle [19]. This line of automata definitions, which were later on referred as "labelled transition systems," emphasises the annihilation of the difference between input and output to enable some form of asynchronous communication between tester and the system under test SUT as well as some rudimentary form of time (the concept supports *silent* τ *actions* to express time elapsing while some *internal* action in the machine is performed). The theory supports in principle that a SUT can non-deterministically decide either to accept input or to emit output; in practical testing scenarios, this possibility is usually ruled out. Formally, an IO-automata is defined as a 5-tuple $(S, S_0, \Sigma, T, Task)$ consisting of: – a (not necessarily finite) set of states S, – a start state (initial state) S_0 which is an element of S, – an alphabet, the *signature* Σ which is partitioned into three disjoint sets of symbols $\Sigma = in_{IOA} \cup out_{IOA} \cup out_{IOA} \cup int_{IOA}$ are called *input* actions, *output* actions, and *internal* actions, – a transition *relation* $T \subseteq S \times \Sigma \times S$, and – a task-partition $Task$ which is defined as an equivalence relation on $out_{IOA} \cup out_{IOA} \cup int_{IOA}$. In contrast to input-output tagged NDA's, where Σ is the *Cartesian product* of input and output, IO Automata construct Σ as *disjoint union*.

The task partition is used to define fairness conditions on an execution of the automaton. These conditions require the automaton to continue giving fair turns to each of its tasks during its execution. This component of the original formulation is often dropped and replaced by other ones in related approaches [15,24].

Symbolic IO Transition Systems. A Symbolic IO Transition System (IOSTS) [22] is a tuple $(D, \Theta, S, S_0, \Sigma, T)$ where – D is a finite set of typed data, partitioned into a set V of variables and a set P of parameters. For $d \in D$, type(d) denotes the type of d. – Θ is the initial condition, a Boolean expression on V, – S is a nonempty, finite set of states and $S_0 \in S$ is the initial state. – Σ is a nonempty, finite set of symbols, which is the disjoint union of a set Σ? of input actions and a set Σ! of output actions. For each action $a \in \Sigma$, its signature $sig(a) = (p_1, \ldots, p_k) \in P^k (k \in \mathbb{N})$ is a tuple of parameters. – T is a set of transitions. Each transition is a tuple (s, a, G, A, s) made of: a location $s \in S$, called the origin of the transition, an action $a \in \Sigma$, called the action of the transition, a Boolean expression G on $V \cup sig(a)$, called the guard, an assignment A, which is a set of expressions of the form $(x := A^x)_{x \in V}$ such that, for each $x \in V$, the right-hand side A^x of the assignment $x := A^x$ is an expression on $V \cup sig(a)$, a location $s \in S$ called the destination of the transition. Similar attempts to generalise IO Automata to symbolic versions of IO-LTL's are [12].

Extended Finite State Machines. An extended finite state machine (EFSM) [7] is a 7-tuple $M = (S, D, I, O, F, U, T)$ where – S is a set of symbolic states, – I is a set of input symbols, – O is a set of output symbols, – D is an n-dimensional linear space $D_1 \times \cdots \times D_n$, – F is a set of enabling functions $f_i : D \to \{0, 1\}$, – U is a set of update functions $u_i : D \to D$, – T is a transition relation, $T : S \times F \times I \to S \times U \times O$ EFSM's have been motivated from the very beginning by (symbolic) testing techniques [7].

Many variants have been discussed in the literature that attempt to give a concrete syntax (e.g., a term-language, just assignments) for F and U; however, we will refrain from this and try to keep our MST framework abstract on the level of functions and not their syntactic representations.

Some Common Notions of Automatons. We distinguish the notion of a *trace*: *Traces*(A) contains the set of lists of symbols $[a_1, a_2, a_3, \ldots]$ in A (which is an arbitrary automaton DA, NDA, DFA, NDFA, . . .), which describe a path in A. Here, we consider the case of an ESFM similar to an input-output tagged DA or NDA. A *run* is a list of triples $[(s_1, a_1, s_2), (s_2, a_2, s_3), \ldots]$ which describes a path in A; *Run*(A) contains the set of runs in A. With *States*$_A(t)$ we denote the set of reachable states after a trace $t \in$ *Trace*(A). If $t \in$ *Trace*(A) (A is an input-output tagged DA or NDA, IO Automaton, IOSTS, EFSM), we denote with *In*$_A(t)$ the set of possible input symbols after t; with *Out*$_A(t)$ the set of possible output symbols. We call an automaton *IO-deterministic*, iff for each trace $t \in$ *Trace*(A), there is at most one reachable state after $t : |States_A(t)| \leq 1$.

For automata A (which is again an input-output tagged DA or NDA, IO Automaton, IOSTS, EFSM), we define the notion of input-sequences of a trace as projection of traces into its input components: if $t = [(i_1, o_1), (i_2, o_2), (i_3, o_3), \ldots]$ is in *Trace*(A), then $[i_1, i_2, i_3, \ldots]$ is the corresponding input-sequence of t.

In other words, the relation between a sequence of input-output pairs and the resulting system state must be a function.

There is a large body of theoretical work replacing the latter testability hypothesis by weaker or alternative ones (and avoiding the strict alternates of

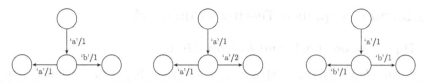

(a) IO-Deterministic SUT. (b) IO-Deterministic SUT. (c) Non-IO-Deterministic SUT.

Fig. 1. IO-Determinism and Non-IO-Determinism

input and output, adding asynchronous communication between tester and SUT, or adding some notion of time), but most practical approaches do assume it as we do throughout this paper. There are approaches (including our own [3]) that allow at least a limited form of access to the final (internal) state of the SUT.

A sequence of input-output pairs through an automaton A is called a *trace*, the set of traces is written *Trace*(A). The function *In* returns for each trace the set of inputs for which A is enabled after this trace; in Fig. 1c for example, *In* [("a", 1)] is just {"b"}, in Fig. 1a, just {"a", "b"}. Dually, *Out* yields for a trace t and input $\iota \in In(t)$ the set of outputs for which A is enabled after t; in Fig. 1b for example, *Out*([("a", 1)],"a") this is just {1, 2}.

3   A Gentle Introduction to Sequence Testing Theory

Sequence testing is a well-established branch of formal testing theory having its roots in automata theory. The methodological assumptions (sometimes called *testability hypothesis* in the literature) are summarised as follows:

1. The tester can reset the system under test (*SUT*) into a known initial state,
2. the tester can stimulate the SUT only via the *operation-calls* and *input* of a known interface; while the internal state of the SUT is hidden to the tester, the SUT is assumed to be *only* controlled by these stimuli,
3. the SUT behaves deterministic with respect to an observed sequence of input-output pairs (it is *IO-deterministic*).

The latter two assumptions assure the reproducibility of test executions. The latter condition does *not* imply that the SUT is deterministic: for a given input ι, and in a given state σ, the SUT may non-deterministically choose between the successor states σ' and σ'', provided that the pairs (o', σ') and (o'', σ'') are distinguishable. Thus, a SUT may behave non-deterministically, but must make its internal decisions observable by appropriate output.

Equipped with these notions, it is possible to formalise the intended *conformance relation* between a system specification (given as automaton SPEC labelled with input-output pairs) and a SUT. The following notions are known in the literature: – *inclusion conformance* [18]: all traces in SPEC must be possible in SUT, – *deadlock conformance* [10]: for all traces $t \in$ *Traces*(SPEC) and $b \notin In(t)$, b must be refused by SUT, and – *input/output conformance* (*IOCO*) [25]: for all traces $t \in$ *Traces*(SPEC) and all $\iota \in In(t)$, the observed output of the SUT must be in *Out*(t, ι).

4   Monadic Sequence Testing Framework

4.1   Higher-Order Logic and Isabelle/HOL

Higher-order logic (HOL) [1,8] is a classical logic based on a simple type system. Types have been extended by Hindley/Milner style polymorphism: they consist of type variables $'\alpha, '\beta, '\gamma, \ldots$ and and type constructors such as $\_ \Rightarrow \_, \_\,\text{set}, \_\,\text{list}, \_ \times \_, \_ + \_, \text{bool}, \text{nat}, \ldots$ (for function space, typed sets, lists, Cartesian products, disjoint sums, Boolean, natural numbers, etc.) with type classes similar to Haskell: $('\alpha : : \text{linorder})\text{list}$ constrains the set of possible types, for example, to those types that posses an ordering symbol which satisfies the properties of a linear order. The simple-typed λ-calculus underlying Isabelle enforces that any λ-expression e must be typed by a type-expression τ; we write $e : : \tau$ for e is well-typed and has type τ. Being based on a polymorphically typed λ-calculus, HOL can be viewed as a combination of a programming language such as SML or Haskell, and a specification language providing powerful logical quantifiers ranging over elementary and function types.

HOL provides the usual logical connectives, e.g., $\_ \wedge \_, \_ \rightarrow \_, \neg\_$ as well as the object-logical quantifiers $\forall x.\ P\,x$ and $\exists x.\ P\,x$; in contrast to first-order logic, quantifiers may range over arbitrary types, including total functions $f : : \alpha \Rightarrow \beta$. HOL is centred around extensional equality $\_ = \_ : : \alpha \Rightarrow \alpha \Rightarrow \text{bool}$.

Isabelle/HOL offers support for extending theories in a logically safe way: a theory extension is *conservative* if the extended theory is consistent provided that the original theory was consistent. Conservative extensions can be *constant definitions, type definitions, datatype definitions, primitive recursive definitions* and *well-founded recursive definitions*.

For example, the polymorphic option-type is defined as:

datatype $'\alpha$ option = None | Some(the:$'\alpha$)

which implicitly introduces the constructors None and Some, the selector the as well as a number of lemmas over this data-type (e.g., None $\neq$ Some x,the (Some x)= x, induction). The option type is also used to model partial functions $'\alpha \rightharpoonup '\beta$ which is synonym to $'\alpha \Rightarrow '\beta$ option.

4.2   Formal Presentations of Automata: Direct Approach

A record of n fields is an n-ary Cartesian where the components have names. Equipped with this machinery, it is for example simple to formalise the concepts of, e.g., NA, NDA, ESFM, as introduced semi-formally in Sect. 2. For example, we can define NA by:

record $('\alpha, '\sigma)$ DA = init   :: $"'\sigma"$
step   :: $"'\sigma \times '\alpha \Rightarrow '\sigma"$
accept :: $"'\sigma$ set$"$

The record specification construct implicitly introduces constructor functions (we may write $(\!|$ init = 0, step = λ(s,a). s + a mod 4, accept = {1,3} $|\!)$ for a an deterministic automaton implicitly typed: (nat, nat) DA) as well as selector and update functions enabling us to write: da(|accept = (accept da) − {1} |).

Constraining the (general, infinite) DA to the more common DFA is straightforward: One can define the type-class of "all finite types" in Isabelle/HOL by

class fin = **assumes** finite: " finite ({x ::'α set. True})"

where the carrier-set of a type 'α is restricted to be finite (finite is a library concept). Thus, it is possible to formalise the DFA by adding type class constraints such as ('α:: fin ,' σ :: fin)DA.

4.3   Formal Presentations of Automata: The Monadic Approach

As shown before, the obvious way to model the state transition relation T of an NDA is by a relation of the type ($\sigma \times (\iota \times o) \times \sigma$) set, (or, for the case of the partial DA: ($\sigma \times \iota(\to o \times \sigma)$) option). Now, types can be *isomorphic*, i.e. there exists a bijection of the underlying carrier-sets. This is the case for types like '$\alpha \times$'β to '$\beta \times$'α (Cartesian isomorphism) as well as: '$\alpha \times$'$\beta \Rightarrow$'γ to '$\alpha \Rightarrow$'$\beta \Rightarrow$'γ (Currying) as well as 'α set to '$\alpha \Rightarrow$bool (foundational in HOL). Thus, one can also model the transition relation isomorphically via:

$$\iota \Rightarrow (\sigma \Rightarrow (o \times \sigma) \text{ set})$$

or for a case of a partial deterministic transition function:

$$\iota \Rightarrow (\sigma \Rightarrow (o \times \sigma) \text{ option})$$

In a theoretic framework based on classical higher-order logic (HOL), the distinction between "deterministic" and "non-deterministic" is actually much more subtle than one might think, and a more detailed discussion is necessary here. First, even in an (infinite) DA setting where the transition is a *function*, the modelled SUT is not necessarily deterministic with respect to its *input sequence*, as the difference between Fig. 1b and c reveals. Actually, provided that sufficient information can be drawn from the output (recall that we assume the SUT to be input-output deterministic), an arbitrary pre-post-condition style specification modelling the input-output relation of a system transition is possible. This is the "usual" kind of non-determinism we need in a specification of a program. We argue therefore that a framework like IOLTS, where systems may non-deterministically decide to accept input or to omit output were an overgeneralisation of little use. Second, a transition function can be under-specified via the Hilbert-choice operator built-in the HOL-logic and ZFC. This classical operator, written SOME x. P(x) chooses an arbitrary element x for which P holds true. We can only infer for y = SOME x. x$\in${a,b,c} that y must be a or b or c.

From the above said, it follows that transition function T in NA or NDA can be isomorphically represented by:

$$step \ \iota \ \sigma = \{(o, \sigma')|\text{post}(\sigma, o, \sigma')\}$$

or respectively:

$$step \ \iota \ \sigma = \text{Some}(\text{SOME}(o, \sigma'). \ \text{post}(\sigma, o, \sigma'))$$

for some post-condition post. In the former "truly non-deterministic" case *step* can and will at run-time choose different results, the latter "under-specified deterministic" version will decide in a given model always the same way: a choice that is, however, unknown at specification level and only declaratively described via post. For many systems (like system scheduler [4], processor models [3], etc.) it was possible to opt for an under-specified deterministic stepping function. The generalisation to a *partial* deterministic transition paves the way to cover EFSM's; their enabling function F, practically equivalent of a pre-condition of the transition, can be represented in a partial function by their non-applicability: $F(x) \equiv x \notin \mathrm{dom}(step)$.

We abbreviate functions of type $\sigma \Rightarrow (o \times \sigma)$ set or $\sigma \Rightarrow (o \times \sigma)$ option $\mathrm{MON_{SBE}}(o, \sigma)$ or $\mathrm{MON_{SE}}(o, \sigma)$, respectively; thus, the aforementioned state transition functions of NDA and DA can be typed by $\iota \rightarrow \mathrm{MON_{SBE}}(o, \sigma)$ for the general and $\iota \rightarrow \mathrm{MON_{SE}}(o, \sigma)$ for the deterministic setting.

If these function spaces were extended by the two operations *bind* and *unit* satisfying three algebraic properties, they form the algebraic structure of a *monad* that is well known to functional programmers as well as category theorists. Popularised by [28], monads became a kind of standard means to incorporate stateful computations into a purely functional world.

Throughout this paper, we will choose as basis for our Monadic Testing Framework under-specified deterministic stepping functions. Consequently, we will concentrate on the $\mathrm{MON_{SE}}(o, \sigma)$ monad which is called the *state-exception monad* in the literature.

The algebraic structure of a Monad comes with two operations *bind* and *unit*; like functional or relational compositions $f \circ g$ resp. $R \circ S$, *bind* can be seen as the "glue" between computations, while *unit* represents a kind of neutral element. *bind* generalizes sequential composition by adding value passing; together with *unit*, which embeds a atomic value into a computation, it can be defined for the special-case of the state-exception monad in HOL as follows:

definition bind$_{\mathrm{SE}}$ :: "('o,'σ)MON$_{\mathrm{SE}}$ $\Rightarrow$('o $\Rightarrow$('o',' σ)MON$_{\mathrm{SE}}$) $\Rightarrow$('o',' σ)MON$_{\mathrm{SE}}$"
where   "bind$_{\mathrm{SE}}$ f g = ($\lambda\sigma$. **case** f σ **of** None $\Rightarrow$None
                                          | Some (out, σ') $\Rightarrow$ g out σ')"
definition unit$_{\mathrm{SE}}$ :: "'o $\Rightarrow$('o, 'σ)MON$_{\mathrm{SE}}$" ("(return _)" 8)
where   "unit$_{\mathrm{SE}}$ e = ($\lambda\sigma$. Some(e,σ))"

Generalizing $f \circ g$, bind$_{\mathrm{SE}}$ takes input and output also into account (in the sense that a later computation may have the output of prior computations as input, and that a prior computation may fail (case None in the case distinction). Following Haskell notation, we will write $x \leftarrow m_1; m_2$ equivalently for bind$_{\mathrm{SE}} m_1 (\lambda x. m_2)$. Moreover, we will write return for unit$_{\mathrm{SE}}$.

This definition of bind$_{\mathrm{SE}}$ and unit$_{\mathrm{SE}}$ satisfy the required monad laws:

    bind_left_unit: (x $\leftarrow$ return c; P x) = P c
    bind_right_unit: (x $\leftarrow$ m; return x) = m
    bind_assoc: (y $\leftarrow$ (x $\leftarrow$m; k x); h y) = (x $\leftarrow$m; (y $\leftarrow$k x; h y))

The concept of a *valid monad execution*, written $\sigma \models m$, can be expressed as follows: an execution of a monad computation m of type (bool, σ) MON$_{\mathrm{SE}}$ is valid iff its execution is performed from the initial state σ, no exception occurs and the result of the computation is true. More formally, $\sigma \models m$ holds iff $(m \ \sigma \neq \text{None} \land \text{fst}(\text{the}(m \ \sigma)))$, where fst and snd are the usual *first* and *second* projection into a Cartesian product.

We define a *valid test-sequence* as a valid monad execution of a particular format: it consists of a series of monad computations $m_1 \ldots m_n$ applied to inputs $\iota_1 \ldots \iota_n$ and a post-condition P wrapped in a return depending on observed output. It is formally defined as follows:

$$\sigma \models o_1 \leftarrow m_1 \ \iota_1; \ldots; o_n \leftarrow m_n \ \iota_n; \text{return}(P \ o_1 \cdots o_n)$$

Since each individual computation m_i may fail, the concept of a valid test-sequence corresponds to a feasible path in an NDA, (partial) DA, ESFM or a GMM, that leads to a state in which the observed output satisfies P.

The notion of a valid test-sequence has two facets: On the one hand, it is executable, i.e., a *program*, iff $m_1, \ldots, m_n, P$ are. Thus, a code-generator can map a valid test-sequence statement to code, where the m_i where mapped to operations of the SUT interface. On the other hand, valid test-sequences can be treated by a particular simple family of symbolic executions calculi, characterised by the schema (for all monadic operations m of a system, which can be seen as the its step-functions):

$$\frac{}{(\sigma \models \text{return} P) = P} \qquad \frac{C_m \ \iota \ \sigma \qquad m \ \iota \ \sigma = \text{None}}{(\sigma \models ((s \leftarrow m \ \iota; m' \ s))) = \text{False}} \qquad (1)$$

$$\frac{C_m \ \iota \ \sigma \qquad m \ \iota \ \sigma = \text{Some}(b, \sigma')}{(\sigma \models s \leftarrow m \ \iota; m' \ s) = (\sigma' \models m' \ b)} \qquad (2)$$

This kind of rules is usually specialised for concrete operations m; if they contain pre-conditions C_m (constraints on ι and state), this calculus will just accumulate them and construct a constraint system to be treated by constraint solvers used to generate concrete input data in a test.

4.4   Example: Bank

To present the effect of the symbolic rules during symbolic execution, we present a model of toy bank that allows for checking the account balance as well as for depositing and withdrawing money. State of the bank system is modelled as a map from client and account information to the account balance:

```
type_synonym client      = string
type_synonym account_no = int
type_synonym data_base   = ( client × account_no) ⇀ int
```

Our Bank example provides only three input actions for checking the *balance* as well as *deposit* and *withdraw* money. Our model can be viewed as a transaction system, in which a series of atomic operations caused by different subjects can be executed in an interleaved way.

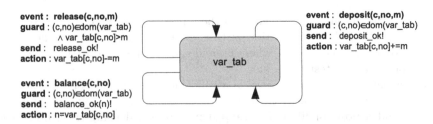

event : release(c,no,m)
guard : (c,no)∈dom(var_tab)
          ∧ var_tab[c,no]>m
send :   release_ok!
action : var_tab[c,no]-=m

event : balance(c,no)
guard : (c,no)∈dom(var_tab)
send :   balance_ok(n)!
action : n=var_tab[c,no]

event : deposit(c,no,m)
guard : (c,no)∈dom(var_tab)
send : deposit_ok!
action : var_tab[c,no]+=m

var_tab

Fig. 2. SPEC: An Extended Finite State Machine for they toy Bank

datatype in_c = deposit client account_no nat
                 | withdraw client account_no nat
                 | balance   client account_no

The output symbols are:

datatype out_c = deposit_ok | withdraw_ok | balance_ok nat

Figure 2 shows an extended finite state-machine (EFSM), the operations of our system model SPEC. A transcription of an EFSM to HOL is straight-forward and omitted here. However, we show a concrete symbolic execution rule derived from the definitions of the SPEC system transition function, e.g., the instance for Eq. 2:

$$\frac{(c, no) \in \operatorname{dom}(\sigma) \qquad \text{SPEC (deposit } c \ no \ m) \ \sigma = \operatorname{Some}(\text{deposit\_ok}, \sigma')}{(\sigma \models s \leftarrow \text{SPEC (deposit } c \ no \ m); m' \ s) = (\sigma' \models m' \ \text{deposit\_ok})}$$

where $\sigma = var\_tab$ and $\sigma' = \sigma((c, no) := (\sigma(c, no) + m))$. Thus, this rule allows for computing σ, σ' in terms of the free variables var_tab, c, no and m. The rules for withdraw and balance are similar. For this rule, SPEC (deposit $c \ no \ m$) is the concrete stepping function for the input event deposit $c \ no \ m$, and the corresponding constraint C_{SPEC} of this transition is $(c, no) \in \operatorname{dom}(\sigma)$.

The symbolic execution is deterministic in the processing of valid test-sequences and computes in one sweep all the different facets: checking enabling conditions, computing constraints for states and input and computing symbolic representations for states and output. Since the core of this calculus is representable by a matching process (rather than a unification process), the deduction aspects can be implemented in systems supporting HOL particularly efficiently.

A Simulation of Test-Driver Generation by Symbolic Execution. We state a family of test conformance relations that link the specification and abstract test drivers. The trick is done by a coupling variable *res* that transport the result of the symbolic execution of the specification SPEC to the attended result of the SUT.

$$\sigma \models o_1 \leftarrow \text{SPEC } \iota_1; \ldots; o_n \leftarrow \text{SPEC } \iota_n; \text{return}(res = [o_1 \cdots o_n])$$
$$\longrightarrow \sigma \models o_1 \leftarrow \text{SUT } \iota_1; \ldots; o_n \leftarrow \text{SUT } \iota_n; \text{return}(res = [o_1 \cdots o_n])$$

Successive applications of symbolic execution rules allow to reduce the premise of this implication to $C_{\mathrm{SPEC}}\ \iota_1\ \sigma_1 \longrightarrow \ldots \longrightarrow C_{\mathrm{SPEC}}\ \iota_n\ \sigma_n \longrightarrow res = [a_1 \cdots a_n]$ (where the a_i are concrete terms instantiating the bound output variables o_i), i.e., the constrained equation $res = [a_1 \cdots a_n]$. The latter is substituted into the conclusion of the implication. In our previous example, case-splitting over input-variables ι_1, ι_2 and ι_3 yields (among other instances) $\iota_1 =$ deposit $c_1\ no_1\ m$, $\iota_2 =$ withdraw $c_2\ no_2\ n$ and $\iota_3 =$ balance $c_3\ no_3$, which allows us to derive automatically the constraint:

$$(c_1, no_1) \in \mathrm{dom}(\sigma) \longrightarrow (c_2, no_2) \in \mathrm{dom}(\sigma') \wedge n < \sigma'(c_2, no_2) \longrightarrow$$
$$(c_3, no_3) \in \mathrm{dom}(\sigma'') \longrightarrow res = [\mathrm{alloc\_ok}, \mathrm{release\_ok}, \mathrm{status\_ok}(\sigma''(c_3, no_3))]$$

where $\sigma' = \sigma((c_1, no_1) := (\sigma(c_1, no_1) + m)))$ and $\sigma'' = \sigma'((c_2, no_2) := (\sigma(c_2, no_2) - n)))$.

In general, the constraint $C_{\mathrm{SPEC}_i}\ \iota_i\ \sigma_i$ can be seen as an *symbolic abstract test execution*; instances of it (produced by a constraint solver such as Z3 integrated into Isabelle) will provide concrete input data for the valid test-sequence statement over SUT, which can therefore be compiled to test driver code. In our example here, the witness $c_1 = c_2 = c_3 = 0$, $c_1 = c_2 = c_3 = 5$, $m = 4$ and $n = 2$ satisfies the constraint and would produce (predict) the output sequence $res = [\mathrm{deposit\_ok}, \mathrm{withdraw\_ok}, \mathrm{balance\_ok}\ 2]$ for SUT according to SPEC. Thus, a resulting (abstract) test-driver is:

$$\sigma \models o_1 \leftarrow \mathrm{SUT}\ \iota_1; o_2 \leftarrow \mathrm{SUT}\ \iota_2; o_3 \leftarrow \mathrm{SUT}\ \iota_3;$$
$$\mathrm{return}([\mathrm{alloc\_ok}, \mathrm{release\_ok}, \mathrm{status\_ok}\ 2] = [o_1, o_2, o_3])$$

A code-generator setup of HOL-TestGen compiles this abstract test-driver to concrete code in C (for example), that is linked to the real SUT implementation.

Experimental Results Gathered from the Example. The traditional way to specify a sequence test scenario in HOL-TestGen looks like this:

test_spec test_balance:
assumes account_def : "$(c_0,no) \in \mathrm{dom}\ \sigma_0$"
and   accounts_pos : "init σ_0" and test_purpose : "test_purpose c_0 no S"
and   sym_exec_spec : "$\sigma_0 \models (s \leftarrow \mathrm{mbind}_{\mathrm{FailStop}}\ S\ \mathrm{SYS}; \mathrm{return}\ (s = x))$"
shows   "$\sigma_0 \models (s \leftarrow \mathrm{mbind}_{\mathrm{FailStop}}\ S\ \mathrm{PUT}; \mathrm{return}\ (s = x))$"

where the assumptions of this scenario (also called *test purposes*) are:

- account_def that the initial system state σ_0 is a map that contains at least a client c_0 with an account no,
- the constraint σ_0 constrains the tests to those σ_0 where all accounts have a positive balance, and
- test_purpose constrains the set of possible input sequences S to those that contain only operations of client $c_)$ and two of his accounts.

We skip the formal definitions of init and test_purpose due to space reasons.

Using explicit test-refinement statements as introduced in Sect. 5, we can state the above scenario equivalently as as inclusion test as follows:

test_spec test_balance3:
"PUT $\sqsubseteq_{IT}\langle\{\sigma.$ init $\sigma \wedge (c_0,no) \in$ dom $\sigma\},\{\iota s.$ test_purpose c_0 no $\iota s\}\rangle$ SYS"
apply(*rule* inclusion_test_I_opt, simp, *erule* conjE)   (* 1 *)
using[[no_uniformity]] **apply**(gen_test_cases 4 1 "PUT")   (* 2 *)
apply(tactic "ALLGOALS(TestGen.REPEAT'(ematch_tac
   [@{**thm** balance.exec_mbindFStop_E},@{**thm** withdraw.exec_mbindFStop_E},
    @{**thm** deposit.exec_mbindFStop_E},@{**thm** valid_mbind'_mt}]))")   (* 3 *)
apply(auto simp: init_def)   (* 4 *)
using[[no_uniformity=false]]
apply(tactic "ALLCASES(uniformityI_tac @{context} [\"PUT\"])")   (* 5 *)
mk_test_suite "bank_simpleNB3"   (* 6 *)
(* ... *)
gen_test_data "bank_simpleNB3"   (* 7 *)

The HOL-TestGen generation process in itself has been described in detail in [6] to which the interested reader is referred. For space reasons, we can only highlight the above test-generation script in the Isar language. It starts with the stages of a test generation from the explicit test-refinement statement over elementary massage involving the test optimisation theorem inclusion_test_I_opt (see Sect. 5) labelled *(* 1 *)*, the splitting-phase of the input sequence labelled *(* 2 *)*, the symbolic execution phase labelled *(* 3 *)*, a simplification of the resulting constraints in *(* 4 *)*, the separation of the constraint systems and test-hypothesises *(* 5 *)* and the generation of the resulting test-theorem. Recall that a test-theorem captures both abstract test-cases and test-hypothesises and links them to the original test specification (see [6]). In *(* 6 *)*, an internal data-structure called *test container*—named "bank_simpleNB3" where this choice has no particular importance—is created into which the test-theorem is stored.

The call of the command **gen_test_data** performs the test-data selection phase (in our example by using Z3) for the test-container "bank_simpleNB3", i.e. it converts abstract test cases in concrete tests by finding ground solutions for the constraints in the abstract test cases. We omit the further phases that compile the test cases to concrete test-oracles in C, which were linked to the implementation of PUT which is just an uninterpreted constant in this specification.

For example, we pick from the list of the abstract test cases:

$$\forall x \in \text{dom } \sigma_0.\ 0 \leq \text{the}(\sigma_0\ x) \longrightarrow \sigma_0\ (c_0,\ no) = \text{Some } y \longrightarrow \text{int } n' \leq y + \text{int } n \longrightarrow$$
$$\sigma_0 \models os \leftarrow \text{mbind}_{\text{FailStop}}[\text{deposit } c_0\ no\ n, \text{withdraw } c_0\ no\ n', \text{balance } c_0\ no]\ \text{PUT};$$
$$\text{unit}_{SE}(os=[\text{deposit\_ok, withdraw\_ok, balance\_ok}(\text{nat}(y+ \text{int } n - \text{int } n'))])$$

This abstract test case says: for any σ_0 which has only positive values, and a y with the balance of the account of client c_0 on his account no, and sufficient money on the account such that the deposit and withdraw operations can both be effectuated (mind the precondition of withdraw that the balance must be sufficiently large for the withdraw), a test-sequence deposit-withdraw-balance must lead to the observable result that all three operations succeed and produce the result value nat(y + int n − int n'), where nat and int are HOL-library coersions between nats and integers. They are a result of our operations in the model that requires at some points natural numbers and at integers on others; this kind of complication is very common in constraints generated from programs or models.

The test-selection phase chooses, e.g., the following concrete tests from the abstract test shown above:

$$(\lambda a.\ \text{Some } 15) \models os \leftarrow \text{mbind}_{\text{FailStop}} \text{ [deposit } c_0 \text{ 6 (nat 17), withdraw } c_0 \text{ 6 (nat 30),}$$
$$\text{balance } c_0 \text{ 6] PUT;}$$
$$\text{unit}_{SE} \text{ (os = [deposit\_ok, withdraw\_ok, balance\_ok(2)]))}$$

This concrete test states: if we start with a system state where any account of any client has the balance 15, then we can run on PUT the sequence: deposit 17 for client c_0 on his account no 6, withdraw 30, and we should observe that all three operations went well and the result of the final one is 2. This concrete test is now finally a computable function, i.e. a *program*; the reader interested in the technical process that compiles it into a test driver in C is referred to Bank.thy in the HOL-TestGen distribution.

In the following, we are interested in a few experimental measurements that we did on a conventional laptop with 2.5 GHz i7 processor and 16 Mb Ram, using Isabelle/HOL-TestGen version 1.8.0. We omit the phases *(* 1 *)* and the test-oracle generation, which were more or less constant and small in the experimental range. We vary over the first parameter of the test-splitting phase, which is 4 in the above test-script and n in the following. It defines the length of the input sequences that were result of the splitting. Since we have 3 different input events in our model (deposit, withdraw, balance), the space of abstract test-cases grows asymptotically with this length by 3^n. We count the number of seconds and the number of abstract/concrete tests found (see Table 1).

Table 1. Run-time and number of test cases of the bank example.

n	(* 2 *)		(* 3 *)		(* 4 *)		(* 5 *)		(* 7 *)	
	sec	no	sec	no	sec	no	sec	no	sec	no
3	$15.1 \cdot 10^0$	7	0.9	7	0.1	7	0.8	7	0.7	7
4	$63.3 \cdot 10^0$	15	1.7	15	2.1	15	2.5	15	1.8	15
5	$7.2 \cdot 10^3$	42	6.1	42	10.3	42	28.0	42	3.8	42
6	$> 88.0 \cdot 10^3$	-	-	-	-	-	-	-	-	-

The splitting phase was not optimised—this is what we usually do in larger case-studies, where we use a number of switches and screws in HOL-TestGen to basically prune the splitting process early[1]. The standard pruning catches already the constraint stemming from test_purpose that a balance-operation has

---

[1] The core-example of [4] can be decomposed into 70000 abstract test-cases in less than two hours on a conventional laptop in HOL-TestGen [6].

to appear at the end and that clients and account numbers are restricted; this explains why the abstract tests indicated here are below 3^n. Note furthermore that the example is somewhat atypical since the generated abstract tests are all feasible and all together represent an easy game for the constraint solver.

5   A Formal Theory on Conformance Relations

This schema of a test-driver synthesis can be refined and optimised: we show three examples of the formalisation of conformance relations as well as formal proofs of their connection possible in our framework. All notions and lemmas mentioned here are formally proven in Isabelle/HOL.

Preliminaries and Observations. First, for iterations of stepping functions an mbind operator can be defined, which is basically a fold over $bind_{SE}$. It takes a list of inputs $\iota s = [i_1, \ldots, i_n]$, feeds it subsequently into SPEC and stops when an error occurs. The standard definition looks as follows:

```
fun    mbind :: "'ι list  ⇒  ('ι ⇒ ('o,' σ) MON_SE) ⇒ ('o list,' σ) MON_SE"
where "mbind [] iostep σ = Some([], σ)"
    | "mbind (a#S) iostep σ =
          (case iostep a σ of
              None  ⇒ Some([], σ)
            | Some (out, σ') ⇒ (case mbind S iostep σ' of
                              None  ⇒ Some([out], σ')
                            | Some(outs, σ") ⇒ Some(out#outs, σ")))"
```

When generalising $bind_{SE}$ to sequences of computations over an input sequence, three different variants are possible:

1. The *failsave* mbind (our default; written $mbind_{FailSave}$ if necessary). This operator has a similar semantics than a sequence of method-calls in Java with a catch-clause at the end: If an exception occurs, the rest of the sequence is omitted, but the state is maintained, and all depends on the computations afterwards in the catch clause.

2. The *failstop* mbind (written $mbind_{FailStop}$). This operator corresponds to a C-like exception handling: System halt and the entire sequence is treated as error. This variant is gained from the above by replacing Some([], σ) in the 5th line of the definition above by None.

3. The *failpurge* mbind. This variant, which we do not detail further in this paper, ignores the failing computations and executes a stuttering step instead. In the modelling of some operating system calls, we found this behaviour useful in situations when atomic actions may fail, report an error, and certain subsequent atomic actions have to be ignored to avoid error-avalanches.

With these mbind operators, valid test sequences for a stepping-function (be it from the specification SPEC or the SUT) evaluating an input sequence ιs and satisfying a post-condition P can be reformulated to:

$$\sigma \models os \leftarrow \text{mbind } \iota s \text{ SPEC; return}(P \iota s \, os)$$

Second, revisiting the animation Sect. 4.4 and abstracting the pattern of the initial test specification, we can now formally define the concept of a test-conformance notion between an implementation I and a specification S:

$$(I \sqsubseteq_{\langle Init, CovCrit, conf \rangle} S) \equiv (\forall \sigma_0 \in Init. \, \forall \iota s \in CovCrit. \, \forall res.$$
$$\sigma_0 \models os \leftarrow \text{mbind } \iota s \, S; \text{ return}(conf \, \iota s \, os \, res)$$
$$\longrightarrow \sigma_0 \models os \leftarrow \text{mbind } \iota s \, I; \text{ return}(conf \, \iota s \, os \, res))$$

Here, $Init$ is a set of initial states, $CovCrit$ a super-set constraining the input sequences (this set can be either considered as "test purpose" or as "coverage criterion"), a *coupling variable res* establishing the link between the possible results of the symbolic execution and their use in a test-oracle of the test-execution. We call *conf* a *conformance characterisation* which represents the exact nature of the test-refinement we want to characterise.

Inclusion Tests and Proven Correct Test-Optimisations. This means we have a precise characterisation of inclusion conformance introduced in the previous section: We constrain the tests to the test sequences where no exception occurred (as result of a violated enabling condition) in the symbolic execution of the model. It suffices to choose for the conformance characterisation:

$$\text{conf}_{\text{IT}} \, \iota s \, os \, res \equiv (\text{length}(\iota s) = \text{length}(os) \wedge res = os)$$

With this conformance characterization, we can *define* our first explicit test-refinement notion formally by instantiating the test-refinement schema above:

$$(I \sqsubseteq_{\text{IT}\langle Init, CC \rangle} S) \equiv (I \sqsubseteq_{\langle Init, CC, \text{conf}_{\text{IT}} \rangle} S)$$

The setting for conf_{IT} (IT for inclusion test) has the consequence that our symbolic executions were only successful iff possible output-sequence are as long as the input sequence. This implies that no exception occurred in possible symbolic runs with possible inputs, i.e., all enabling conditions have to be satisfied.

Now, it can be sformally proven by induction that:

$$\sigma \models os \leftarrow \text{mbind}_{\text{FailSave}} \, \iota s \, f; \text{return}(\text{length}(\iota s) = \text{length}(os) \wedge P \, \iota s \, os) =$$
$$\sigma \models os \leftarrow \text{mbind}_{\text{FailStop}} \, \iota s \, f; \text{return}(P \, \iota s \, os)$$

This means that in inclusion test-refinements, both $\text{mbind}_{\text{FailSave}}$-occurrences can be replaced by $\text{mbind}_{\text{FailStop}}$. This has a minor and a major advantage:

– At test-execution time, the generated code is slightly more efficient (less cases to check, simpler oracle).

– At symbolic execution time, drastically simpler constraints can be generated: While mbind$_{\text{FailSave}}$ generates disjunctions for both normal behaviour (enabling condition satisfied) as well as exceptional behaviour (enabling condition violated) were generated, while mbind$_{\text{FailStop}}$ generates constraints only for normal behaviour, which are therefore simpler to solve in the test-data selection phase by a constraint solver.

A consequence is the following theorem `inclusion_test_I_opt`, which reads presented as natural deduction rule as follows:

$$\dfrac{\left[\begin{array}{l}\sigma_0 \in \text{Init}, \iota s \in CC, \\ \sigma_0 \vDash os \leftarrow \text{mbind}_{\text{FailStop}}\ \iota s\ S; \text{unit}_{\text{SE}}(os = res)\end{array}\right]_{\sigma_0\ \iota s\ res} \\ \vdots \\ \sigma_0 \vDash os \leftarrow \text{mbind}_{\text{FailStop}}\ \iota s\ I; \text{unit}_{\text{SE}}(os = res)}{I \sqsubseteq_{IT\langle \text{Init}, CC\rangle} S}$$

Deadlock-Inclusion. Using pre-and postcondition predicates, it is straightforward to characterise deadlock conformance: in this kind of test, we investigate that the SUT blocks (in the sense: enabling condition violated) exactly when it should according to the specification. Such test scenarios arise, for example, if a protocol is checked that it *only* does what the specification admits. In other words, we test the absence of back-doors in the implementation of a protocol.

This kind of test is expressed in our framework by the conformance characterisation:

$$\text{conf}_{\text{DF}}\ pre\ \iota s\ os\ res = (\text{length}(\iota s) = \text{length}(os) - 1 \wedge res = os \wedge \neg pre(\text{last}(\iota s))$$

With this conformance characterisation, we can define our second explicit test-refinement notion formally by instantiating the test-refinement schema:

$$(I \sqsubseteq_{\text{DF}\langle \text{Init}, CC\rangle} S) \equiv (I \sqsubseteq_{\langle \text{Init}, CC, \text{conf}_{\text{DF}}\ pre_S\rangle} S)$$

where $pre_S\ \iota$ is the enabledness condition of S for some input ι. Here, we assume that pre_S only depends on the input and not on the state after the execution of the input sequence. However, this can be easily remedied by a slightly more powerful pattern.[2]

The Connection to "traditional" IO Conformance. Another application of our formalisation is the possibility to actually put standard notions based on automata-theoretic notion into relation with our MST Framework. Of natural interest is the IO-Conformance relation mentioned earlier. We pick from a wealth of alternative definitions [23].

However, recall that our framework assumes synchronous communication between tester and SUT; and so far ignores concepts such as quiescence.

---

[2] The `Monads.thy`-library provides the assert$_{SE}$-operator for this purpose.

An equivalence between a ioco in the sense of [23] and IOCO in the sense of our MST Framework is therefore only possible for IO-LTS specifications of a particular form. Formalising an IO-LTS in this sense results in:

record $('\iota,\ 'o,\ '\sigma)$ io_lts $=$
    init   :: "$'\sigma$ set"
    trans :: "$('\sigma \times ('\iota +'o) \times'\sigma)$ set"

This version of [23] just possesses a disjoint sum of input and output actions; other versions of the same author provide also one or several internal actions $'\tau$; this would result in $('\iota + 'o + '\tau)$.

We skip the straight-forward definitions for "Straces", "out" and "after" (synonym to "States" in Sect. 2) and define:

definition out :: "$[('\iota,'o,'\sigma)$ io_lts $,'\sigma$ set$] \Rightarrow ('o)$ set"
where   "out TS ss $\equiv$ {a. $\exists$ s $\in$ ss. $\exists$ s'. (s,Inr a,s') $\in$ (trans TS)}"

definition ioco :: "$[('\iota,'o,'\sigma)$io_lts $,('\iota,'o,'\sigma)$io_lts$] \Rightarrow$ bool" (**infixl** "ioco" 200)
where   "i ioco s $\equiv (\forall$ t $\in$ Straces(s). out i (i after t) $\subseteq$ out s (s after t))"

On the other hand, we may formalise our own notion of IOCO conformance and relate these two. To this end we specify a conformance characterisation and the resulting third explicit test-refinement notion:

$$\text{conf}_{IOCO}\ post\ \iota s\ os\ res \equiv (res = os \wedge \text{length}(\iota s) = \text{length}(os) \wedge post\ (\text{last} \iota s))$$

$$(I \sqsubseteq_{IOCO\langle Init, CC\rangle} S) \equiv (I \sqsubseteq_{\langle Init, CC, \text{conf}_{IOCO}\ post_S\rangle} S)$$

For the following main result of this paper, we introduce an auxiliary notion: we call an io_lts A *strictly IO-alternating* iff all $t \in Straces(A)$ that finish in an input action ι all prolongations in t' (that is: $t@t' \in Straces(A)$ start with an output action[3]). Moreover, we define a function two_step that serves essentially as wrapper interface to SUT that sends an input action, waits for the returned output-action and binds the latter to the rest of the computation (rather than comparing them to a pre-conceived o and stating "inconclusive" if the observed output does not match to the pre-computed one as in [23].) This enables us to prove the following theorem that links Tretmanns ioco with ours by:

theorem ioco_VS_IOCO:
  assumes "strictly_IO_alternating S" and "io_deterministic S"
  shows "$\exists$ S'. I ioco S = ((two_step I) $\sqsubseteq_{IOCO\langle\{x.True\},\{x.True\}\rangle}$ S'"

Proof Sketch: We give an existential witness for S' by defining a conversion function convert2SE that converts S into its monadic counterpart. This is done by constructing the Runs of S which must have the form $[...,(\ \sigma_n, \iota_m, \sigma_{n+1}), (\sigma_{n+1},'o_{m+1},\sigma_{n+2}),...]$. Thus, from the set of Runs, the relation $('\iota \times ('\sigma \rightarrow ('o \times '\sigma))$ can be reconstructed, which under the assumptions strictly_IO_alternating and io_deterministic represents a function.

---

[3] In a definition variant with $'\tau$, these actions must be skipped.

6   Conclusion and Future Work

We see several conceptual and practical advantages of a *monadic approach* to sequence testing, the MST Framework:

1. MST's generalise GMM's, io-tagged DA's and NDA's, as well as EFSM's; they are equivalent to particular forms of IO-LTL's and IO-STS's in IOCO conformance settings.
2. MST's can cope with non-deterministic system models (provided they are input-output-deterministic, which we consider a reasonable requirement for system testability).
3. In case of under-specification-non-determinism, substantial case-studies of substantial complexities show the feasibility of our approach [4].
4. the monadic theory models explicitly the difference between input and output, between data under control of the tester and results under control of the SUT,
5. the theory lends itself for a theoretical and practical framework of numerous conformance notions, even non-standard ones, and which gives
6. ways to new calculi for efficient symbolic evaluation enabling symbolic states (via invariants) and input events (via constraints) as well as a seamless, theoretically founded transition from system models to test-drivers.

We see several directions for future work: On the model level, the formal theory of sequence testing should be further explored and extended. It is particularly tempting to incorporate in our MST theory partial-order reduction techniques for further test refinement optimisations.

Acknowledgement. This work was partially supported by the Euro-MILS project funded by the European Union's Programme [FP7/2007-2013] under grant agreement number ICT-318353.

References

1. Andrews, P.B.: Introduction to Mathematical Logic and Type Theory: To Truth through Proof, 2nd edn. Kluwer Academic Publishers, Dordrecht (2002)
2. Brucker, A.D., Brügger, L., Wolff, B.: Formal firewall conformance testing: An application of test and proof techniques. Softw. Testing Verif. Reliab. (STVR) **25**(1), 34–71 (2015)
3. Brucker, A.D., Feliachi, A., Nemouchi, Y., Wolff, B.: Test program generation for a microprocessor. In: Veanes, M., Viganò, L. (eds.) TAP 2013. LNCS, vol. 7942, pp. 76–95. Springer, Heidelberg (2013)
4. Brucker, A.D., Havle, O., Nemouchi, Y., Wolff, B.: Testing the IPC protocol for a real-time operating system. In: Gurfinkel, A., Seshia, S.A. (eds.) VSTTE 2015. LNCS, vol. 9593, pp. 40–60. Springer, Heidelberg (2016). doi:10.1007/978-3-319-29613-5_3
5. Brucker, A.D., Wolff, B.: Test-sequence generation with Hol-TestGen with an application to firewall testing. In: Gurevich, Y., Meyer, B. (eds.) TAP 2007. LNCS, vol. 4454, pp. 149–168. Springer, Heidelberg (2007)

6. Brucker, A.D., Wolff, B.: On theorem prover-based testing. Formal Aspects Comput. (FAC) **25**(5), 683–721 (2013)
7. Cheng, K.T., Krishnakumar, A.S.: Automatic functional test generation using the extended finite state machine model. In: International Design Automation Conference, DAC 1993, pp. 86–91. ACM, New York (1993)
8. Church, A.: A formulation of the simple theory of types. J. Symbolic Logic **5**(2), 56–68 (1940)
9. D'Antoni, L., Veanes, M.: Minimization of symbolic automata. In: Jagannathan, S., Sewell, P. (eds.) The 41st Annual ACM SIGPLAN-SIGACT Symposium on Principles of Programming Languages, POPL, pp. 541–554. ACM (2014)
10. Feliachi, A., Gaudel, M., Wenzel, M., Wolff, B.: The circus testing theory revisited in Isabelle/HOL. In: Formal Methods and Software Engineering, pp. 131–147 (2013)
11. Fraenkel, A., Bar-Hillel, Y.: Foundations of Set Theory. Studies in Logic and the Foundations of Mathematics. North-Holland, Amsterdam (1958)
12. Frantzen, L., Tretmans, J., Willemse, T.A.C.: A symbolic framework for model-based testing. In: Havelund, K., Núñez, M., Roşu, G., Wolff, B. (eds.) FATES 2006 and RV 2006. LNCS, vol. 4262, pp. 40–54. Springer, Heidelberg (2006)
13. Gill, A.: Introduction to the Theory of Finite-State Machines. McGraw-Hill, New York (1962)
14. Halmos, P.: Naive Set Theory. Undergraduate Texts in Mathematics. Springer, New York (1974)
15. Jard, C., Jéron, T.: TGV: theory, principles and algorithms. STTT **7**(4), 297–315 (2005)
16. Jéron, T.: Symbolic model-based test selection. Electr. Notes Theor. Comput. Sci. **240**, 167–184 (2009)
17. Kalaji, A.S., Hierons, R.M., Swift, S.: Generating feasible transition paths for testing from an extended finite state machine (EFSM) with the counter problem. In: Third International Conference on Software Testing, Verification and Validation, ICST, pp. 232–235. IEEE Computer Society (2010)
18. Ponce de León, H., Haar, S., Longuet, D.: Conformance relations for labeled event structures. In: Brucker, A.D., Julliand, J. (eds.) TAP 2012. LNCS, vol. 7305, pp. 83–98. Springer, Heidelberg (2012)
19. Lynch, N., Tuttle, M.: An introduction to input/output automata. CWI-Quarterly **2**(3), 219–246 (1989)
20. Mealy, G.H.: A method for synthesizing sequential circuits. Bell Syst. Tech. J. **34**(5), 1045–1079 (1955)
21. Moore, E.F.: Gedanken-experiments on sequential machines. In: Shannon, C., McCarthy, J. (eds.) Automata Studies, pp. 129–153. Princeton University Press, Princeton (1956)
22. Rusu, V., Marchand, H., Jéron, T.: Automatic verification and conformance testing for validating safety properties of reactive systems. In: Fitzgerald, J.S., Hayes, I.J., Tarlecki, A. (eds.) FM 2005. LNCS, vol. 3582, pp. 189–204. Springer, Heidelberg (2005)
23. Tretmanns, J., Belifante, Z.: Automatic testign with formal methods. In: 7th European International Conference on Software Testing, Analysis and Review (EuroSTAR 1999) (1999)
24. Tretmans, J.: Test generation with inputs, outputs and repetitive quiescence. Soft. Concepts Tools **17**(3), 103–120 (1996)

25. Tretmans, J.: Model based testing with labelled transition systems. In: Hierons, R.M., Bowen, J.P., Harman, M. (eds.) FORTEST. LNCS, vol. 4949, pp. 1–38. Springer, Heidelberg (2008)
26. Veanes, M., Bjørner, N.: Alternating simulation and IOCO. STTT **14**(4), 387–405 (2012)
27. Veanes, M., Bjørner, N.: Symbolic automata: the toolkit. In: Flanagan, C., König, B. (eds.) TACAS 2012. LNCS, vol. 7214, pp. 472–477. Springer, Heidelberg (2012)
28. Wadler, P.: Comprehending monads. Math. Struct. Comput. Sci. **2**(4), 461–493 (1992)

Advances in Property-Based Testing for αProlog

James Cheney[1]([✉]), Alberto Momigliano[2], and Matteo Pessina[2]

[1] University of Edinburgh, Edinburgh, UK
jcheney@inf.ed.ac.uk
[2] Università degli Studi di Milano, Milan, Italy
momigliano@di.unimi.it, matteo.pessina3@studenti.unimi.it

Abstract. αCheck is a light-weight property-based testing tool built on top of αProlog, a logic programming language based on nominal logic. αProlog is particularly suited to the validation of the meta-theory of formal systems, for example correctness of compiler translations involving name-binding, alpha-equivalence and capture-avoiding substitution. In this paper we describe an alternative to the negation elimination algorithm underlying αCheck that substantially improves its effectiveness. To substantiate this claim we compare the checker performances w.r.t. two of its main competitors in the logical framework niche, namely the QuickCheck/Nitpick combination offered by Isabelle/HOL and the random testing facility in PLT-Redex.

1 Introduction

Formal compiler verification has come a long way from McCarthy and Painter's "Correctness of a Compiler for Arithmetic Expression" (1967), as witnessed by the success of *CompCert* and subsequent projects [21,35]. However outstanding these achievements are, they are not a magic wand for every-day compiler writers: not only CompCert was designed with verification in mind, whereby the implementation and the verification were a single process, but there are only a few dozen people in the world able and willing to carry out such an endeavour. By verification, CompCert means the preservation of certain simulation relations between source, intermediate and target code; however, the translations involved are relatively simple compared to those employed by modern optimizing compilers. Despite some initial work [1,7], handling more realistic optimizations seems even harder, e.g. the verification of the *call arity* analysis and transformation in the Glasgow Haskell Compiler (GHC):

> "The [Nominal] Isabelle development corresponding to this paper, including the definition of the syntax and the semantics, contains roughly 12,000 lines of code with 1,200 lemmas (many small, some large) in 75 theories, created over the course of 9 months" (page 11, [7]).

For the rest of us, hence, it is back to compiler testing, which is basically synonymous with passing a hand-written fixed validation suite. This is not completely satisfactory, as the coverage of those tests is difficult to assess and

B.K. Aichernig and C.A. Furia (Eds.): TAP 2016, LNCS 9762, pp. 37–56, 2016.
DOI: 10.1007/978-3-319-41135-4_3

because, being fixed, these suites will not uncover new bugs. In the last few years, *randomized differential testing* [24] has been suggested in combination with automatic generation of (expressive) test programs, most notably for C compilers with the *Csmith* tool [36] and to a lesser extent for GHC [30]. The oracle is *comparison checking*: Csmith feeds randomly generated programs to several compilers and flags the minority one(s), that is, those reporting different outputs from the majority of the other compilers under test, as incorrect. Similarly, the outcome of GHC on a random program with or without an optimization enabled is compared.

Property-based testing, as pioneered by QuickCheck [12], seems to leverage the automatic generation of test cases with the use of *logical specifications* (the properties), making validation possible not only in a differential way, but internally, *w.r.t.* (an abstraction of) the behavior of the source and intermediate code. In fact, compiler verification/validation is a prominent example of the more general field of verification of the *meta-theory* of formal systems. For many classes of (typically) shallow bugs, a tool that automatically finds counterexamples can be surprisingly effective and can complement formal proof attempts by warning when the property we wish to prove has easily-found counterexamples. The beauty of such *meta-theory model checking* is that, compared to other general forms of system validation, the properties that should hold are already given by means of the theorems that the calculus under study is supposed to satisfy. Of course, those need to be fine tuned for testing to be effective, but we are mostly free of the thorny issue of specification/invariant generation.

In fact, such tools are now gaining traction in the field of semantics engineering, see in particular the QuickCheck/Nitpick combination offered in Isabelle/HOL [4] and random testing in PLT-Redex [18]. However, a particular dimension to validating for example optimizations in a compiler such as GHC, whose intermediate language is a variant of the polymorphically typed λ-calculus, is a correct, simple and effective handling of *binding signatures* and associated notions such as α-equivalence and capture avoiding substitutions. A small but not insignificant part of the success of the CompCert project is due to not having to deal with any notion of binder[1]. The ability to encode possibly non-algorithmic relations (such as typing) in a declarative way would also be a plus.

The nominal logic programming language αProlog [11] offers all those facilities. Additionally, it was among the first to propose a form of property based testing for language specifications with the *αCheck* tool [9]. In contrast to QuickCheck/Nitpick and PLT Redex, our approach supports binding syntax directly and uses logic programming to perform *exhaustive symbolic* search for counterexamples. Systems lacking this kind of support may end up with ineffective testing capabilities or requiring an additional amount of coding, which needs to be duplicated in every case study:

---

[1] X. Leroy, personal communication. In fact, the encoding in [22] does not respect α-equivalence, nor does it implement substitutions in a capture avoiding way.

"Redex offers little support for handling binding constructs in object languages. It provides a generic function for obtaining a fresh variable, but no help in defining capture-avoiding substitution or α-equivalence [...] In one case [...] managing binders constitutes a significant portion of the overall time spent [...] Generators derived from grammars [...] require substantial massaging to achieve high test coverage. This deficiency is particularly pressing in the case of typed object languages, where the massaging code almost duplicates the specification of the type system" (page 5, [18]).

αCheck extends αProlog with tools for searching for counterexamples, that is, substitutions that makes the antecedent of a specification true and the conclusion false. In logic programming terms this means fixing a notion of *negation*. To begin with, αCheck adopted the infamous *negation-as-failure* (NF) operation, "which put pains thousandfold upon the" logic programmers. As many good things in life, its conceptual simplicity and efficiency is marred by significant problems:

- the lack of an agreed intended semantics against which to carry a soundness proof: this concern is significant because the semantics of negation as failure has not yet been investigated for nominal logic programming;
- even assuming such a semantics, we know that *NF* is unsound for non-ground goals; hence all free variables must be instantiated before solving the negated conclusion. This is obviously exponentially expensive in an exhaustive search setting and may prevent optimizations by goal reordering.

To remedy this αCheck also offered *negation elimination* (NE) [3,26], a source-to-source transformation that replaces negated subgoals to calls to equivalent positively defined predicates. *NE* by-passes the previous issues arising for *NF* since, in the absence of local (existential) variables, it yields an ordinary (α)Prolog program, whose intended model is included in the complement of the model of the source program. In particular, it avoids the expensive term generation step needed for *NF*, it has been proved correct, and it may open up other opportunities for optimization. Unfortunately, in the experiments reported in our initial implementation of αCheck [9], *NE* turned out to be slower than *NF*.

Perhaps to the reader's chagrin, this paper does not tackle the validation of compiler optimizations (yet). Rather, it lays the foundations by:

1. describing an alternative implementation of negation elimination, dubbed *NEs*—"s" for simplified: this improves significantly over the performance of *NE* as described in [9] by producing negative programs that are equivalent, but much more succinct, so much as to make the method competitive *w.r.t. NF*;
2. and by evaluating our checker in comparison with some of its competitors in the logical framework niche, namely QuickCheck/Nitpick [4] and PLT-Redex [18]. To the best of our knowledge, this is the first time any of these three tools have been compared experimentally.

In the next section we give a tutorial presentation of the tool and move then to the formal description of the logical engine (Sect. 3). In Sect. 4, we detail the

NEs algorithm and its implementation, whereas Sect. 5 carries out the promised comparison on two case studies, a prototypical λ-calculus with lists and a basic type system for secure information flow. The sources for αProlog and αCheck can be found at https://github.com/aprolog-lang/aprolog. Supplementary material, including the full listing of the case studies presented here and an online appendix containing additional experiments and some formal notions used in Sect. 3, but omitted here for the sake of space, are available at [10]. We assume some familiarity with logic programming.

2 A Brief Tour of αCheck

We specify the formal systems and the properties we wish to check as Horn logic programs in αProlog [11], a logic programming language based on *nominal logic*, a first-order theory axiomatizing names and name-binding introduced by Pitts [32].

In αProlog, there are several built-in types, functions, and relations with special behavior. There are distinguished *name types* that are populated with infinitely many *name constants*. In program text, a lower-case identifier is considered to be a name constant by default if it has not already been declared as something else. Names can be used in *abstractions*, written a\M in programs, considered equal up to α-renaming of the bound name. Thus, where one writes $\lambda x.M$, $\forall x.M$, etc. in a paper exposition, in αProlog one writes lam(x\M), forall(x\M), etc. In addition, the *freshness* relation a # t holds between a name a and a term t that does not contain a free occurrence of a. Thus, $x \notin FV(t)$ is written in αProlog as x # t; in particular, if t is also a name then freshness is name-inequality. For convenience, αProlog provides a function-definition syntax, but this is just translated to an equivalent (but more verbose) relational implementation via *flattening*.

Horn logic programs over these operations suffice to define a wide variety of object languages, type systems, and operational semantics in a convenient way. To give a feel of the interaction with the checker, here we encode a simply-typed λ-calculus augmented with constructors for integers and lists, following the PLT-Redex benchmark sltk.lists.rkt from http://docs.racket-lang.org/redex/benchmark.html, which we will examine more deeply in Sect. 5.1. The language is formally declared as follows:

$$\begin{array}{lll}
\text{Types} & A, B ::= int \mid ilist \mid A \rightarrow B \\
\text{Terms} & M \quad ::= x \mid \lambda x{:}A.\ M \mid M_1\ M_2 \mid c \mid err \\
\text{Constants } c & \quad ::= n \mid nil \mid cons \mid hd \mid tl \\
\text{Values} & V \quad ::= c \mid \lambda x{:}A.\ M \mid cons\ V \mid cons\ V_1\ V_2
\end{array}$$

We start (see the top of Fig. 1) by declaring the syntax of terms, constants and types, while we carve out values *via* an appropriate predicate. A similar predicate is_err characterizes the threading in the operational semantics of the *err* expression, used to model run time errors such as taking the head of an empty list.

```
ty: type.
intTy: ty.            funTy: (ty,ty) -> ty.       listTy: ty.
cst: type.
toInt: int -> cst.  nil: cst.  cons: cst.  hd: cst.  tl: cst.
id: name_type.
exp: type.
var: id -> exp.      lam: (id\exp,ty) -> exp.  app: (exp,exp) -> exp.
c: cst -> exp.       err: exp.

type ctx = [(id,ty)].

pred tc (ctx,exp,ty).
tc(_,err,T).
tc(_,c(C),T)                           :- tcf(C) = T.
tc([(X,T)|G],var(X),T).
tc([(Y,_)|G],var(X),T)                 :- X # Y, tc(G,var(X),T).
tc(G,app(M,N),U)                       :- tc(G,M,funTy(T,U)), tc(G,N,T).
tc(G,lam(x\M,T),funTy(T,U))            :- x # G, tc([(x,T) |G],M,U).

pred step(exp,exp).
step(app(c(hd),app(app(c(cons),V),VS)),V) :- value(V), value(VS).
step(app(c(tl),app(app(c(cons),V),VS)),VS):- value(V), value(VS).
step(app(lam(x\M,T),V), subst(M,x,V))     :- value(V).
step(app(M1,M2),app(M1',M2))              :- step(M1,M1').
step(app(V1,M2),app(M1,M2'))              :- value(V1), step(M2,M2').

pred is_err(exp).
is_err(err).
is_err(app(c(hd),c(nil)))).
is_err(app(c(tl),c(nil)))).
is_err(app(E1,E2))                        :- is_err(E1).
is_err(app(V1,E2))                        :- value(V1), is_err(E2).
```

Fig. 1. Encoding of the example calculus in αProlog

We follow this up (see the remainder of Fig. 1) with the static semantics (predicate tc) and dynamic semantics (one-step reduction predicate step), where we omit the judgments for the value predicate and subst function, which are analogous to the ones in [9]. Note that *err* has any type and constants are typed *via* a table tcf, also omitted.

Horn clauses can also be used as specifications of desired program properties of such an encoding, including basic lemmas concerning substitution as well as main theorems such as preservation, progress, and type soundness. This is realized *via* checking *directives*

```
#check "spec" n : H1, ..., Hn => A.
```

where spec is a label naming the property, n is a parameter that bounds the search space, and H1 through Hn and A are atomic formulas describing the preconditions and conclusion of the property. As with program clauses, the specification formula is implicitly universally quantified. Following the PLT-Redex development, we concentrate here only on checking that preservation and progress hold.

```
#check "pres" 7 : tc([],E,T), step(E,E') => tc([],E',T).
#check "prog" 7 : tc([],E,T) => progress(E).
```

Here, `progress` is a predicate encoding the property of "being either a value, an error, or able to make a step". The tool will not find any counterexample, because, well, those properties are (hopefully) true of the given setup. Now, let us insert a typo that swaps the range and domain types of the function in the application rule, which now reads:

```
tc(G,app(M,N),U) :- tc(G,M,funTy(T,U)), tc(G,N,U). % was funTy(U,T)
```

Does any property become false? The checker returns immediately with this counterexample to progress:

```
E = app(c(hd),c(toInt(N)))
T = intTy
```

This is abstract syntax for *hd n*, an expression erroneously well-typed and obviously stuck. Preservation meets a similar fate: $(\lambda x{:}T \to int.\ x\ err)\ n$ steps to an ill-typed term.

```
E = app(lam(x\app(var(x),err),funTy(T,intTy)),c(toInt(N)))
E' = app(c(toInt(N)),err)
T = intTy
```

3   The Core Language

In this section we give the essential notions concerning the core syntax, to which the surface syntax used in the previous section desugars, and semantics of αProlog programs.

An αProlog *signature* is composed by sets Σ_D and Σ_N of, respectively, base types δ, which includes a type o of *propositions*, and name types ν; a collection Σ_P of *predicate symbols* $p : \tau \to o$ and one Σ_F of *function symbol* declarations $f : \tau \to \delta$. Types τ are formed as specified by the following grammar:

$$\tau ::= \delta \mid \tau \times \tau' \mid \mathbf{1} \mid \nu \mid \langle \nu \rangle \tau$$

where $\delta \in \Sigma_D$ and $\nu \in \Sigma_N$ and $\mathbf{1}$ is the unit type. Given a signature, the language of *terms* is defined over sets $V = \{X, Y, Z, \ldots\}$ of logical variables and sets $A = \{\mathsf{a}, \mathsf{b}, \ldots\}$ of names:

$$t, u ::= \mathsf{a} \mid \pi \cdot X \mid \langle \rangle \mid \langle t, u \rangle \mid \langle \mathsf{a} \rangle t \mid f(t)$$

$$\pi ::= \mathsf{id} \mid (\mathsf{a}\ \mathsf{b}) \circ \pi$$

where π are permutations, which we omit in case $\mathsf{id} \cdot X$, $\langle \rangle$ is unit, $\langle t, u \rangle$ is a pair and $\langle \mathsf{a} \rangle t$ is the abstract syntax for name-abstraction. The result of applying the permutation π (considered as a function) to a is written $\pi(\mathsf{a})$. Typing for these terms is standard, with the main novelty being that name-abstractions $\langle a \rangle t$ have abstraction types $\langle \nu \rangle \tau$ provided $a : \nu$ and $t : \tau$.

The *freshness* ($s \#_\tau u$) and *equality* ($t \approx_\tau u$) constraints, where s is a term of some name type ν, are the new features provided by nominal logic. The former relation is defined on ground terms by the following inference rules, where $f : \tau \to \delta \in \Sigma_F$:

$$\frac{a \neq b}{a \#_\nu b} \qquad \frac{}{a \#_1 \langle \rangle} \qquad \frac{a \#_\tau t}{a \#_\delta f(t)} \qquad \frac{a \#_{\tau_1} t_1 \quad a \#_{\tau_2} t_2}{a \#_{\tau_1 \times \tau_2} \langle t_1, t_2 \rangle} \qquad \frac{a \#_{\nu'} b \quad a \#_\tau t}{a \#_{\langle \nu' \rangle \tau} \langle b \rangle t} \qquad \frac{}{a \#_{\langle \nu' \rangle \tau} \langle a \rangle t}$$

In the same way we define the equality relation, which identifies terms modulo α-equivalence, where $(a \ b) \cdot u$ denotes *swapping* two names in a term:

$$\frac{}{a \approx_\nu a} \qquad \frac{}{\langle \rangle \approx_1 \langle \rangle} \qquad \frac{t_1 \approx_{\tau_1} u_1 \quad t_2 \approx_{\tau_2} u_2}{\langle t_1, t_2 \rangle \approx_{\tau_1 \times \tau_2} \langle u_1, u_2 \rangle} \qquad \frac{t \approx_\tau u}{f(t) \approx_\delta f(u)}$$

$$\frac{a \approx_\nu b \quad t \approx_\tau u}{\langle a \rangle t \approx_{\langle \nu \rangle \tau} \langle b \rangle u} \qquad \frac{a \#_\nu b \quad a \#_\nu u \quad t \approx_\tau (a \ b) \cdot u}{\langle a \rangle t \approx_{\langle \nu \rangle \tau} \langle b \rangle u}$$

Given a signature, *goals* G and *program clauses* D have the following form:

$$A ::= t \approx u \mid t \# u$$
$$G ::= \bot \mid \top \mid A \mid p(t) \mid G \wedge G' \mid G \vee G' \mid \exists X{:}\tau.\ G \mid \mathsf{N}a{:}\nu.\ G \mid \forall^* X{:}\tau.\ G$$
$$D ::= \top \mid p(t) \mid D \wedge D' \mid G \supset D \mid \forall X : \tau.\ D \mid \bot \mid D \vee D'$$

The productions shown in black yield a fragment of nominal logic called N-goal clauses [11], for which resolution based on nominal unification is sound and complete. This is in contrast to the general case where the more complicated *equivariant unification* problem must be solved [8]. We rely on the fact that D formulas in a program Δ can always be normalized to sets of clauses of the form $\forall \boldsymbol{X}{:}\boldsymbol{\tau}.\ G \supset p(t)$, denoted $\mathrm{def}(p, \Delta)$. The *fresh-name* quantifier N, firstly introduced in [32], quantifies over names not occurring in a formula (or in the values of its variables). The extensions shown in red here in the language BNF (and in its proof-theoretic semantics in Fig. 2) instead are constructs brought in from the negation elimination procedure (Sect. 4.1) and which will not appear in any source programs. In particular, an unusual feature is the *extensional* universal quantifier $\forall^*$ [15]. Differently from the *intensional* universal quantifier $\forall$, for which $\forall X{:}\tau.\ G$ holds if and only if $G[x/X]$ holds, where x is an eigenvariable representing any terms of type τ, $\forall^* X{:}\tau.\ G$ succeeds if and only if $G[t/X]$ does for *every* ground term of type τ.

Constraints are G-formulas of the following form:

$$C ::= \top \mid t \approx u \mid t \# u \mid C \wedge C' \mid \exists X{:}\tau.\ C \mid \mathsf{N}a{:}\nu.\ C$$

We write $\mathcal{K}$ for a set of constraints and Γ for a context keeping track of the types of variables and names. Constraint-solving is modeled by the judgment $\Gamma; \mathcal{K} \models C$, which holds if for all maps θ from variables in Γ to ground terms if $\theta \models \mathcal{K}$ then $\theta \models C$. The latter notion of satisfiability is standard, modulo handling of names: for example $\theta \models \mathsf{И}a{:}\nu.\ C$ iff for some b fresh for θ and C, $\theta \models C[\mathsf{b}/\mathsf{a}]$.

$$\frac{\Gamma;\mathcal{K} \models A}{\Gamma;\Delta;\mathcal{K} \Rightarrow A}\ con \qquad \frac{\Gamma;\Delta;\mathcal{K} \Rightarrow G_1 \quad \Gamma;\Delta;\mathcal{K} \Rightarrow G_2}{\Gamma;\Delta;\mathcal{K} \Rightarrow G_1 \wedge G_2}\ \wedge R$$

$$\frac{\Gamma;\Delta;\mathcal{K} \Rightarrow G_i}{\Gamma;\Delta;\mathcal{K} \Rightarrow G_1 \vee G_2}\ \vee R_i \qquad \frac{\Gamma;\mathcal{K} \models \exists X{:}\tau.\ C \quad \Gamma,X{:}\tau;\Delta;\mathcal{K},C \Rightarrow G}{\Gamma;\Delta;\mathcal{K} \Rightarrow \exists X{:}\tau.\ G}\ \exists R$$

$$\frac{\Gamma;\mathcal{K} \models \mathsf{И}a{:}\nu.\ C \quad \Gamma\#a{:}\nu;\Delta;\mathcal{K},C \Rightarrow G}{\Gamma;\Delta;\mathcal{K} \Rightarrow \mathsf{И}a{:}\nu.\ G}\ \mathsf{И}R$$

$$\frac{}{\Gamma;\Delta;\mathcal{K} \Rightarrow \top}\ \top R \qquad \frac{\Gamma;\Delta;\mathcal{K} \xrightarrow{D} Q \quad D \in \Delta}{\Gamma;\Delta;\mathcal{K} \Rightarrow Q}\ sel$$

$$\frac{\bigwedge\{\Gamma,X{:}\tau;\Delta;\mathcal{K},C \Rightarrow G \mid \Gamma;\mathcal{K} \models \exists X{:}\tau.\ C\}}{\Gamma;\Delta;\mathcal{K} \Rightarrow \forall^* X{:}\tau.\ G}\ \forall^*\omega$$

....

$$\frac{\Gamma;\mathcal{K} \models t \approx u}{\Gamma;\Delta;\mathcal{K} \xrightarrow{p(t)} p(u)}\ hyp \qquad \frac{\Gamma;\Delta;\mathcal{K} \xrightarrow{D_i} Q}{\Gamma;\Delta;\mathcal{K} \xrightarrow{D_1 \wedge D_2} Q}\ \wedge L_i$$

$$\frac{\Gamma;\Delta;\mathcal{K} \xrightarrow{D} Q \quad \Gamma;\Delta;\mathcal{K} \Rightarrow G}{\Gamma;\Delta;\mathcal{K} \xrightarrow{G \supset D} Q}\ \supset L$$

$$\frac{\Gamma;\mathcal{K} \models \exists X{:}\tau.\ C \quad \Gamma,X{:}\tau;\Delta;\mathcal{K},C \xrightarrow{D} Q}{\Gamma;\Delta;\mathcal{K} \xrightarrow{\forall X{:}\tau.\ D} Q}\ \forall L$$

$$\frac{}{\Gamma;\Delta;\mathcal{K} \xrightarrow{\perp} Q}\ \perp L \qquad \frac{\Gamma;\Delta;\mathcal{K} \xrightarrow{D_1} Q \quad \Gamma;\Delta;\mathcal{K} \xrightarrow{D_2} Q}{\Gamma;\Delta;\mathcal{K} \xrightarrow{D_1 \vee D_2} Q}\ \vee L$$

Fig. 2. Proof search semantics of αProlog programs

We can describe an idealized interpreter for αProlog with the "amalgamated" proof-theoretic semantics introduced in [11] and inspired by similar techniques stemming from CLP [20] — see Fig. 2, sporting two kind of judgments, goal-directed proof search $\Gamma;\Delta;\mathcal{K} \Rightarrow G$ and focused proof search $\Gamma;\Delta;\mathcal{K} \xrightarrow{D} Q$. This semantics allows us to concentrate on the high-level proof search issues, without requiring to introduce or manage low-level operational details concerning constraint solving. We refer the reader to [11] for more explanation and ways to make those judgments operational. Note that the rule $\forall^*\omega$ says that goals of the form $\forall^* X{:}\tau.G$ can be proved if $\Gamma,X{:}\tau;\Delta;\mathcal{K},C \Rightarrow G$ is provable for every constraint C such that $\Gamma;\mathcal{K} \models \exists X{:}\tau.\ C$ holds. Since this is hardly practical, the number of candidate constraints C being infinite, we approximate it by modifying the interpreter so as to perform a form of case analysis: at every stage, as dictated by the type of the quantified variable, we can either instantiate X by performing a one-layer type-driven case distinction and further recur to expose the next layer by introducing new $\forall^*$ quantifiers, or we can break the recursion by instantiation with an eigenvariable.

4   Specification Checking

Informally, #check specifications correspond to specification formulas of the form

$$\mathsf{И a}.\forall X.\ G \supset A \tag{1}$$

where G is a goal and A an atomic formula (including equality and freshness constraints). Since the И-quantifier is self-dual, the negation of (1) is of the form $\mathsf{И a}.\exists X.G \wedge \neg A$. A *(finite) counterexample* is a closed substitution θ providing values for X such that $\theta(G)$ is derivable, but the conclusion $\theta(A)$ is not. Since we live in a logic programming world, the choice of what we mean by "not holding" is crucial, as we must choose an appropriate notion of *negation*.

In αCheck the reference implementation reads negation as *finite failure* (*not*):

$$\mathsf{И a}.\exists X{:}\tau.\ G \wedge gen[\![\tau]\!](X) \wedge not(A) \tag{2}$$

where $gen[\![\tau]\!]$ are type-indexed predicates that *exhaustively* enumerate the inhabitants of τ. For example, $gen[\![ty]\!]$ yields the predicate:

```
gen_ty(intTy).          gen_ty(listTy).
gen_ty(funTy(T1,T2)) :- gen_ty(T1), gen_ty(T2).
```

A check such as (2) can simply be executed as a goal in the αProlog interpreter, using the number of resolution steps permitted to solve each subgoal as a bound on the search space. This method, combined with a complete search strategy such as iterative deepening, will find a counterexample, if one exists. This realization of specification checking is simple and effective, while not escaping the traditional problems associated with such an operational notion of negation.

4.1   Negation Elimination

Negation Elimination [3,26] is a source-to-source transformation that replaces negated subgoals with calls to a combination of equivalent positively defined predicates. In the absence of local (existential) variables, *NE* yields an ordinary (α)Prolog program, whose intended model is included in the complement of the model of the source program. In other terms, a predicate and its complement are mutually *exclusive*. *Exhaustivity*, that is whether a program and its complement coincide with the Herbrand base of the program's signature may or may not hold, depending on the decidability of the predicate in question; nevertheless, this property, though desirable, is neither frequent nor necessary in a model checking context. When local variables are present, the derived positivized program features the *extensional* universal quantifier presented in the previous section.

The generation of complementary predicates can be split into two phases: *term complementation* and *clause complementation.*

Term Complementation. A cause of atomic goal failure is when its arguments do not unify with any of the program clause heads in its definition. The idea is then to generate the complement of the term structure in each clause head by constructing a set of terms that differ in at least one position. However, and similarly to the higher-order logic case, the complement of a nominal term containing free or bound names cannot be represented by a *finite* set of nominal terms. For our application nonetheless, we can pre-process clauses so that the standard complementation algorithm for (linear) first order terms applies [19]. This forces terms in source clause heads to be linear and free of names (including swapping and abstractions), by replacing them with logical variables, and, in case they occurred in abstractions, by constraining them in the clause body by a *concretion* to a fresh variable. A concretion, written $t@a$, is the elimination form for abstractions and can be implemented by translating a goal G with an occurrence of $[t@a]$ (notation $G[t@a]$) to $\exists X.t \approx \langle a \rangle X \wedge G[X]$. For example, the clause for typing lambdas is normalized as:

```
tc(G,lam(M,T),funTy(T,U)):- new x. tc([(x,T) |G],M@x,U).
```

Hence, we can use a type-directed version of first-order term complementation, $not[\![\tau]\!] : \tau \to \tau$ *set* and prove its correctness in term of *exclusivity* following [3,27]: the intersection of the set of ground instances of a term and its complement is empty. *Exhaustivity* also holds, but will not be needed. The definition of $not[\![\tau]\!]$ is in the appendix [10], but we offer the following example:

$$not[\![\mathsf{exp}]\!](\mathsf{app}(\mathsf{c}(\mathsf{hd}),\_)) =$$
$$\{\mathsf{lam}(\_,\_), \mathsf{err}, \mathsf{c}(\_), \mathsf{var}(\_), \mathsf{app}(\mathsf{c}(\mathsf{tl}),\_), \mathsf{app}(\mathsf{c}(\mathsf{nil}),\_), \mathsf{app}(\mathsf{c}(\mathsf{toInt}(\_)),\_),$$
$$\mathsf{app}(\mathsf{var}(\_),\_), \mathsf{app}(\mathsf{err},\_), \mathsf{app}(\mathsf{lam}(\_,\_),\_), \mathsf{app}(\mathsf{app}(\_,\_),\_)\}$$

Clause Complementation. The idea of the clause complementation algorithm is to compute the complement of each head of a predicate definition using term complementation, while clause bodies are negated pushing negation inwards until atoms are reached and replaced by their complement and the negation of constraints is computed. The contributions (in fact a disjunction) of each of the original clauses are finally merged. The whole procedure can be seen as a negation normal form procedure, which is consistent with the operational semantics of the language.

The first ingredient is complementing the equality and freshness constraints, yielding (α-)inequality $neq[\![\tau]\!]$ and non-freshness $nfr[\![\nu, \delta]\!]$: we implement these

$$not^G(\top) = \bot$$
$$not^G(\bot) = \top$$
$$not^G(p(t)) = p^\neg(t)$$

$$not^D(\top) = \bot$$
$$not^D(\bot) = \top$$
$$not^D(G \supset p(t)) = \bigwedge\{\forall(p^\neg(u)) \mid u \in not[\![\tau]\!](t)\} \wedge (not^G(G) \supset p^\neg(t))$$

$$not^G(t \approx_\tau u) = neq[\![\tau]\!](t, u)$$
$$not^G(a \#_\tau u) = nfr[\![\nu, \tau]\!](a, u)$$
$$not^G(G \wedge G') = not^G(G) \vee not^G(G') \quad not^D(D \wedge D') = not^D(D) \vee not^D(D')$$
$$not^G(G \vee G') = not^G(G) \wedge not^G(G') \quad not^D(D \vee D') = not^D(D) \wedge not^D(D')$$
$$not^G(\forall^* X{:}\tau.\ G) = \exists X{:}\tau.\ not^G(G) \quad not^D(\forall X{:}\tau.\ D) = \forall X{:}\tau.\ not^D(D)$$
$$not^G(\exists X{:}\tau.\ G) = \forall^* X{:}\tau.\ not^G(G)$$
$$not^G(\mathsf{N}a{:}\nu.\ G) = \mathsf{N}a{:}\nu.\ not^G(G) \quad not^D(\Delta) = not^D(\mathrm{def}(p, \Delta))$$

Fig. 3. Negation of a goal and of clause

using type-directed code generation within the αProlog interpreter and refer again to the appendix [10] for their generic definition.

Figure 3 shows goal and clause complementation: most cases of the former, *via* the not^G function, are intuitive, being classical tautologies. Note that the self-duality of the N-quantifier allows goal negation to be applied recursively. Complementing existential goals is where we introduce *extensional* quantification and invoke its proof-theory.

Clause complementation is where things get interesting and differ from the previous algorithm [9]. The complement of a clause $G \supset p(t)$ must contain a "factual" part, built *via* term complementation, motivating failure due to clash with (some term in) the head. We obtain the rest by negating the body with $not^G(G)$. We take clause complementation *definition-wise*, that is the negation of a program is the conjunction of the negation of all its predicate definitions. An example may help: negating the typing clauses for constants and application (tc from Fig. 2) produces the following disjunction:

```
(not_tc(_,err,_) /\ not_tc(_,var(_),_) /\ not_tc(_,app(_,_),_) /\
  not_tc(_,lam(_,_),_):- neq(tcf(C), T))
 \/
(not_tc(_,err,_) /\ not_tc(_,var(_),_) /\ not_tc(_,c(_),_) /\
  not_tc(_,lam(_,_),_) /\
 not_tc(G,app(M,N),U):- forall* T. not_tc(G,M,funTy(T,U)) /\
 not_tc(G,app(M,N),U):- forall* T. not_tc(G,N,T))
```

Notwithstanding the top-level disjunction, we are *not* committing to any form of disjunctive logic programming: the key observation is that '$\vee$' can be restricted to a program constructor *inside* a predicate definition; therefore it can be eliminated by simulating unification in the definition:

$$(G_1 \supset Q_1) \vee (G_2 \supset Q_2) \equiv \theta(G_1 \wedge G_2 \supset Q_1)$$

where $\theta = \mathrm{mgu}(Q_1, Q_2)$. Because $\vee$ is commutative and associative we can perform this merging operation in any order. However, as with many bottom-up operations, merging tends to produce a lot of redundancies in terms of clauses that are instances of each other. We have implemented *backward* and *forward* subsumption [23], by using an extension of the αProlog interpreter itself to check entailment between newly generated clauses and the current database (and vice-versa). Despite the fact that this subsumption check is *partial*, because the current unification algorithm does not handle equivariant unification with mixed prefixes [25] and extensional quantification [8], it makes all the difference: the `not_is_err` predicate definition decreases from an unacceptable 128 clauses to a much more reasonable 18. The final definition of `not_tc` follows, where we (as in Prolog) use the semicolon as concrete syntax for disjunction in the body:

```
not_tc(_,c(C),T)             :- neq_ty(tcf(C),T).
not_tc([],var(_),_).
not_tc([(X,T)|G],var(X'),T') :- (neq_ty(T,T'); fresh_id(X,X')),
                                 not_tc(G,var(X'),T').
not_tc(G,app(M,N),U)         :- forall* T:ty. not_tc(G,M,funTy(T,U));
                                              not_tc(G,N,T).
not_tc(G,app(M,N),listTy)    :- forall* T:ty. not_tc(G,M,funTy(T,listTy));
                                              not_tc(G,N,T).
not_tc(G,app(M,N),intTy)     :- forall* T:ty. not_tc(G,M,funTy(T,intTy));
                                              not_tc(G,N,T).
not_tc(_,lam(_),listTy).
not_tc(_,lam(_),intTy).
not_tc(G,lam(M,T),funTy(T,U)):- new x:id. not_tc([(x,T)|G],M@x,U).
```

Regardless of the presence of two subsumed clauses in the `app` case that our approach failed to detect, it is a big improvement in comparison to the 38 clauses generated by the previous algorithm [9]. And in exhaustive search, every clause counts.

Having synthesized the negation of the `tc` predicate, αCheck will use it internally while searching, for instance in the preservation check, for

$$\exists E. \exists T.\ \mathsf{tc}([], E, T), \mathsf{step}(E, E'), \mathsf{not\_tc}([], E', T)$$

Soundness of clause complementation is crucial for the purpose of model checking; we again express it in terms of exclusivity. The proof follows the lines of [26].

Theorem 1 (Exclusivity). *Let $\mathcal{K}$ be consistent. It is not the case that:*

- $\Gamma; \Delta; \mathcal{K} \Rightarrow G$ *and* $\Gamma; not^D(\Delta); \mathcal{K} \Rightarrow not^G(G)$;
- $\Gamma; \Delta; \mathcal{K} \xrightarrow{D} Q$ *and* $\Gamma; not^D(\Delta); \mathcal{K} \xrightarrow{not^D(D)} not^G(Q)$.

5 Case Studies

We have chosen as case studies here the *Stlc* benchmark suite, introduced in Sect. 2, and an encoding of the Volpano et al. security type system [34], as suggested in [5]. For the sake of space, we report *at the same time* our comparison between the various forms of negation, in particular *NEs* vs. *NE, and* the other systems of reference, accordingly, PLT-Redex and Nitpick.

PLT-Redex [13] is an executable DSL for mechanizing semantic models built on top of *DrRacket*. Redex has been the first environment to adopt the idea of random testing a la QuickCheck for validating the meta-theory of object languages, with significant success [18]. As we have mentioned, the main drawbacks are the lack of support for binders and low coverage of test generators stemming from grammar definitions. The user is therefore required to write her own generators, a task which tends to be demanding.

The system where proofs and disproofs are best integrated is arguably Isabelle/HOL [4]. In the appendix [10] we report some comparison with its version of QuickCheck, but here we concentrate on *Nitpick* [5], a higher-order model finder in the *Alloy* lineage supporting (co)inductive definitions. Nitpick works translating a significant fragment of HOL into first-order relational logic and then invoking Alloy's SAT-based model enumerator. The tool has been used effectively in several case studies, most notably weak memory models for C++ [6]. It would be natural to couple Isabelle/HOL's QuickCheck and/or Nitpick's capabilities with *Nominal* Isabelle [33], but this would require strengthening the latter's support for computation with names, permutations and abstract syntax modulo α-conversion. So, at the time of writing, αCheck is unique as a model checker for binding signatures and specifications.

All test have been performed under Ubuntu 15.4 on a Intel Core i7 CPU 870, 2.93 GHz with 8 GB RAM. We time-out the computation when it exceeds 200 seconds. We report 0 when the time is <0.01. These tests must be taken with a lot of salt: not only is our tool under active development but the comparison with the other systems is only roughly indicative, having to factor differences between logic and functional programming (PLT-Redex), as well as the sheer scale and scope of counter-examples search in a system such as Isabelle/HOL.

5.1   Head-to-Head with PLT-Redex

We first measure the amount of *time to exhaust the search space* (TESS) using the three versions of negations supported in αCheck, over a bug-free version of the *Stlc* benchmark for $n = 1, 2, \ldots$ up to the point where we time-out. This gives some indication of how much of the search space the three techniques explore, keeping in mind that what is traversed is very different in shape; hence the more reliable comparison is between *NE* and *NEs*. As the results depicted in Fig. 4 suggests,

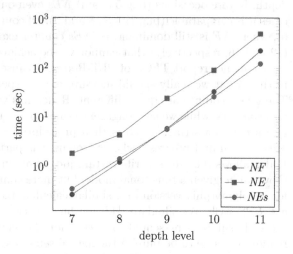

Fig. 4. Loglinear-plot of TESS on prog theorem

Table 1. TFCE on the *stlc* benchmark, Redex-style encoding

bug	check	NF	NE	NEs	cex	Description/Class
1	pres	0.3 (7)	1 (7)	0.37 (7)	$(\lambda x.xerr)n$	range of function in app rule
	prog	0 (5)	3.31 (9)	0.27 (5)	$hd\ n$	matched to the arg. (S)
2	prog	0.27 (8)	t.o. (11)	85.3 (12)	*(cons n) nil*	value *(cons v)* v omitted (M)
3	pres	0.04 (6)	0.04 (6)	0.3 (6)	$(\lambda x.n)m$	order of types swapped in func-
	prog	0 (5)	3.71 (9)	0.27 (8)	$hd\ n$	tion pos of app (S)
4	prog	t.o	t.o	t.o	?	The type of cons is incorrect (S)
5	pres	t.o. (9)	t.o. (10)	41.5 (10)	$tl\ ((cons\ n)\ err)$	tail red. returns the head (S)
6	prog	29.8 (11)	t.o. (11)	t.o. (12)	$hd\ ((cons\ n)\ nil)$	hd red. on part. appl. cons (M)
7	prog	1.04 (9)	18.5 (10)	1.1 (9)	$hd((\lambda x.err)n)$	no eval for argument of app (M)
8	pres	0.02 (5)	0.03 (5)	0.1 (5)	$(\lambda x.x)nil$	lookup always returns int (U)
9	pres	0 (5)	0.02 (5)	0.1 (5)	$(\lambda x.y)n$	vars do not match in lookup (S)

NEs shows a clear improvement over *NE*, while *NF* holds its ground, however hindered by the explosive exhaustive generation of terms.

However, our mission is finding counterexamples and so we compare the *time to find counterexamples* (TFCE) using *NF*, *NE*, *NEs* on the said benchmarks. We list in Table 1 the 9 mutations from the cited site. Every row describes the mutation inserted with an informal classification inherited from ibidem—(S)imple, (M)edium or (U)nusual, better read as artificial. We also list the counterexamples found by αCheck under *NF* (NE(s) being analogous but less instantiated) and the depths at which those are found or a time-out occurred.

The results in Table 1 show a remarkable improvement of *NEs* over *NE*, in terms of counter-examples that were timed-out (bug 2 and 5), as well as major speedups of more than an order of magnitude (bugs 3 (ii) and 7). Further, *NEs* never under-performs *NE*, probably because it locates counterexample at a lower depth. In rare occasions (bug 5 again) *NEs* even outperforms *NF* and in several cases it is comparable (bug 1, 3, 7, 8 and 9). Of course there are occasions (2 and 6), where *NF* is still dominant, as *NEs* counter-examples live at steeper depths (12 and 16, respectively) that cannot yet be achieved within the time-out.

We do not report TFCE of PLT-Redex, because, being based on randomized testing, what we really should measure is time spent *on average* to find a bug. The two encodings are quite different: Redex has very good support for evaluation contexts, while we use congruence rules. Being untyped, the Redex encoding treats *err* as a string, which is then procedurally handled in the statement of preservation and progress, whereas for us it is part of the language. Since [18], Redex allows the user to write certain judgments in a declarative style, provided they can be given a functional mode, but more complex systems, such as typing for a polymorphic version of a similar calculus, require very indirect encoding, e.g. CPS-style. We simulate addition on integers with numerals (omitted from the code snippets presented in Sect. 2 for the sake of space), as we currently require our code to be pure in the logical sense, as opposed to Redex that maps integers to Racket's ones. *W.r.t.* lines of code, the size of our encoding is roughly

1/4 of the Redex version, not counting Redex's built-in generators and substitution function. The adopted checking philosophy is also somewhat different: they choose to test preservation and progress together, using a cascade of three built-in generators and collect all the counterexamples found within a timeout.

The performance of the negation elimination variants in this benchmark is not too impressive. However, if we adopt a different style of encoding (let's call it PCF, akin to what we used in [9]), where constructors such as hd are *not* treated as constants, but are first class, e.g.:

```
tc(G,hd(E),intTy)        :- tc(G,E,listTy).
step(hd(cons(H,Tl)), H) :- value(H),value(Tl).
```

then all counter-examples are found very quickly, as reported in Table 2. In bug 4, *NEs* struggles to get at depth 13: on the other hand PLT-Redex fails to find that very bug. Bug 6 as well as several counterexamples disappear as not well-typed. This improved efficiency may be due to the reduced amount of nesting of terms, which means lower depth of exhaustive exploration. This is not a concern for random generation and (compiled) functional execution as in PLT-Redex.

Table 2. TFCE on the *Stlc* benchmark, PCF-style encoding. *NEs* cex shown

bug#	check	NF	NE	NEs	cex
1	pres	0.05 (5)	2.79 (5)	0.04 (5)	$(\lambda x.hdx)N$
2	prog	0 (4)	7.76 (9)	0.8 (7)	*(cons N) nil*
3	pres	0 (4)	0.05 (4)	0 (4)	$(\lambda x.nil)nil$
4	prog	0.15 (7)	t.o. (10)	199.1 (12)	*N + (cons N nil)*
5	pres	0(4)	0.04 (4)	0(4)	*tl (cons N) nil*
7	prog	5.82 (9)	151.2 (11)	19.54. (10)	$(\lambda x.nil)(N+M)$
8	pres	0.01 (4)	0.04 (4)	0.1 (4)	$(\lambda x.x)nil$
9	pres	0 (4)	0.04 (4)	0.1 (4)	$(\lambda x.y)\ N$

5.2 Nitpicking Security Type Systems

To compare Nitpick with our approach, we use the security type system due to Volpano, Irvine and Smith [34], whereby the basic imperative language *IMP* is endowed with a type system that prevents information flow from private to public variables[2]. For our test, we actually selected the more general version of the type system formalized in [28], where the security levels are generalized from *high* and *low* to natural numbers. Given a fixed assignment *sec* of such security levels to variables, then lifted to arithmetic and Boolean expressions, the typing judgment $l \vdash c$ reads as "command c does not contain any information flow to

---

[2] For an interesting case study regarding instead *dynamic* information flow and carried out in Haskell, see [17]. A large part of the paper is dedicated to the fine tuning of custom generators and shrinkers.

variables $< l$ and only safe flows to variables $\geq l$." Following [28], we call this system *syntax-directed*.

The main properties of interest relate states that agree on the value of each variable (strictly) *below* a certain security level, denoted as $\sigma_1 \approx_{<l} \sigma_2$ iff $\forall x.\ sec\ x < l \rightarrow \sigma_1(x) = \sigma_2(x)$. Assume a standard big-step evaluation semantics for IMP, relating an initial state σ and a command c to a final state τ:

Confinement If $\langle c, \sigma \rangle \downarrow \tau$ and $l \vdash c$ then $\sigma \approx_{<l} \tau$;
Non-interference If $\langle c, \sigma \rangle \downarrow \sigma'$, $\langle c, \tau \rangle \downarrow \tau'$, $\sigma \approx_{\leq l} \tau$ and $0 \vdash c$ then $\sigma' \approx_{\leq l} \tau'$;

We extend this exercise by considering also a *declarative* version (std) $l \vdash_d c$ of the syntax directed system, where anti-monotonicity is taken as a primitive rule instead of an admissible one as in the previous system; finally we encode also a syntax-directed *termination-sensitive* (stT) version $l \vdash_{\Downarrow} c$, where non-terminating programs do not leak information and its declarative cousin $(stTd)$ $l \vdash_{\Downarrow d} c$. We then insert some mutations in all those systems, as detailed in Table 3 and investigate whether the following equivalences among those systems still hold:

st↔std $l \vdash c$ iff $l \vdash_d c$ and **stT↔stTd** $l \vdash_{\Downarrow} c$ iff $l \vdash_{\Downarrow d} c$.

Again the experimental evidence is quite pleasing as far as *NE* vs. *NEs* goes, where the latter is largely superior (5 (ii), 1 (i), 7 (ii)). In one case *NEs* improves on *NF* (1 (ii)) and in general competes with it save for 4 (ii) and 5 (i) and (ii). To have an idea of the counterexamples found by αCheck, the command $(\texttt{SKIP}; \texttt{x}:=1), sec\ \texttt{x} = 0, \texttt{l} = 1$ and state σ mapping x to 0 falsifies confinement 1 (i); in fact, this would not hold were the typing rule to check the second premise. A not too dissimilar counterexample falsifies non-interference 1 (ii): c is $(\texttt{SKIP}; \texttt{x}:=\texttt{y}), sec\ \texttt{x}, \texttt{y} = 0, 1, \texttt{l} = 0$ and σ maps y to 0 and x undefined

Table 3. αCheck vs. Nitpick on the Volpano benchmark suite. (sp) indicates that Nitpick produced a spurious counterexample.

bug	check	Nitpick	NF	NE	NEs	Description
1	conf	(sp)	0.03 (5)	4.4 (8)	2.1 (7)	second premise of seq rule omitted
	non-inter	t.o.	9.13 (8)	6.71 (8)	6.1 (8)	ditto
2	non-inter	(sp)	3.3 (8)	2.1 (8)	1.9 (8)	var swap in $\leq$ premise of assn rule
3	st→std	0.95	t.o	t.o	t.o	inversion of $\leq$ in antimono rule ditto
	std→st	0.75	0.8 (7)	0.3 (7)	0.3 (7)	
4	st→std					$\leq$ assumption omitted in IF: **true**
	std→st	1.3	0.9 (7)	t.o.	t.o	ditto
5	st→std	5.1(sp)	24.5 (11)	t.o	t.o	as 2 but on decl. version of the rule
	std→st	1.1	0.2 (7)	t.o.	24.6 (11)	ditto
6	stT→stTd	5.1(sp)	t.o	t.o	t.o	as 2 but on term. version of the rule
	stTd→stT	1.0	0.01 (5)	0.32 (7)	0.05 (6)	ditto
7	stT→stTd					as 4 but on term-decl. rule: **true**
	stTd→stT	1.6	1.7 (8)	12.5 (9)	1.2(8)	ditto

(i.e. to a logic variable), while τ maps y to 1 and keeps x undefined. We note in passing that here extensional quantification is indispensable, since ordinary generic quantification is unable to instantiate security levels so as to find the relevant bugs.

The comparison with Nitpick[3] is more mixed. On one hand Nitpick fails to find 1 (ii) within the timeout and in other four cases it reports *spurious* counterexamples, which on manual analysis turn out to be good. On the other it nails down, quite quickly, two other cases where αCheck fails to converge at all (3 (i), 6 (i)). This despite the facts that relations such as evaluations, $\vdash_d$ and $\vdash_{\Downarrow d}$, are reported not well founded requiring therefore a problematic unrolling.

The crux of the matter is that differently from Isabelle/HOL's mostly functional setting (except for inductive definition of evaluation and typing), our encoding is fully relational: states and security assignments cannot be seen as partial functions but are reified in association lists. Moreover, we pay a significant price in not being able to rely on built-in types such as integers, but have to deploy our clearly inefficient versions. This means that to falsify simple computations such as $n \leq m$, we need to provide a derivation for that failure. Finally, this case study does not do justice to the realm where αProlog excels, namely it does not exercise binders intensely: we are only using nominal techniques in representing program variables as names and freshness to guarantee well-formedness of states and of the table encoding the variable security settings. Yet, we could not select more binding intensive examples due to the current difficulties with running Nitpick under *Nominal* Isabelle.

6   Conclusions and Future Work

We have presented a new implementation of the *NE* algorithm underlying our model checker αCheck and experimental evidence showing satisfying improvements *w.r.t.* the previous incarnation, so as to make it competitive with the *NF* reference implementation. The comparison with PLT-Redex and Nitpick, systems of considerable additional maturity, is also, in our opinion, favourable: αCheck is able to find similar counterexamples in comparable amounts of time; it is able to find some counterexamples that Redex or Nitpick respectively do not; and in no case does it report spurious counterexamples. Having said that, our comparison is at most just suggestive and certainly partial, as many other proof assistants have incorporated some notion of PBT, e.g. [29,31]. A notable absence here is a comparison with what at first sight is a close relative, the Bedwyr system [2], a logic programming engine that allows a form of model checking directly on syntactic expressions possibly containing binding. Since Bedwyr uses depth-first search, checking properties for infinite domains should be approximated by writing logic programs encoding generators for a finite portion of that model. Our initial experiments in encoding the *Stlc* benchmark in Bedwyr have failed to find any counterexample, but this could be imputed simply to

---

[3] Settings: `[sat_solver=MiniSat_JNI,max_threads=1,timeout=200]`.

our lack of experience with the system. Recent work about "augmented focusing systems" [16] could overcome this problem.

All the mutations we have inserted so far have injected faults in the specifications, not in the checks. This make sense for our intended use; however, it would be interesting to see how our tool would fare *w.r.t.* mutation testing of *theorems*.

Exhaustive term generation has served us well so far, but it is natural to ask whether *random* generation could have a role in αCheck, either by simply randomizing term generation under *NF* or more generally the logic programming interpreter itself, in the vein of [14]. More practically, providing generators and reflection mechanism for built-in datatypes and associated operators is a priority.

Finally, we would like to implement improvements in nominal equational unification algorithms, which would make subsumption complete, *via equivariant* unification [8], and more ambitiously introduce *narrowing*, so that functions could be computed rather then simulated relationally. In the long run, this could open the door to use αCheck as a light-weight model checker for (a fragment) of Nominal Isabelle.

References

1. Aspinall, D., Beringer, L., Momigliano, A.: Optimisation validation. Electron. Notes Theor. Comput. Sci. **176**(3), 37–59 (2007)
2. Baelde, D., Gacek, A., Miller, D., Nadathur, G., Tiu, A.F.: The Bedwyr system for model checking over syntactic expressions. In: Pfenning, F. (ed.) CADE 2007. LNCS (LNAI), vol. 4603, pp. 391–397. Springer, Heidelberg (2007)
3. Barbuti, R., Mancarella, P., Pedreschi, D., Turini, F.: A transformational approach to negation in logic programming. J. Log. Program. **8**, 201–228 (1990)
4. Blanchette, J.C., Bulwahn, L., Nipkow, T.: Automatic proof and disproof in Isabelle/HOL. In: Tinelli, C., Sofronie-Stokkermans, V. (eds.) FroCoS 2011. LNCS, vol. 6989, pp. 12–27. Springer, Heidelberg (2011)
5. Blanchette, J.C., Nipkow, T.: Nitpick: a counterexample generator for higher-order logic based on a relational model finder. In: Kaufmann, M., Paulson, L.C. (eds.) ITP 2010. LNCS, vol. 6172, pp. 131–146. Springer, Heidelberg (2010)
6. Blanchette, J.C., Weber, T., Batty, M., Owens, S., Sarkar, S.: Nitpicking C++ concurrency. In: Schneider-Kamp, P., Hanus, M. (eds.) Proceedings of the 13th International ACM SIGPLAN Conference on Principles and Practice of Declarative Programming, pp. 113–124. ACM (2011)
7. Breitner, J.: Formally proving a compiler transformation safe. In: Proceedings of the 2015 ACM SIGPLAN Symposium on Haskell, Haskell 2015, pp. 35–46. ACM, New York (2015)
8. Cheney, J.: Equivariant unification. J. Autom. Reasoning **45**(3), 267–300 (2010)
9. Cheney, J., Momigliano, A.: Mechanized metatheory model-checking. In: Leuschel, M., Podelski, A. (eds.) PPDP, pp. 75–86. ACM (2007)
10. Cheney, J., Momigliano, A., Pessina, M.: Appendix to Advances in property-based testing for αProlog (2016). http://momigliano.di.unimi.it/alphaCheck.html
11. Cheney, J., Urban, C.: Nominal logic programming. ACM Trans. Program. Lang. Syst. **30**(5), 26 (2008)

12. Claessen, K., Hughes, J.: QuickCheck: a lightweight tool for random testing of Haskell programs. In: Proceedings of the 2000 ACM SIGPLAN International Conference on Functional Programming (ICFP 2000), pp. 268–279. ACM (2000)

13. Felleisen, M., Findler, R.B., Flatt, M.: Semantics Engineering with PLT Redex. The MIT Press, Massachusetts (2009)

14. Fetscher, B., Claessen, K., Pałka, M., Hughes, J., Findler, R.B.: Making random judgments: automatically generating well-typed terms from the definition of a type-system. In: Vitek, J. (ed.) ESOP 2015. LNCS, vol. 9032, pp. 383–405. Springer, Heidelberg (2015)

15. Harland, J.: Success and failure for hereditary Harrop formulae. J. Log. Program. **17**(1), 1–29 (1993)

16. Heath, Q., Miller, D.: A framework for proof certificates in finite state exploration. In: Kaliszyk, C., Paskevich, A. (eds.) Proceedings Fourth Workshop on Proof eXchange for Theorem Proving, PxTP 2015, Berlin, Germany, 2–3 Aug 2015, vol. 186. EPTCS, pp. 11–26 (2015)

17. Hritcu, C., Hughes, J., Pierce, B.C., Spector-Zabusky, A., Vytiniotis, D., Azevedo de Amorim, A., Lampropoulos, L.: Testing noninterference, quickly. In: Proceedings of the 18th ACM SIGPLAN International Conference on Functional Programming, ICFP 2013, pp. 455–468. ACM, New York (2013)

18. Klein, C., Clements, J., Dimoulas, C., Eastlund, C., Felleisen, M., Flatt, M., McCarthy, J.A., Rafkind, J., Tobin-Hochstadt, S., Findler, R.B.: Run your research: on the effectiveness of lightweight mechanization. In: Proceedings of the 39th Annual ACM SIGPLAN-SIGACT Symposium on Principles of Programming Languages, POPL 2012, pp. 285–296. ACM, New York (2012)

19. Lassez, J.-L., Marriott, K.: Explicit representation of terms defined by counter examples. J. Autom. Reasoning **3**(3), 301–318 (1987)

20. Leach, J., Nieva, S., Rodríguez-Artalejo, M.: Constraint logic programming with hereditary Harrop formulas. TPLP **1**(4), 409–445 (2001)

21. Leroy, X.: Formal verification of a realistic compiler. CACM **52**(7), 107–115 (2009)

22. Leroy, X., Grall, H.: Coinductive big-step operational semantics. Inf. Comput. **207**(2), 284–304 (2009)

23. Loveland, W.D., Nadathur, G.: Proof procedures for logic programming. Technical report, Durham, NC, USA (1994)

24. McKeeman, W.M.: Differential testing for software. Digit. Tech. J. **10**(1), 100–107 (1998)

25. Miller, D.: Unification under a mixed prefix. J. Symb. Comput. **14**(4), 321–358 (1992)

26. Momigliano, A.: Elimination of negation in a logical framework. In: Clote, P.G., Schwichtenberg, H. (eds.) CSL 2000. LNCS, vol. 1862, p. 411. Springer, Heidelberg (2000)

27. Momigliano, A., Pfenning, F.: Higher-order pattern complement and the strict lambda-calculus. ACM Trans. Comput. Log. **4**(4), 493–529 (2003)

28. Nipkow, T., Klein, G.: Concrete Semantics-with Isabelle/HOL. Springer, Heidelberg (2014)

29. Owre, S.: Random testing in PVS. In: Workshop on Automated Formal Methods (AFM) (2006)

30. Palka, M.H., Claessen, K., Russo, A., Hughes, J.: Testing an optimising compiler by generating random lambda terms. In: AST 2011, pp. 91–97. ACM (2011)

31. Paraskevopoulou, Z., Hritcu, C., Dénès, M., Lampropoulos, L., Pierce, B.C.: Foundational property-based testing. In: Urban, C., Zhang, X. (eds.) Interactive Theorem Proving. LNCS, vol. 9236, pp. 325–343. Springer, Heidelberg (2015)

32. Pitts, A.M.: Nominal logic, a first order theory of names and binding. Inf. Comput. **183**, 165–193 (2003)
33. Urban, C., Kaliszyk, C.: General bindings and alpha-equivalence in nominal Isabelle. Log. Methods Comput. Sci. **8**(2), 1–35 (2012)
34. Volpano, D., Irvine, C., Smith, G.: A sound type system for secure flow analysis. J. Comput. Secur. **4**(2–3), 167–187 (1996)
35. Ševčík, J., Vafeiadis, V., Zappa Nardelli, F., Jagannathan, S., Sewell, P.: CompCertTSO: a verified compiler for relaxed-memory concurrency. J. ACM **60**(3), 22:1–22:50 (2013)
36. Yang, X., Chen, Y., Eide, E., Regehr, J.: Finding and understanding bugs in c compilers. In: PLDI 2011, pp. 283–294. ACM, New York (2011)

Tests and Proofs for Enumerative Combinatorics

Catherine Dubois[1], Alain Giorgetti[2(✉)], and Richard Genestier[2]

[1] Samovar (UMR CNRS 5157), ENSIIE, Évry, France
catherine.dubois@ensiie.fr
[2] FEMTO-ST Institute (UMR CNRS 6174 - UBFC/UFC/ENSMM/UTBM),
University of Franche-Comté, Besançon, France
{alain.giorgetti,richard.genestier}@femto-st.fr

Abstract. In this paper we show how the research domain of enumerative combinatorics can benefit from testing and formal verification. We formalize in Coq the combinatorial structures of permutations and maps, and a couple of related operations. Before formally proving soundness theorems about these operations, we first validate them, by using logic programming (Prolog) for bounded exhaustive testing and Coq/QuickChick for random testing. It is an experimental study preparing a more ambitious project about formalization of combinatorial results assisted by verification tools.

1 Introduction

Enumerative combinatorics is the branch of mathematics studying discrete structures of finite cardinality when some of their parameters are fixed. One of its objectives is counting, i.e. determining these cardinalities. This research domain also studies non-trivial structural bijections between two families of structures and algorithms for exhaustive generation up to some size. In this paper we show how the research domain of enumerative combinatorics can benefit from testing and formal verification. In enumerative combinatorics we target combinatorial maps, defined as a pair of permutations acting transitively on a set. In software engineering we focus on automated testing and interactive deductive verification with the Coq proof assistant [2].

We formalize in Coq the notions of permutation and combinatorial map, two operations on permutations, and two operations on combinatorial maps. Technically we first define these operations on functions. Then we formally prove that they can be restricted to permutations, and finally to maps for the last two. In other words we prove that they respectively preserve permutations and the map structure.

Unless the proof is trivial, it is common to test lemmas and theorems before proving. Main validation methods are random(ized) testing, bounded exhaustive testing (BET) [5] and finite model finding [3]. In the following we deal with random testing and BET. BET checks a formula for all its possible inputs up to a given small size. It is often sufficient to detect many errors, while providing counterexamples of minimal size. A challenge for BET is to design and implement

© Springer International Publishing Switzerland 2016
B.K. Aichernig and C.A. Furia (Eds.): TAP 2016, LNCS 9762, pp. 57–75, 2016.
DOI: 10.1007/978-3-319-41135-4_4

efficient algorithms to generate the data. We address it in a lightweight way by exploiting the features of logic programming implemented in a Prolog system. Prolog is well suited for algorithm prototyping due to its closeness to first-order logic specifications. Thanks to backtracking, characteristic predicates written in Prolog can often be used for free as bounded exhaustive generators.

We present a successful application of random and bounded exhaustive testing to debug Coq specifications of combinatorial structures. Our original approach of both case studies (permutations and maps) also is a contribution in formalization of mathematics. In comparison with other approaches [8,10,16], our formalization is very close to the mathematical definition of a map, as a transitive pair of permutations. Our work is freely available at http://members. femto-st.fr/alain-giorgetti/en/coq-unit-testing. It has been developed with Coq 8.4 and SWI-Prolog 5.10.4 [28].

The paper is organized as follows. Section 2 presents the testing methodology on the simple example of permutations. Section 3 introduces the notion of rooted map, its formalization in Coq, correctness theorems, and random and bounded exhaustive testing performed before trying to prove them. Section 4 describes related work and Sect. 5 concludes.

2 Testing Coq Conjectures

This section presents our methodology for testing Coq specifications. Before investing time in proving false lemmas we want to check their validity. Property-based testing (PBT) is popular for functional languages, as exemplified by Quick-Check [7] in Haskell. QuickCheck like approach has also been adopted by proof assistants, e.g. Isabelle [1], Agda [12], PVS [22], FoCaLiZe [6] and more recently Coq [23]. We consider here two kinds of PBT: random testing (in Sect. 2.2) and bounded exhaustive testing (in Sect. 2.3). They are illustrated by the running example of permutations on a finite set presented in Sect. 2.1.

2.1 Permutations in Coq

Permutations on a finite set form an elementary but central combinatorial family. In particular, permutations are the core of the definition of combinatorial maps. It is well known that any injective endofunction on a finite domain is a permutation. However, as far as we know, no popular Coq library defines permutations as injective endofunctions supporting the two operations of insertion and direct sum that we introduce here for their interest in the formal study of rooted maps in Sect. 3. In the following the reader is required to have some basic knowledge about Coq.

Listing 1.1 shows our Coq formalization of permutations. A permutation is defined as an injective function from an interval of natural numbers (whose lower bound is 0) to itself. In Coq the inductive type nat of Peano natural numbers is predefined, with the constructors 0 for zero and S for the successor function. We manipulate functions defined on nat (later called *natural functions*) but we only impose constraints for the elements in the interval, whatever the definition outside the interval. The predicates is_endo and is_inj respectively define the properties of being an endofunction and injectivity. Then a permutation is a *record* structure composed of a natural function and the proofs that the latter satisfies the two previous properties. For convenience we also consider their conjunction is_permut.

```
Definition is_endo (n : nat) (f : nat → nat) := ∀ x, x < n → f x < n.
Definition is_inj (n : nat) (f : nat → nat) := ∀ x y,
  x < n → y < n → x ◇ y → f x ◇ f y.
Record permut (n : nat) : Set := MkPermut {
  fct : nat → nat;
  endo : is_endo n fct;
  inj : is_inj n fct }.
Definition is_permut n f := is_endo n f ∧ is_inj n f.
```

Listing 1.1. Permutations as injective endofunctions in Coq.

We can define a more concrete encoding of permutations: a permutation p on $\{0, \ldots, n-1\}$ may also be represented by the list $[p(0); p(1); \ldots; p(n-1)]$ of its images, called its *one-line notation* in combinatorics. For instance the list $[1; 0; 3; 2; 6; 4; 5]$ represents the permutation $p = \begin{pmatrix} 0\ 1\ 2\ 3\ 4\ 5\ 6 \\ 1\ 0\ 3\ 2\ 6\ 4\ 5 \end{pmatrix}$. We'll generate permutations as lists and go from this representation to the functional one with the help of the function list2fun defined by

```
Definition list2fun (l:list nat) : nat → nat := fun (n:nat) ⇒ nth n l n.
```

The function nth in Coq standard library is such that (nth n l d) returns the n-th element of l if it exists, and d otherwise.

Let f be a function defined on $\{0, \ldots, n-1\}$ and i a natural number. The *insertion before i in f* is the function f' defined on $\{0, \ldots, n\}$ as follows: (a) it is f if $i > n$; (b) it is f extended with the fixed-point $f(n) = n$ if $i = n$; (c) if $i < n$ then $f'(n) = i$, $f'(j) = n$ if $f(j) = i$, and $f'(j) = f(j)$ if $0 \le j \le n-1$ and $f(j) \ne i$. The operation of insertion in a natural function is defined in Coq by

```
Definition insert_fun n (f : nat → nat) (i : nat) : nat → nat :=
fun x ⇒ if le_lt_dec i n then
        match nat_compare x n with
          Eq ⇒ i
        | Lt ⇒ if eq_nat_dec (f x) i then n else f x
        | Gt ⇒ x
        end
      else x.
```

The *direct sum* of a function f_1 defined on $\{0, \ldots, n_1 - 1\}$ and a function f_2 defined on $\{0, \ldots, n_2 - 1\}$ is the function f on $\{0, \ldots, n_1 + n_2 - 1\}$ such that $f(x) = f_1(x)$ if $0 \le x < n_1$ and $f(x) = f_2(x - n_1) + n_1$ if $n_1 \le x < n_1 + n_2$. It is an extension of the well-known *direct sum* on permutations [18, p. 57]. The direct sum is defined in Coq on natural functions by

```
Definition sum_fun n1 f1 n2 f2 : nat → nat := fun x ⇒
if lt_ge_dec x n1 then f1 x else
if lt_ge_dec x (n1+n2) then (f2 (x−n1)) + n1 else x.
```

Listing 1.2 states that both operations preserve permutations. To validate these lemmas, we define Boolean versions is_endob, is_injb and is_permutb of the logical properties is_endo, is_inj and is_permut. Listing 1.3 shows the functions is_endob and is_permutb. An evaluation of (is_endob n f) returns true iff the function f is an endofunction on $\{0, \ldots, n-1\}$. The lemma is_endo_dec states that the Boolean function is_endob is a correct implementation of the predicate is_endo. Similar lemmas are proved for the other two Boolean functions. If the correlation between is_endo and is_endob is quite immediate, it is not the case for is_inj and is_injb. To define is_injb, we rely on another lemma we have proved: a function f is injective on $\{0, 1, \ldots, n\}$ iff the list $[f(0); f(1); \ldots; f(n)]$ of its images has no duplicate.

```
Lemma insert_permut: ∀ (n : nat) (p : permut n) (i : nat),
  is_permut (S n) (insert_fun n (fct p) i).
Lemma sum_permut: ∀ n1 (p1 : permut n1) n2 (p2 : permut n2),
  is_permut (n1 + n2) (sum_fun n1 (fct p1) n2 (fct p2)).
```

Listing 1.2. Preservation properties of the insertion and sum operations.

```
Fixpoint is_endob_aux n f m := match m with
   0 ⇒ if (lt_dec (f 0) n) then true else false
 | S p ⇒ if (lt_dec (f m) n) then is_endob_aux n f p else false
end.
Definition is_endob n f := match n with
   0 ⇒ true
 | S p ⇒ is_endob_aux n f p
end.
Lemma is_endo_dec : ∀ n f, (is_endob n f = true ↔ is_endo n f).
Definition is_permutb n f := (is_endob n f) && (is_injb n f).
```

Listing 1.3. Boolean functions for permutations.

2.2 Random Testing

QuickChick [17] is a random testing plugin for Coq. It allows us to check the validity of executable conjectures with random inputs. QuickChick is mainly a generic framework providing combinators to write testing code, in particular random generators. The general workflow that we follow to validate by testing a conjecture like ∀ x: T, precondition x → conclusion (f x), where precondition and conclusion are logical predicates, starts with the definition of a random generator gen_T of values of type T that satisfy the property precondition. Then we have to turn conclusion into a Boolean function conclusionb – if it is possible, otherwise QuickChick does not apply – that we prove semantically equivalent to the logical predicate. The test is run by using the following command which generates a fixed number of inputs using the generator gen_T and for each one applies the function f and verifies the property under test (conclusion):

QuickCheck (forAll gen_T (fun x ⇒ conclusionb (f x)).

In this approach we rely on the generator which is here part of the trusted code. QuickChick proposes some theorems (or axioms) about its different combinators which could be used to prove that the generator is correct, but it may be hard work. In the following we propose to test that the generator produces correct outputs. For that purpose, we implement the same approach: turning the logical property precondition into an executable one preconditionb.

We now illustrate QuickChick features on permutations encoded as natural functions. However, QuickChick cannot deal with functions so we generate permutations as lists and then transform them into functions, as detailed in Sect. 2.1. Let us notice that QuickChick heavily uses monads. However, in the following we explain very informally some piece of code.

We first define a generator for permutations on $\{0, \ldots, n-1\}$, as lists without any duplicate containing $0, 1, \ldots n - 1$ in any order:

```
Fixpoint gen_permutl (n : nat) : G (list nat) := match n with
  0 ⇒ returnGen nil
| S p ⇒ do! m ← choose (0, n); liftGen (insert_pos p m) (gen_permutl p)
end.
```

If n is 0, the output is the empty list. Otherwise (n is the successor of p) the recursive call (gen_permutl p) generates a list encoding a permutation on $\{0, \ldots, p-1\}$ and the function inserts p in the latter at a position m which is randomly chosen (using the combinator choose). The combinator liftGen applies a function, here insert_pos p m, to the result of a generator. To have confidence in this generator, we test that the outputs do not contain any duplicate, that their length is n and that their elements are natural numbers less than n. These three conditions are implemented by the Boolean predicate list_permutb.

```
QuickCheck (sized (fun n ⇒ forAll (gen_permutl n) (list_permutb n))).
+++ OK, passed 10000 tests
```

The maximal number of tests (10000 here) can be adjusted by the user. We iterate over different values for n thanks to the use of the combinator sized.

We can follow the same process to validate that permutations as natural functions are obtained by applying the translation function list2fun on lists generated by the previous generator gen_permutl:

```
Definition fun_permutb n l := is_permutb n (list2fun l).
QuickCheck (sized (fun n ⇒ forAll (gen_permutl n) (fun_permutb n))).
+++ OK, passed 10000 tests
```

We are now ready to test the conjectures formulated in Listing 1.2, following the same methodology: (i) when a natural function representing a permutation is to be generated, we use the list generator gen_permutl; (ii) the logical property under test is turned into its Boolean version composed with the translation function list2fun. For example testing Lemma insert_permut is obtained by

```
QuickCheck (sized (fun n ⇒ forAll (gen_permutl n)
              (fun l ⇒ (forAll arbitraryNat
                (fun i ⇒ let f := list2fun l in
                  is_permutb (S n) (insert_fun n f i)))))).
```

This QuickCheck command has the same structure as the previous ones except that we use two generators, one for permutations and another one for arbitrary natural numbers, named arbitraryNat. This command passed 10000 tests. If we inject a fault in the definition of insert_fun, e.g. replacing the result n by S n in the Lt case, we get a counterexample, e.g. $l = [0; 1]$ and $i = 0$ for $n = 2$.

2.3   Bounded Exhaustive Testing

For testing Coq specifications we also advocate in favor of bounded exhaustive
testing (BET) and its lightweight support with logic programs, for many reasons.
Firstly BET is especially well adapted to enumerative combinatorics, because
it corresponds to the familiar research activity of generation of combinatorial
objects in this domain. Secondly BET provides the author of a wrong lemma
with the smallest combinatorial structure revealing her error. Thirdly the combinatorial structures formalized in Coq as inductive structures with properties are
often easy to formalize in first-order logic with Prolog predicates. Fourthly the
Prolog backtracking mechanism often provides bounded exhaustive generators
for free. All these advantages are illustrated in this paper.

In order to make the validation tasks easier, we extend a Prolog validation
library created by Valerio Senni [27] and previously applied to the validation of
algorithms on words encoding rooted planar maps [14]. The library provides full
automation for symmetric bounded exhaustive comparison for increasing bound
values. It returns counterexamples whenever validation fails (so the debugging
process is guided by those counterexamples), and it collects statistics such as
generation time and memory consumption. We illustrate some of the validation
library features on the example of permutations. The reader is assumed to be
familiar with logic programming, or can otherwise read a short summary in [14].

We encode a function f on $\{0, \ldots, n-1\}$ by the Prolog list of its images
$[f(0), \ldots, f(n-1)]$, its one-line notation. A list is *linear* if it has no duplicates.
Listing 1.4 shows a Prolog predicate `line` such that the formula `line(L,N)` (resp.
`line(L,K,N)`) holds iff L is a linear list of length N (resp. K) with elements in
$\{0, \ldots, N-1\}$. We then say for short that L is a *permutation list*. In other words,
this characteristic predicate of permutations corresponds to (is_permut n) in Coq.
The predicate is parameterized by the list length. This is not strictly required for
formal specification but useful for generation purposes. The formula `in(K,I,J)`
holds iff the integer K is in the interval $[I..J]$.

```
line([],0,_).
line([Y|P],K,N) :- K > 0, Km1 is K-1, Nm1 is N-1, in(Y,0,Nm1),
  line(P,Km1,N), \+ member(Y,P).
line(P,N) :- line(P,N,N).
```

Listing 1.4. Permutations in Prolog.

A clear advantage of logic programming is that the predicate `line` works in
two ways: as an *acceptor* of permutation lists, and as a *generator* enumerating
permutation lists of a given length. For a characteristic predicate p and a given
size n the query scheme

Q: $p(L, n)$, `write_coq(L)`, `fail`.

indeed allows the enumeration of all the accepted data of size n. The query
forces the construction of a first datum L of size n accepted by p, its output
on a stream, and the failure of the proof mechanism by using the built-in `fail`.
Since the proof fails, the backtracking mechanism recovers the last choice-point
(necessarily in p) and triggers the generation of a new datum, until there are
no more choice-points. Here the predicate `write_coq` is defined by the user to

output (as side-effect) a test case in Coq syntax. For instance, it can easily be defined so that the query

```
line(L,3), write_coq(3), fail.
```

writes one Coq line such as

Eval compute in (is_permutb 3 (list2fun [2;0;1])) .

for each permutation list of length 3. These lines constitute a test suite for the Coq function is_permutb, under the assumptions that the Coq function list2fun and the Prolog program in Listing 1.4 are correct. The latter can be checked in two ways: by visual inspection of the lists it generates, or by counting. For counting, the library provides the predicate iterate so that the query

```
:- iterate(0,6,line).
```

outputs the numbers 1, 1, 2, 6, 24, 120 and 720 of distinct lists of length n from 0 to 6 accepted by the predicate line. We then easily recognize the first numbers $n!$ of permutations of length n.

We can now adapt the predicate write_coq of the query Q to the BET of the lemmas in Listing 1.2. For Lemma insert_permut the query evaluation can generate in a Coq file all the Coq lines of the form

Eval compute in (is_permutb $(n+1)$ (insert_fun n (list2fun l) i)).

for n up to some bound, for $0 \le i \le n$ and for any list l (of length n) satisfying line(l, n). Then we check that the compilation of the generated Coq file always produces true. We proceed similarly with the lemma sum_permut.

As mentioned before about the property is_inj, it may be hard to write a Boolean version of a property and to prove its correctness. In that case BET sometimes remains possible, as illustrated by the following example. Suppose that we find no implementation of the property is_permut. Then we generate a non-computational proof generalizing the following example

```
Goal is_permut 3 (list2fun (2::0::1:: nil )). unfold is_permut.
unfold list2fun. unfold list2funX. split.
- unfold is_endo. intros x Hx. assert (x = 0 ∨ x = 1 ∨ x = 2). omega.
  firstorder; subst; simpl; omega.
- unfold is_inj. intros x y Hx Hy Hxy.
  assert (x = 0 ∨ x = 1 ∨ x = 2). omega.
  assert (y = 0 ∨ y = 1 ∨ y = 2). omega.
  firstorder; subst; simpl; omega. Qed.
```

The proof first splits into one subproof for the property is_endo and one for is_inj. Each subproof works by enumeration of the possible values of x (and y for injectivity). This approach holds whenever the property is universally quantified with variables i of type nat upper bounded by some number b. Then the tactic enumerates all the possible values of i. The assertion is proved by the tactic omega which implements a decision procedure for linear arithmetics (the Omega test [24]). The proof is then decomposed into cases by the firstorder tactic. In the subproof for injectivity each case contains hypotheses x =... and y =... assigning values to both variables. After replacement of x and y with their values the Omega test ends the proof.

3   Case Study of Rooted Maps

It is now time to apply our test methodology to more challenging Coq theorems. As case study we consider the combinatorial family of rooted maps, formalized in Coq as transitive permutations (Sect. 3.1). Then we introduce two operations that should construct a map from one or two smaller ones by edge addition (Sect. 3.2). Both operations are defined as combinations of the two operations of insertion and direct sum defined in Sect. 2. Finally we check by testing and then prove formally that both operations preserve permutations and transitivity (Sect. 3.3). Section 3.4 reports some testing and proving statistics.

3.1   Definitions and Formalization

A *topological map* is a cellular embedding of a connected graph (possibly with loops and multiple edges) into a compact, oriented surface without boundary [19]. A *face* of a topological map is a connected component of the complement of the graph in the surface. By definition each face is homeomorphic to an open disc. Figure 1(a) shows a topological map. It is drawn on the plane for convenience, but should be considered as drawn on the sphere, so that the *outer face* (the infinite white piece of the plane) becomes homeomorphic to an open disk. We admit the existence of a map containing a single vertex, no edges, and a single face, called the *vertex map*. Any other map contains at least one edge.

A half-edge, i.e. an edge equipped with one of its two possible orientations, is usually called a *dart*. The other dart on the same edge is called the *opposite dart*. The vertex at the source of a dart and the face to the right of a dart are said to be *incident* to that dart. A *loop* is an edge whose two associated darts are incident to the same vertex. We only consider *labeled* topological maps, whose darts are identified by a unique label. In the drawings the label of a dart is always written in its incident face and near its incident vertex. For instance, the dart 11 in Fig. 1(a) is incident to the outer face, it is incident to the same vertex as the darts 3 and 4, and its opposite dart is labeled by 10.

Edmonds [13] reduced topological maps to their combinatorial structure, defined as follows. A *(combinatorial) labeled map* with n edges is a triple (D, R, L)

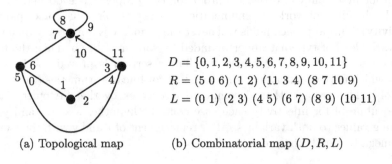

(a) Topological map   (b) Combinatorial map (D, R, L)

$D = \{0, 1, 2, 3, 4, 5, 6, 7, 8, 9, 10, 11\}$
$R = (5\ 0\ 6)\ (1\ 2)\ (11\ 3\ 4)\ (8\ 7\ 10\ 9)$
$L = (0\ 1)\ (2\ 3)\ (4\ 5)\ (6\ 7)\ (8\ 9)\ (10\ 11)$

Fig. 1. Two representations of a rooted map.

where D is a finite set of even cardinality $2n$, R is a permutation of D and L is a fixed-point free involution of D such that the group $\langle R, L \rangle$ generated by R and L acts transitively on D. This transitivity means that any element of D can be obtained from any other element of D by finitely many applications of the permutations R, L and their inverse. Figure 1(b) shows the combinatorial map (D, R, L) corresponding to the topological map in Fig. 1(a). More generally the one-to-one correspondence between topological and combinatorial labeled maps works as follows. An element of the set D is a dart of the topological map. The permutations R and L respectively encode its vertices and edges. An orbit of the permutation R lists the darts encountered when turning counterclockwise around a vertex. The involution L exchanges each dart with its opposite on the same edge. For instance, the orbit (5 0 6) of R encodes the leftmost vertex in Fig. 1(a) and the orbit (8 9) of L encodes the loop in Fig. 1(a). The transitive action of the permutations R and L corresponds to the connexity of the embedded graph.

A *rooting* of a map is essentially the choice of one of its darts, called its *root*. The edge which includes the root dart is called the *root edge*. By convention, the vertex map is also considered to be rooted. In the drawings the root dart is indicated by an arrow, as the dart 11 in Fig. 1(a). Two labeled maps (D, R, L) and (D', R', L') are *isomorphic* if there is a bijection θ from D to D' such that $R' = \theta^{-1} R\, \theta$ and $L' = \theta^{-1} L\, \theta$. This bijection is called a *labeled map isomorphism*. For a predefined root $d \in D$, two labeled maps (D, R, L) and (D, R', L') with the same set of darts D are *root-preserving isomorphic* if they are isomorphic and their isomorphism preserves the root d. A *rooted combinatorial map* (or *map* for short) is an equivalence class for the relation of root-preserving isomorphism between labeled maps. For the purpose of enumeration, the special virtue of rooted maps is that they have no symmetries, in the sense that the automorphism group of any rooted map is trivial.

In order to simplify the formalization and formal reasoning we refine the usual definition of a combinatorial labeled map. In the usual definition of a labeled map $M = (D, R, L)$ the set of darts D is any finite set and the permutation L is any fixed-point free involution on D. Here we fix D to $\{0, \ldots, 2e - 1\}$ for any map with e edges. Since rooted maps are defined modulo conjugation, we also fix L to the fixed-point free involution that swaps $2i$ and $2i + 1$ for all $0 \le i < e$. This involution is formalized in Coq by

```
Definition opp (n:nat) : nat := if (even_odd_dec n) then (n+1) else (n-1).
```

Such a map is said to be *local*. For instance, the combinatorial map in Fig. 1(b) is local. A local map can be represented using only its vertex permutation R, called its *rotation*. To root a local map, we always choose the largest element $(2e - 1)$ of D.

We now define the transitivity of any function f on some set D so that a triple (D, R, opp) is a local map iff its rotation R is transitive. We say that there is a *step* between two elements x and y of D by a function f iff $f(x) = y$, $f(y) = x$ or $\mathsf{opp}(x) = y$. Two numbers x and y are *connected* by f iff there is a path (i.e. a sequence of steps) from x to y. Finally, a function f is *transitive* on D if any two elements of D are connected by f.

```
Inductive connected n (f : nat → nat) : nat → nat → nat → Prop :=
 | c0    : ∀ x y, x < n → y < n → x = y → connected n f 0 x y
 | cfirst : ∀ l x y z, x < n → y < n → z < n →
     f x = y ∨ f y = x ∨ opp x = y →
     connected n f l y z → connected n f (S l) x z.
Definition is_transitive_fun (n: nat) (f : nat → nat) : Prop :=
 ∀ x, x < n → ∀ y, y < n → ∃ m, connected n f m x y.
Definition transitive_fun (n: nat) (f : nat → nat) : Prop :=
 ∀ y, y < n → ∀ x, x < y → ∃ m, connected n f m x y.
Definition is_transitive n (p : permut n) := transitive_fun n (fct p).
```

Listing 1.5. Definition of transitivity.

Listing 1.5 shows a Coq formalization of transitivity on $\{0, \ldots, n-1\}$ of a natural function. The connectivity property is specified by the inductive predicate connected so that (connected n f l x y) holds iff the natural numbers x and y are related by exactly l steps of f. The constructor cfirst states that a path between x and y can be decomposed into its first step and its end, while the constructor c0 expresses the trivial case where $x = y$. This definition is completed by three lemmas (not shown here): one lemma decomposing a path into its beginning and its last step and two lemmas respectively proving the symmetry and the transitivity of the binary relation (connected n f l). The definitions is_transitive_fun and transitive_fun implement two versions of the property of transitivity of a function. Decompositions into cases in several proofs are dramatically shortened by using the second definition transitive_fun of transitivity considering only numbers x strictly smaller than y. Using symmetry of the predicate connected we prove that both definitions of transitivity are equivalent. The predicate is_transitive defines the transitivity of a permutation as the transitivity of its associated function.

All the maps considered hereafter are local and are encoded by their transitive rotation. A local map (D, R, opp) with e edges is formalized in Coq by a record composed of its vertex permutation of length 2e (its rotation) and the property that this permutation is transitive, as follows:

```
Record map (e : nat) : Set := {
 rotation : permut (2*e);
 transitive : is_transitive rotation }.
```

3.2   Map Construction Operations

An edge is an *isthmus* if both of its associated darts are incident to the same face. A map is *isthmic* (resp. *non-isthmic*) if it is not the vertex map and its root edge is (resp. not) an isthmus. We define here an operation c_I constructing an isthmic map from two maps and a family of operations c_N^k (indexed by a number k) constructing a non-isthmic map from one map. Both operations proceed by addition of one edge.

Isthmic Operation. The operation c_I is illustrated by an example in Fig. 2. It adds an isthmic edge between a local map M_1 with e_1 edges and a local map M_2 with e_2 edges. The result is a map $M = c_I(M_1, M_2)$ with $e_1 + e_2 + 1$ edges.

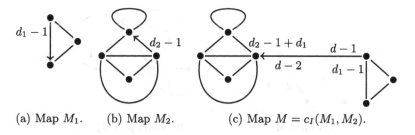

(a) Map M_1.   (b) Map M_2.   (c) Map $M = c_I(M_1, M_2)$.

Fig. 2. Example of construction of an isthmic map.

Let $d_1 = 2e_1$, $d_2 = 2e_2$ and $d = 2e_1 + 2e_2 + 2$ be the numbers of darts of M_1, M_2 and M. The additional edge is composed of the two darts $d - 1$ ($= d_1 + d_2 + 1$) and $d - 2$ ($= d_1 + d_2$). The root of M is the dart $d - 1$, while its opposite dart $\text{opp}(d - 1)$ is $d - 2$.

```
Definition isthmic_fun d1 (r1 : nat → nat) d2 (r2 : nat → nat) : nat → nat
:= match d1 with
| 0 ⇒ match d2 with
        | 0 ⇒ insert_fun 1 (insert_fun 0 r2 0) 1
        | S d2m1 ⇒ insert_fun (d2+1) (insert_fun d2 r2 d2m1) (d2+1)
      end
| S d1m1 ⇒ match d2 with
             | 0 ⇒ insert_fun (d1+1) (insert_fun d1 r1 d1) d1m1
             | S d2m1 ⇒
             insert_fun (d1+d2+1)
               (insert_fun (d1+d2) (sum_fun d1 r1 d2 r2) (d1m1+d2))
             d1m1
           end end.
```

Listing 1.6. Isthmic operation in Coq.

Listing 1.6 presents a Coq function isthmic_fun implementing this operation on two natural functions r1 and r2 representing the rotations R_1 and R_2 of M_1 and M_2. If R_1 and R_2 represent the vertex map ($d_1 = d_2 = 0$) then the resulting map M reduced to one non-loop edge and the resulting rotation R is the permutation (0) (1). If M_1 is the vertex map ($d_1 = 0$) and M_2 is not empty ($d_2 \neq 0$) then the dart $d - 2$ ($= d_2$) is added just before the dart $d_2 - 1$ in its orbit in R_2 and then the dart $d - 1$ ($= d_2 + 1$) is added as a fixed-point of R. If M_1 is not empty ($d_1 \neq 0$) and M_2 is the vertex map ($d_2 = 0$) then the dart $d - 2$ ($= d_1$) is added as a fixed-point, and then the dart $d - 1$ ($= d_1 + 1$) is added just before the dart $d_1 - 1$ in its orbit. Otherwise, when M_1 and M_2 are not the vertex map, the direct sum $R' = sum(R_1, R_2)$ is computed thanks to a call to the function sum_fun. Then the dart $d_1 + d_2$ is inserted just before the dart $d_2 - 1 + d_1$ in its orbit in R', and finally the dart $d_1 + d_2 + 1$ is inserted just before the dart $d_1 - 1$ in its orbit in the resulting permutation.

Non-isthmic Operation. For $0 \leq k \leq 2e$ the operation c_N^k adds a non-isthmic edge in a local map M with e edges (represented by its rotation R of length $d = 2e$) to obtain a local map M' with $e + 1$ edges represented by its rotation R' of length $d' = 2e + 2$. The resulting permutation R' is obtained by insertion

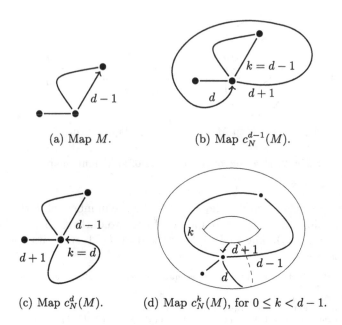

(a) Map M.   (b) Map $c_N^{d-1}(M)$.

(c) Map $c_N^d(M)$.   (d) Map $c_N^k(M)$, for $0 \le k < d-1$.

Fig. 3. Examples of construction of non-isthmic maps.

of the new root $d+1$ and its opposite d in R. If M is the vertex map, the new edge is added – as a loop – in a unique way to obtain M'. Otherwise, there are $d+1$ ways to add the new edge, distinguished by the value of k between 0 and d. Figure 3 shows a map M with three edges (in Fig. 3(a)) and three maps obtained by application of the operation c_N^k on M, for different values of k. Two of them are planar maps whereas the last one in Fig. 3(d) is a toroidal map (a map on a torus). When $k = d-1$ and $k = d$ the added edge is a loop. These cases are respectively illustrated in Fig. 3(b) and (c). Note that the order of insertion of darts is important: in Fig. 3(b), the dart d is inserted just before the dart $d-1$ but then the dart $d+1$ is inserted just before the dart $k = d-1$, so that the dart d finally is just before $d+1$ in its orbit in the rotation R' of M'. In all the other cases, the dart d is just before the dart $d-1$ in R'. Figure 3(d) shows a case $0 \le k < d-1$ where the dart k is not incident to the same face as $d-1$. In this case, the new edge can only be added through a hole perfored in the surface.

Listing 1.7 presents a Coq function non_isthmic_fun implementing this operation on a natural function r representing the vertex permutation R of a local map with d darts, when k is d or less. When $d = 0$ the rotation R represents the vertex map, the new edge is a loop and the resulting function is the permutation (0 1). Otherwise, the dart d is inserted just before the root $d-1$ of M in its orbit in R. Let us denote here by Q the resulting permutation. Then the dart $d+1$ is inserted just before the dart k in its orbit of Q.

```
Definition non_isthmic_fun (d:nat) (r:nat → nat) (k:nat)
(k_le_d:k ≤ d) : nat → nat :=
match d with
| 0      ⇒ insert_fun 1 (insert_fun 0 r 0) 0
| S dm1 ⇒ insert_fun (S d) (insert_fun d r dm1) k
end.
```

Listing 1.7. Non-isthmic operation in Coq.

3.3   Validation and Proof

We have separately formalized combinatorial maps and two map constructions as operations on natural functions. It remains to prove that each operation preserves transitive permutations. We proceed in two steps. The first step consists in checking and proving that both operations preserve permutations. The second step concerns transitivity.

Preservation of Permutations. The proof that the construction operations preserve permutations is decomposed into intermediate lemmas. For example, one of them

```
Lemma isthmic_endo : ∀ d1 (r1:permut d1) d2 (r2:permut d2),
 is_endo (S (S (d1 + d2))) (isthmic_fun d1 (fct r1) d2 (fct r2)).
```

states that the isthmic operation preserves endofunctions, and

```
Lemma non_isthmic_inj: ∀ d (r:permut d) k (k_le_d:k ≤ d),
 is_inj (S (S d)) (non_isthmic_fun d (fct r) k k_le_d).
```

states that the non-isthmic operation preserves injectivity.

As in Sect. 2.3, we validate by BET that the isthmic and non-isthmic operations preserve permutations. In the non-isthmic case, we meet a specificity of testing with dependent types. The non-isthmic operation is indeed parameterized by a proof. So the BET has to generate such a proof for each test input. It can be automated only if all these proofs share a common pattern (notion of *uniform* proof). In the present case we need a uniform proof of $x \leq y$ for any pair of natural numbers x and y. Fortunately the Coq predicate $\leq$ is reflected by the Boolean function leb:nat→nat→bool through the lemma

```
Lemma leb_complete : ∀ m n, leb m n = true → m ≤ n.
```

so that the term (leb_complete x y eq_refl) is a uniform Coq proof of $x \leq y$. For the preservation of permutations by the non-isthmic operation the BET generates test cases such as

```
Eval compute in (
 let proof := leb_complete 2 3 eq_refl
 in is_permutb 5 (non_isthmic_fun 3 (list2fun [0;0;0]) 2 proof)).
```

for $x = 2$ and $y = 3$. After this validation we have proved all the permutation preservation lemmas.

Random testing also allows us to validate the preservation of permutations by the isthmic operation. The following QuickCheck command randomly generates a first natural number d1, a permutation list l1 of length d1 and then a second number d2 together with a permutation list of length d2 and checks if the isthmic operation builts a permutation from the corresponding natural functions.

```
QuickCheck (forAll arbitraryNat (fun d1 ⇒
  forAll (gen_permutl d1) (fun l1 ⇒ let f1 := list2fun l1 in
    forAll arbitraryNat (fun d2 ⇒
      forAll (gen_permutl d2) (fun l2 ⇒ let f2 := list2fun l2 in
        is_permutb (S (S (d1 + d2))) (isthmic_fun d1 f1 d2 f2 )))))).
```

Unfortunately for non_isthmic_fun, this process is not applicable. We could follow the same process: generate a natural number d, a permutation list of length d and a number k less than d and so on. Thanks to the choose combinator provided by QuickChick, it is easy to provide such a k. However, we are not able to produce a proof term for k ≤ d which is an argument required by non_isthmic_fun because QuickChick does not provide a correctness proof for choose. A solution could be to rewrite non_isthmic_fun without this proof argument.

Preservation of Transitivity. We first validate and then demonstrate that the isthmic and non-isthmic operations preserve transitive permutations and therefore can be considered as operations on (local) maps. These properties are formalized by the two theorems presented in Listing 1.8. Theorem isthmic_trans (resp. non_isthmic_trans) states that the isthmic (resp. non-isthmic) operation preserves the transitivity when acting on two permutations (resp. one permutation) of even length.

```
Theorem isthmic_trans: ∀ d1 (r1: permut d1) d2 (r2: permut d2),
  even d1 → even d2 → is_transitive r1 → is_transitive r2 →
    is_transitive (isthmic_permut r1 r2).
Theorem non_isthmic_trans: ∀ d (r: permut d) k (k_le_d: k ≤ d),
  even d → is_transitive r → is_transitive (non_isthmic_permut r k_le_d ).
```

Listing 1.8. Preservation of transitivity by the isthmic and non-isthmic operations.

```
Fixpoint nlist n (f:nat → nat) : nat → list nat := fun x ⇒ match n with
  0   ⇒ (opp x):: nil
| S m ⇒ elimDup ((nlist m f x) ++
    (if eq_nat_dec (f m) x then m:: nil else nil) ++
    (if eq_nat_dec x m then (f m):: nil else nil))
end.
Fixpoint dfs (g:nat → list nat) (n:nat) (v: list nat) (x:nat) :=
if (in_dec eq_nat_dec x v) then v else match n with
  0 ⇒ v
| S n' ⇒ fold_left (dfs g n') (g x) (x:: v)
end.
Definition is_transitive_funb n f := if
  eq_nat_dec n (length (dfs (nlist n f) n nil 0)) then true else false.
```

Listing 1.9. Boolean function for transitivity.

For testing we propose in Listing 1.9 an implementation of the transitivity predicate defined in Listing 1.5. It is based on a depth-first search in the graph where a directed edge goes from x to y if $f(x) = y$, $f(y) = x$ or opp$(x) = y$, for any two vertices x and y in $\{0, \ldots, n-1\}$. The call (nlist n f x) returns the list of neighbors of x in this graph. The auxiliary function elimDup eliminates duplicates in a list. The depth-first search is implemented by the function dfs inspired by the function with the same name in [21]. The function fold_left is such that (fold_left f [x1;..;xk] a) computes f (.. (f (f a x1) x2) ..) xk.

Proving the soundness of this implementation wrt. its specification in Listing 1.5 is not an easy task and is therefore left as a future work. The soundness of is_transitive_funb can however be checked, for instance by counting the first numbers of transitive permutations. The number $t(e)$ of transitive permutations of length $2e$ is indeed equal to the number of rooted maps, multiplied by the number $2^{e-1}(e - 1)!$ of isomorphic local labeled maps in a rooted map if $e > 0$ (Remember that a rooted map is an equivalence class of isomorphic labeled maps, for root-preserving isomorphisms). The first numbers of rooted maps and many references about them can be found in [29].

Let d = 2e be an even natural Coq number and let I be a Coq list of all the permutation lists of length d. The Coq code

```
Definition is_transitive_listb d I := is_transitive_funb d (list2fun I).
Eval compute in (length (filter (is_transitive_listb d) I).
```

computes the length of the list obtained by filtering the transitive permutation lists. Thus it should compute $t(e)$. The list I is generated by the Prolog-based BET presented in Sect. 2. This validation is feasible only for $e = 0, 1, 2, 3$. It correctly counts $t(e) = 1, 2, 20, 592$ after examining $(2e)!$ permutations. For $e = 4$ the Coq compilation runs out of memory. After this validation by counting, we use the Boolean function is_transitive_funb to test the theorems in Listing 1.8.

The isthmic operation combines insertion and direct sum. One could think that it preserves transitivity because these two operations also do. In fact, it is not so simple. In particular, the direct sum operation does not preserve transitivity. It can be understood by coming back to its definition. But it can also be quickly invalidated by BET on an executable version of the wrong property:

```
Theorem sum_transitive: ∀ d1 r1 d2 r2, even d1 → even d2 →
    is_permut d1 r1 → is_transitive_fun d1 r1 →
    is_permut d2 r2 → is_transitive_fun d2 r2 →
    is_transitive_fun (d1 + d2) (sum_fun d1 r1 d2 r2).
```

The BET provides us with the smallest counterexample where r1 and r2 are the function (list2fun [1; 0]) encoding the transposition exchanging 0 and 1.

Random testing also allows us to invalidate this conjecture and obtain some counterexamples. For some executions, we retrieve exactly the previous smallest one. As a process for generating transitive permutations is lacking, we generate permutations as functions (as previously) and filter those which are transitive using the Boolean predicate is_transitive_funb. The following QuickCheck command does the job. If f1 (or f2) is not transitive, the test case is discarded (it is done by the combinator written as ⟹).

```
QuickCheck (forAll gen_even (fun d1 ⇒
    forAll (gen_permutl d1) (fun l1 ⇒ let f1 := list2fun l1 in
    is_transitive_funb d1 f1⟹
        forAll gen_even (fun d2 ⇒
        forAll (gen_permutl d2) (fun l2 ⇒ let f2 := list2fun l2 in
        is_transitive_funb d2 f2⟹
            is_transitive_funb (d1 + d2) (sum_fun d1 f1 d2 f2)))))).
2 [0;1] 4 [2;0;1;3] *** Failed! After 3 tests and 0 shrinks
```

Each transitivity preservation proof reduces to the preservation of connectivity between any two numbers (darts) x and y with $x < y$. For instance the most complex case in the proof of Theorem isthmic_trans is $0 \le x < d_1$ $(x \in R_1)$ and $d_1 \le y < d_1 + d_2$ $(y \in R_2)$. Its proof constructs a path between x and y by concatenation of a path from the dart x to the root $d_1 - 1$ of R_1, a step between $d_1 - 1$ and the root $d - 1 = d_1 + d_2 + 1$, a step between the root $d - 1$ and its opposite $d - 2 = d_1 + d_2$ through the fixed-point free involution opp, a step from $d - 2$ to the root $d_2 - 1$ of R_2, relabelled $d_1 + d_2 - 1$, and finally a path from that dart $d_1 + d_2 - 1$ to y in the relabelling of R_2.

3.4   Some Metrics

The case study is composed of 80 definitions, 185 lemmas and 2 theorems, for a total of 5580 lines of Coq code. Among them around 280 lines are dedicated to validation. These lines contain 23 definitions and 4 lemmas. They include Boolean versions of some logical definitions used by both random testing and BET, e.g. the Boolean function is_permutb, their corresponding correctness proofs, and the generators required by QuickChick. The Prolog code for BET is composed of 44 lines added to the validation library and 860 lines whose execution generates test suites for the case study.

All the validations by counting and BET presented in the paper are executed with lists up to length 4, in less that 21 s on a PC Intel Core i5-2400 3.10 GHz × 4 under Linux Ubuntu 14.04 (the time for test generation is neglictible). The QuickChick random tests (10000 test cases for each validation step except for the wrong conjecture) are generated and executed in less than 54 s. These are reasonable times for thousands of automatically generated tests. For a comparison the Coq compilation time is around 20 s.

4   Related Work

Several techniques and tools help strengthening the trust in programs manipulating structured data. Randomized property-based testing (RPBT) consists in random generation of test data to validate given assertions about programs. RPBT has gained much popularity since the appearance of QuickCheck for Haskell [7], followed by e.g. Quickcheck for Isabelle [5]. In RPBT a random data generator can be defined by filtering the output of another one, in a similar way as an exhaustive generator can be defined by filtering another exhaustive generator in BET. A more generic approach is type-targeted testing [26], wherein types are converted into queries to SMT solvers whose answers provide counterexamples. SmallCheck and Lazy SmallCheck [25] are two Haskell libraries for property-based testing, allowing an automatic exhaustive testing for small values. In Coq, as far as we know, there is no equivalent to the Haskell library SmallCheck.

The theory of combinatorial maps was developed from the early 1970's. Tutte [30,31] proposed the most advanced work in this direction, developing an axiomatic theory of combinatorial maps without referencing topology.

More recently Lazarus [20] conducted a computational approach on graphs and surfaces based on combinatorial maps. He notably proposed a formal definition of the basic operation of edge deletion on combinatorial labeled maps. An advanced formalization related to maps is that of combinatorial hypermaps to state and prove the Four Colour Theorem in the Coq system [15,16]. Note that combinatorial hypermaps generalize combinatorial maps by allowing an arbitrary permutation L (i.e., not necessarily a fixed-point free involution). This formalization does not explicitly state that L and R are bijective, but adopt the alternative definition of a hypermap as a *triple* of endofunctions that compose to the identity [15, p. 19]. It would be interesting to investigate this idea with local maps rather than hypermaps, and to determine to what extent it could simplify our formalization. Some formal proofs about combinatorial maps or variants have already been carried out in the domain of computational geometry. Dufourd et al. have developed a large Coq library specifying hypermaps used to prove some classical results such as Euler formula for polyhedra [10], Jordan curve theorem [11], and also some algorithms such as convex hull [4] and image segmentation [9]. In these papers, a combinatorial map or hypermap is represented by an inductive type with some constraints. Its constructors are related to the insertion of a dart or the links of two darts. This representation differs from ours that relies on permutations. In [8], Dubois and Mota proposed a formalization of generalized maps using the B formalism, very close to the mathematical presentation with permutations and involutions. Here we simplify the structure by fixing the involution.

5   Conclusion

We have shown how to use random testing and bounded exhaustive testing to validate Coq definitions and theorems. The bounded exhaustive testing is based on logical specifications. It is assisted by a validation library in Prolog. We have applied these methods on two case studies. The second case study is also an original formalization of rooted maps with an interactive theorem prover. It directly encodes the combinatorial definition of a rooted map (as a transitive pair of injective endofunctions) and two basic operations for constructing them from smaller ones. The properties that these operations preserve permutations and transitivity are formalized, validated by random and bounded exhaustive testing, and then proved with some interactivity.

These two case studies about combinatorial structures show that logic programming features make Prolog an effective tool for prototyping and validating this kind of Coq code. Our focus is more on the design and validation methodology than on the resulting algorithms. The present work is intended to serve as a methodological guideline for further studies, in particular with other families of combinatorial objects.

Acknowledgments. The authors warmly thank the anonymous referees for suggestions, Noam Zeilberger for fruitful discussions and Valerio Senni for advice about his validation library.

References

1. Berghofer, S., Nipkow, T.: Random testing in Isabelle/HOL. In: Cuellar, J., Liu, Z. (eds.) Software Engineering and Formal Methods (SEFM 2004), pp. 230–239. IEEE Computer Society (2004)
2. Bertot, Y., Castéran, P.: Interactive Theorem Proving and Program Development: Coq'Art: The Calculus of Inductive Constructions. Texts in Theoretical Computer Science. Springer, New York (2004)
3. Blanchette, J.C., Nipkow, T.: Nitpick: a counterexample generator for higher-order logic based on a relational model finder. In: Kaufmann, M., Paulson, L.C. (eds.) ITP 2010. LNCS, vol. 6172, pp. 131–146. Springer, Heidelberg (2010)
4. Brun, C., Dufourd, J., Magaud, N.: Designing and proving correct a convex hull algorithm with hypermaps in Coq. Comput. Geom. **45**(8), 436–457 (2012)
5. Bulwahn, L.: The new quickcheck for Isabelle - Random, exhaustive and symbolic testing under one roof. In: Hawblitzel, C., Miller, D. (eds.) CPP 2012. LNCS, vol. 7679, pp. 92–108. Springer, Heidelberg (2012)
6. Carlier, M., Dubois, C., Gotlieb, A.: Constraint Reasoning in FOCALTEST. In: International Conference on Software and Data Technologies (ICSOFT 2010), Athens, July 2010
7. Claessen, K., Hughes, J.: QuickCheck: a lightweight tool for random testing of Haskell programs. In: Proceedings of the Fifth ACM SIGPLAN International Conference on Functional Programming, SIGPLAN Not., vol. 35, pp. 268–279. ACM, New York (2000)
8. Dubois, C., Mota, J.M.: Geometric modeling with B: formal specification of generalized maps. J. Sci. Pract. Comput. **1**(2), 9–24 (2007)
9. Dufourd, J.: Design and formal proof of a new optimal image segmentation program with hypermaps. Pattern Recogn. **40**(11), 2974–2993 (2007)
10. Dufourd, J.: Polyhedra genus theorem and Euler formula: a hypermap-formalized intuitionistic proof. Theor. Comput. Sci. **403**(2–3), 133–159 (2008)
11. Dufourd, J.: An intuitionistic proof of a discrete form of the Jordan curve theorem formalized in Coq with combinatorial hypermaps. J. Autom. Reasoning **43**(1), 19–51 (2009)
12. Dybjer, P., Haiyan, Q., Takeyama, M.: Combining testing and proving in dependent type theory. In: Basin, D., Wolff, B. (eds.) TPHOLs 2003. LNCS, vol. 2758, pp. 188–203. Springer, Heidelberg (2003)
13. Edmonds, J.R.: A combinatorial representation for oriented polyhedral surfaces. Notices Amer. Math. Soc. **7**, 646 (1960)
14. Giorgetti, A., Senni, V.: Specification and Validation of Algorithms Generating Planar Lehman Words, June 2012. https://hal.inria.fr/hal-00753008
15. Gonthier, G.: A computer checked proof of the Four Colour Theorem (2005). http://research.microsoft.com/gonthier/4colproof.pdf
16. Gonthier, G.: The four colour theorem: engineering of a formal proof. In: Kapur, D. (ed.) ASCM 2007. LNCS (LNAI), vol. 5081, pp. 333–333. Springer, Heidelberg (2008)
17. Hritcu, C., Lampropoulos, L., Dénès, M., Paraskevopoulou, Z.: Randomized property-based testing plugin for Coq. https://github.com/QuickChick
18. Kitaev, S.: Patterns in Permutations and Words. Springer, New York (2011)
19. Lando, S.K., Zvonkin, A.K.: Graphs on Surfaces and Their Applications. Springer, New York (2004)

20. Lazarus, F.: Combinatorial graphs and surfaces from the computational and topological viewpoint followed by some notes on the isometric embedding of the square flat torus (2014). http://www.gipsa-lab.grenoble-inp.fr/~francis.lazarus/Documents/hdr-Lazarus.pdf

21. Mathematical Components team: Library mathcomp.ssreflect.fingraph. http://math-comp.github.io/math-comp/htmldoc/mathcomp.ssreflect.fingraph.html

22. Owre, S.: Random testing in PVS. In: Workshop on Automated Formal Methods (AFM) (2006)

23. Paraskevopoulou, Z., Hritcu, C., Dénès, M., Lampropoulos, L., Pierce, B.C.: Foundational property-based testing. In: Urban, C., Zhang, X. (eds.) ITP 2015. LNCS, vol. 9236, pp. 325–343. Springer, Heidelberg (2015)

24. Pugh, W.: The Omega test: A fast and practical integer programming algorithm for dependence analysis. In: Proceedings of the 1991 ACM/IEEE Conference on Supercomputing, Supercomputing 1991, pp. 4–13. ACM, New York (1991)

25. Runciman, C., Naylor, M., Lindblad, F.: Smallcheck and lazy smallcheck: automatic exhaustive testing for small values. In: Proceedings of the 1st ACM SIGPLAN Symposium on Haskell, Haskell 2008, Victoria, BC, Canada, 25 September 2008, pp. 37–48 (2008). http://doi.acm.org/10.1145/1411286.1411292

26. Seidel, E.L., Vazou, N., Jhala, R.: Type targeted testing. In: Vitek, J. (ed.) ESOP 2015. LNCS, vol. 9032, pp. 812–836. Springer, Heidelberg (2015)

27. Senni, V.: Validation library. https://subversion.assembla.com/svn/validation/

28. SWI: Prolog. http://www.swi-prolog.org/

29. The OEIS Foundation Inc: The On-Line Encyclopedia of Integer Sequences. https://oeis.org/A000698

30. Tutte, W.T.: What is a map? In: Harary, F. (ed.) New Directions in the Theory of Graphs: Proceedings, pp. 309–325. Academic Press, New York (1973)

31. Tutte, W.T.: Combinatorial oriented maps. Canad. J. Math. **31**(5), 986–1004 (1979)

Classifying Test Suite Effectiveness via Model Inference and ROBBDs

Hermann Felbinger[1]([⊠]), Ingo Pill[2], and Franz Wotawa[2]

[1] Virtual Vehicle Research Center, Graz, Austria
hermann.felbinger@v2c2.at
[2] Institute for Software Technology, TU Graz, Inffeldgasse 16b/II, 8010 Graz, Austria
{ipill,wotawa}@ist.tugraz.at

Abstract. Deciding whether a given test suite is effective enough is certainly a challenging task. Focusing on a software program's functionality, we propose in this paper a new method that leverages Boolean functions as abstract reasoning format. That is, we use machine learning in order to infer a special binary decision diagram from the considered test suite and extract a total variable order, if possible. Intuitively, if an ROBDD derived from the Boolean functions representing the program under test's specification actually coincides with that of the test suite (using the same variable order), we conclude that the test suite is effective enough. That is, any program that passes such a test suite should clearly show the desired input-output behavior. In our paper, we provide the corresponding algorithms of our approach and their respective proofs. Our first experimental results illustrate our approach's practicality and viability.

Keywords: Software testing · Machine learning · BDD · ROBDD

1 Introduction

Test suite generation and in turn the decision whether a test suite is good enough are certainly quite complex tasks. In this paper, we focus on the latter and in particular on the functional aspect. That is, we would like to know whether a given test suite examines the functionality of our p rogram to the best of our knowledge. Certainly, a test suite examining all possible input combinations would be an assuring approach, but exhaustive testing of the entire I/O space is certainly impossible in most cases due to the sheer number of required tests.

Now, let us consider the example of a Boolean function as illustrated in Fig. 1. The function has $n = 3$ input variables, and let us assume that we have an exhaustive test suite TS containing 2^n test cases s.t. all input combinations are tested. While TS certainly is effective due to checking the entire I/O space, for a subset $T \subseteq TS$, T's effectiveness is unclear. If we assume there to be, e.g., 40 inputs, exhaustive testing with 2^{40} test cases is however certainly impossible. Our idea now is to learn a canonical representation from T that we then compare

© Springer International Publishing Switzerland 2016
B.K. Aichernig and C.A. Furia (Eds.): TAP 2016, LNCS 9762, pp. 76–93, 2016.
DOI: 10.1007/978-3-319-41135-4_5

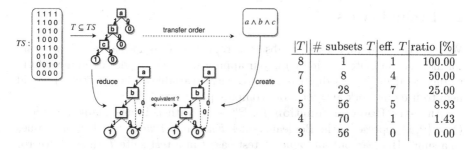

Fig. 1. An illustration of our approach for a simple Boolean function, and a table reporting on the performance of several test suites $T \subseteq TS$.

$|T|$	# subsets T	eff. T	ratio [%]
8	1	1	100.00
7	8	4	50.00
6	28	7	25.00
5	56	5	8.93
4	70	1	1.43
3	56	0	0.00

to a corresponding representation derived from the program under test's specification, in order to check whether they are equivalent. In case of equivalence, we then assume that the test suite captures the same behavior as the program. This leads us to the immediate and important question: What is an attractive canonical representation suitable for a test suite *and* the tested program?

As described in Sect. 3, we use reduced ordered binary decision diagrams (ROBDDs) as our canonical format. In particular, like illustrated in Fig. 1, we infer a binary decision tree DT from the considered test suite T via machine learning. In the learning algorithm proposed in Sect. 3.1, similar to the algorithm C4.5 (see Sect. 2) we take the local information gain into account when choosing the next decision variable. Consequently, the variable order in DT's individual paths is determined via the entropy of the local situations in order to come up with a "good" order. Our next step is to derive an ordering graph O for DT as described Sect. 3.2, and if it is cycle-free, we extract a total variable order and reduce DT to an ROBDD (for the latter see Sect. 3.3). Afterwards we derive an ROBDD for the system under test (SUT) from its Boolean functions' specification with the concept described in Sect. 3.4.

Our argument is that if the two ROBDDs coincide, then a program satisfying T should implement the desired I/O behavior. Our experiments reported in Sect. 4 show an excellent correlation between our classification and fault identification capabilities. Note that if O features cycles, then there are contradicting variable orders in DT's paths (see Sect. 3.2) that we would need to resolve by reordering the variables in some paths (this is not implemented yet).

Now let us come back to our example. If we consider the table in Fig. 1, we can see, e.g., that for a subset size of 4 ($=n+1$), out of the $\binom{2^n}{n+1} = 70$ subsets, there is a single one that we would consider to be effective, and that the likelihood of achieving this with some $T \subseteq TS$ increases with a higher subset size. While our approach cannot yet be used to derive *missing* test cases, it can serve for adding a quality label to some existing test suite T.

Please note that we chose a single Boolean function as example out of simplicity, but our approach can consider any number of outputs (a set of Boolean functions, or a Boolean formula) as long as the test cases provide values for all input variables and the outputs' values are deterministic for a test case.

2 Preliminaries

We use Boolean functions as abstract representation format for a program (or also a combinatorial circuit) in our approach. Static Single Assignment form as discussed in [3] and digitizing non-Boolean variables (via predicates) would help to use our work also for more complex programs.

An n-ary **Boolean function** $f : \mathbb{B}^n \to \mathbb{B}$ with n inputs maps n Boolean ($\mathbb{B} = \{0, 1\}$ represents the Boolean values *False* and *True* as usual) input values to a single Boolean output value. A test case t in a test suite T thus is a vector $(x_1, .., x_{n+1})$ defining n input values and f's expected output when executing t. For our implementation, we consider the following unary and binary standard operators in a Boolean function: $\neg$ (not), $\wedge$ (and), $\vee$ (or), and $\oplus$ (xor).

An essential ingredient of our approach is that we **learn a decision tree** from a test suite. As depicted in more detail in Sect. 3.1, we use an altered version of the widely used **C4.5 algorithm** [15] for this. The algorithm computes the *entropy* and *information gain* when selecting nodes/variables while growing the tree. So let us first define these two terms.

In information theory, entropy is commonly used as a measure of purity or impurity of an arbitrary set of examples, and we would like to choose an optimal next decision variable in this respect. In our case, for a test suite T, we take a Boolean output variable (if there are more, we have to choose one) and can derive the entropy $E(T)$ with respect to this variable according to Eq. 1. In this equation, p_t represents the proportion of test cases s.t. the considered output variable's value is *True*, and p_f gives the same proportion for *False* ($p_t + p_f = 1$). If all test cases result in the same output value, then entropy is 0, while an entropy of 1 indicates $p_t = p_f = 0.5$. In general, we have $0 \leq E(T) \leq 1$.

$$E(T) \equiv -p_t \log_2 p_t - p_f \log_2 p_f. \tag{1}$$

When growing the tree, the variables for nodes $n \in N$ are selected by investigating the effectiveness of the various input variables in classifying the test cases. Informally, the *information gain* of a variable reports the expected reduction in entropy caused by partitioning the test suite according to this variable. Formally, the information gain $Gain(T, v)$ of variable v for a set of test cases T is computed as of Eq. 2, where $Values(v)$ returns the domain of variable v (which is $\mathbb{B}$ in our case) and $T_b \subseteq T$ denotes T's subset s.t. v has value $b \in Values(v)$. Coming back to the learning algorithm, it selects a variable with the highest information gain. If there is no variable v s.t. $Gain(T, v) > 0$, the current node becomes a leaf labeled by $b \in \mathbb{B}$ s.t. b is the most probable classification of the inputs leading to this leaf. Consequently, there can still be misclassifications.

$$Gain(T, v) \equiv E(T) - \sum_{b \in Values(v)} \frac{|T_b|}{|T|} E(T_b). \tag{2}$$

We use special **binary decision diagrams (BDDs)** [1] as canonical format for our comparison. A BDD describes a Boolean function f via a rooted, directed acyclic graph. In particular, the BDD consists of nodes N for representing the consideration of a Boolean variable, two nodes L representing f's two possible outcomes *False* and *True*, and directed edges E connecting the nodes as follows. Each node $n \in N$ is labeled by a variable $var(n)$ and has *a pair* of outgoing edges $e_0(n)$ and $e_1(n)$ leading to a child node for the corresponding evaluation (the i of $e_i(n)$) of variable $var(n)$. Nodes in L have no outgoing edge.

A canonical variant of BDDs are reduced ordered binary decision diagrams (ROBDD)s [5]. A specific feature of an ROBDD is that it implements a certain variable order in the graph, i.e., there is a total order s.t. for $n, n' \in N$ we have that if $v_1 = var(n)$ appears before $v_2 = var(n')$ in some path, then this is the case for all paths Π^k in the BDD (the BDD is an OBDD then) s.t. both variables appear in them. Furthermore, an ROBDD is reduced, which means that each node in the OBDD represents a different Boolean function. Due to the resulting canonicity of an ROBBD, we can easily decide **equivalence**:

Definition 1. *Two ROBDDs A and B are* equivalent *iff their root nodes are equivalent. Two nodes $n_1 \in A$ and $n_2 \in B$ are equivalent if they are either*

1. *leaf nodes with the same label, or*
2. *non-leaf nodes that have the same label and the pairs of outgoing edges $(e_0(n_1), e_0(n_2))$ and $(e_1(n_1), e_1(n_2))$ lead to equivalent nodes respectively.*

Determining two ROBDDs' equivalence is linear in the size of the smaller (if not equivalent) ROBDD where its size is given by the number of its nodes.

3   Classifying Test Suite Effectiveness

Via comparing the canonical representations of the test suite and the program under test, we aim to decide whether a test suite is effective enough. The basic steps of our approach at achieving this are illustrated in Fig. 2.

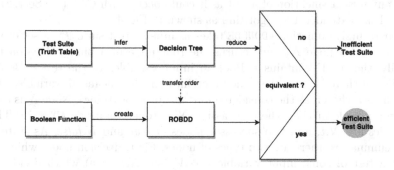

Fig. 2. Process of our test suite classification approach.

Our initial step is to learn a decision tree DT from the considered test suite T, where we report on the details of this step in Subsect. 3.1. An important prerequisite here is that the test cases in T are unique, since duplicates affect the information gain as computed for selecting the next decision variable in a tree. Like we mentioned in the introduction, furthermore the output variables' values have to be deterministic for the input values (as provided by some $t \in T$).

As depicted in Subsect. 3.2, we then investigate the variable orders in the individual paths in DT and derive a total variable order if possible, i.e., if DT is ordered. If there is such a total variable order Ψ, we reduce DT to an $ROBDD$ as described in Subsect. 3.3. Furthermore, we derive an ROBDD for the program or system under test as depicted in Subsect. 3.4, using the same order Ψ.

In our last step, we finally compare the two resulting ROBDDs according to Definition 1, using the recursive algorithm isEqual given in Fig. 3.

1: **function** IsEqual($Node\, n_1, Node\, n_2$)
2:     **if** isLeaf(n_1) and isLeaf(n_2) and label(n_1) == label(n_2) **then**
3:         **return** *True*
4:     **else if** isLeaf(n_1) or isLeaf($n2$) **then**
5:         **return** *False*
6:     **else**
7:         **return** label(n_1) == label(n_2) and isEqual(true(n_1), true(n_2)) and isEqual(false(n_1), false(n_2))
8:     **end if**
9: **end function**

Fig. 3. Function to decide whether two ROBDDs are equivalent.

3.1   Learning a Decision Tree from a Test Suite

Aiming at deriving a representative ROBDD for T, we certainly would like to avoid any misclassification of a test as it could occur with C4.5 (see Sect. 2). To this end, we extended the algorithm as shown in Fig. 4.

Our recursive function ADDNODE takes as input a test suite TS, a set of variables V, and a node N, and returns the root node of a binary decision tree. Initially, the set V contains n Boolean input variables of the tested Boolean function (if there is more than one function, then this means all variables other than the one chosen as the considered output during learning). Node N is a new and empty node in DT, where we assign N's properties inside ADDNODE. These properties are $N.v$, and two successor nodes $N.true$ and $N.false$. As stated in the preliminaries, there are two types of nodes. First, decision nodes which represent a test of some input variable $v \in V$ (s.t. $N.v = v$) which divides the local TS' into two subsets TS'_{v_t} and TS'_{v_f} according to the value of variable v. Correspondingly, each such decision node has exactly two successor nodes. Then there are leaf nodes, reporting the output's value of the test cases classified to this node (thus $N.v \in \mathbb{B}$). A leaf node does not have any successor nodes.

```
 1: function ADDNODE(TS, V, N)
 2:     v, g ← MAX_IG(TS, V, E(TS))
 3:     if g > 0 then
 4:         N.v ← v
 5:         N.true ← ADDNODE(TS_{v_t} ⊆ TS, V' ← V \ {v}, N' ← new_node())
 6:         N.false ← ADDNODE(TS_{v_f} ⊆ TS, V', N' ← new_node())
 7:     else
 8:         if E(TS) > 0 then
 9:             v ← V.head
10:             N.v ← v
11:             N.true ← ADDNODE(TS_{v_t} ⊆ TS, V' ← V \ {v}, N' ← new_node())
12:             N.false ← ADDNODE(TS_{v_f} ⊆ TS, V', N' ← new_node())
13:         else
14:             N.name ← OUT(TS)
15:         end if
16:     end if
17:     return N
18: end function
```

Fig. 4. Function to learn a decision tree from a test-suite TS.

In line 2, the function MAX_IG returns a variable v and its information gain g s.t. g is the maximum gain of all $v \in V$ (obviously there could be more than one such v). If there is such a variable with $g > 0$, we select it and recursively update $N.v$ and the *true* and *false* successor nodes. The two recursive calls of ADDNODE use as input $TS_{v_t} \subseteq TS$ s.t. v is *True* (or the complement TS_{v_f} for *False*), the variable set $V' \leftarrow V\backslash\{v\}$ s.t. v was removed from V, and a fresh new node N'.

If there is no variable with $g > 0$, our adaption takes control. That is, if there are still different output values for TS indicated by entropy $E(TS) > 0$, we select the first variable from V ($V.head$) as decision variable and proceed like for a decision variable selected as of above (with corresponding recursive calls for the successor nodes). If all expected outcomes for the tests in TS coincide ($E(TS) = 0$), N is a leaf node to be assigned this expected outcome OUT(TS).

Note that we assume the test suites to be deterministic. Thus the algorithm in Fig. 4 derived from C4.5 is guaranteed to terminate without misclassifications.

3.2   Isolating a Total Variable Order from *DT*

Two crucial questions for our approach are whether there is a total variable order fitting the learned decision tree DT, and in turn how to extract such an order so as to use it for generating an ROBDD for the SUT. For tackling these questions, we start by constructing an *ordering graph* as of Definition 3. But let us first define a path Π in DT and its variable sequence $\Phi = var(\Pi)$, as well as DT's alphabet.

Definition 2. *A path Π of length $|\Pi| = n$ in a decision tree DT is a sequence of nodes $\pi_0...\pi_{n-1}$ such that there is an edge from π_i to π_{i+1} (π_i is parent of*

π_{i+1}) *for* $0 \le i < n-2$. *The path of some node s in DT is the node sequence from DT's root node r to s.* $\Phi = var(\Pi)$ *is the sequence of variables* ϕ_i *considered at the individual nodes* π_i *in* Π *s.t.* $\phi_i = var(\pi_i)$. *For the leaves, that per definition have no variable* label *but are labeled either False or True, we have* $\epsilon = var(\pi_i)$ *s.t. in this case we have* $|\Phi| = |\Pi| - 1$. *The alphabet* $\Sigma = alphabet(DT)$ *is the union of the variables considered at the individual nodes in DT.*

Definition 3. *An ordering graph O for a decision tree DT is a directed graph represented by the tuple* $(Q, q_0, T \subseteq Q \times Q, \Sigma, l : Q \to \Sigma, \lambda : \Sigma \to Q)$ *such that*

- $\Sigma = alphabet(DT)$ *is a finite alphabet inherited from DT*
- Q *is a finite set of nodes, where* $|Q| = |\Sigma|$ *and for each* $\sigma \in \Sigma$ *there is some* $q_\sigma \in Q$ *s.t.* $l(q_\sigma) = \sigma$
- q_0 *is the root node, where* $l(q_0) = var(r)$ *such that r is DT's root node*
- T *is the transition relation, where* $(q_\sigma, q_\delta) \in T$ *iff DT features two nodes s and d s.t. (1) s is a parent of d, and (2)* $l(q_\sigma) = var(s)$ *and* $l(q_\delta) = var(d)$.
- l *is a labeling function that assigns each* $q \in Q$ *some* $\sigma \in \Sigma$.
- λ *is a function that returns for some* $\sigma \in \Sigma$ *a* $q_\sigma \in Q$ *such that* $l(q_\sigma) = \sigma$.

Corollary 1. *Due to* $|Q| = |\Sigma|$ *and the definition of Q, we have that for every* $\sigma \in \Sigma$ *there is a* unique $q \in Q$ *such that* $l(q) = \sigma$.

When deriving an ordering graph for a given decision tree, the construction of Q, q_0, l and λ is straightforward, and for T we can use the algorithm CREATET given in Fig. 5. This algorithm's idea is to traverse the whole tree from the leaves towards the root, and whenever we end up at the root or some state that we have visited before, we proceed with the next leaf. For each node visited in this process, we add its *incoming* edge to T, so that we end up with the edge collection required by Definition 3. It is easy to see that the algorithm terminates and that its run-time is linear in the amount of nodes in DT.

Via the following Theorem 1, we can then decide whether there is a total variable order that aggregates the individual partial orders as defined via $var(\Pi)$ by the available paths Π in DT. For our investigations it will suffice to focus on the leaves' paths since all other paths are contained in them.

Theorem 1. *For a decision tree DT with alphabet* Σ *there exists a total variable order that does not contradict any path from the root to some leaf if and only if there is no cycle in the corresponding ordering graph O as of Definition 3.*

Proof (Sketch). A basic observation about ordering graphs is that for any edge in DT from s to d s.t. $var(s) = \sigma \in \Sigma$ and $var(d) = \delta \in \Sigma$, there is also a directed edge from q_σ to q_δ in O s.t. $l(q_\sigma) = \sigma$ and $l(q_\delta) = \delta$. It is important to note that, according to Definition 3, O does not contain any other edges.

Now, let us assume that the partial variable orders as defined by the individual paths in DT contradict each other. That is, there are some variables σ and δ in Σ s.t. in some path Π^1 we have $i < j$ for $\sigma = var(\pi^1_i)$ and $\delta = var(\pi^1_j)$, but there is also some path Π^2 s.t. $j < i$ for $\sigma = var(\pi^2_i)$ and $\delta = var(\pi^2_j)$. Since for any such edge in DT, there is a corresponding

```
 1: function CREATET(DT)
 2:     unmark(DT.nodes)
 3:     T ← ∅
 4:     L ←list of DT's leaves, e.g., sorted according to depth.
 5:     while |L| > 0 do
 6:         node ← L.pop()
 7:         node ← node' = parent of node // skip leaf (has no variable label)
 8:         next ← False
 9:         while (!next) do
10:             if marked(node) then // proc. w. next leaf
11:                 next ← True
12:             else if node has parent node' then
13:                 T ← T ∪ {(node.variable, node'.variable)}
14:                 node ← node'
15:             else
16:                 mark(node)
17:             end if
18:         end while
19:     end while
20:     return T
21: end function
```

Fig. 5. Function to create T of an ordering graph for a binary tree DT.

directed edge in O, this means that $q_\delta = \lambda(\delta)$ is reachable from $q_\sigma = \lambda(\sigma)$ via the node sequence $\lambda(var(\pi^1{}_i))\ldots\lambda(var(\pi^1{}_j))$, while q_σ is reachable from q_δ via the sequence implied by Π^2 (i.e., $\lambda(var(\pi^2{}_j))\ldots\lambda(var(\pi^2{}_i))$). Consequently, O has a cycle.

Now let us assume that for any two variables σ and δ in Σ and the paths Π^k that consider *both* variables, we have for $\sigma = var(\pi^k{}_i)$ and $\delta = var(\pi^k{}_j)$ that either $i < j$ for all k or $j < i$ for all k. In other words, there are no contradictions between the individual partial orders of DT's paths. Without losing generality let us assume $i < j$. Consequently, q_δ is reachable from q_σ via any sequence implied by some path Π^k in DT that features σ and δ. However, q_σ is unreachable from q_δ. That is, due to our observation on O's edges, this would require the presence of a path in DT where we would consider q_δ before q_σ, but which contradicts our assumption. With the definition of Q, we thus cannot have a cycle in O, so that O is indeed a directed acyclic graph (DAG).

For identifying cycles in a directed graph, we can use, e.g., the STRONG-CONNECT algorithm depicted in [19].

If the ordering graph is indeed a DAG, we can retrieve *some* total order Ψ (as a sequence of $\psi_i \in \Sigma$) via the topological sorting algorithm variant CREATEORDER given in Fig. 6. The underlying idea is as follows: It is easy to see that we have that for every $\sigma \in \Sigma$, the source nodes q_α of q_σ's incoming edges define the complete set of variables $\alpha \in \Sigma$ that are considered *right* before σ for some path in DT. Consequently these variables also have to appear before

σ in a total order, and we have to consider this property in a recursive way (reasoning again from α). For easy access, we thus store T's edges in a fashion that every $q \in Q$ has a list of parents $q.inlist$ and a list of children $q.outlist$. Now, if we traverse O starting with q_0, and follow the outgoing edges of some q_σ only whenever all of q_σ's incoming edges have been followed, we can establish a total order by appending $\sigma \in \Sigma$ to the order (once) whenever the outgoing edges of q_σ "become available". If O is indeed a DAG, we can do so in a breadth-first manner (for a cycle this obviously would not work).

```
1: function CREATEORDER(O)
2:     assert isDAG(O)
3:     Ω ← ∅
4:     Ψ ← [l(q₀)]
5:     for all qᵢ ∈ q₀.outlist do
6:         remove q₀ from qᵢ.inlist
7:         Ω ← Ω ∪ {qᵢ}
8:     end for
9:     while |Ω| > 0 do
10:         pop q_σ from Ω such that |q_σ.inlist| = 0
11:         for all qᵢ ∈ q_σ.outlist do
12:             remove q_σ from qᵢ.inlist
13:             if qᵢ ∉ Ω then
14:                 Ω ← Ω ∪ {qᵢ}
15:             end if
16:         end for
17:         Ψ.append((q_σ))
18:     end while
19:     return Ψ
20: end function
```

Fig. 6. Function to derive a total order Ψ of an acyclic ordering graph O.

In our algorithm, thus, whenever we add a variable δ to Ψ (line 17), we *remove* the obligation of δ having to appear prior to σ for all σ s.t. $\lambda(\sigma)$ is a child of $\lambda(\delta)$ in line 12 (or 6 for q_0's children). Obviously, whenever all obligations have been met for some σ s.t. $|\lambda(\sigma).inlist| = 0$, we can select σ (line 10) and append it to Ψ (line 17). Since there is no reason to search for such a σ in the whole Σ, we keep a worklist Ω containing those $\lambda(\sigma)$ for which some of σ's obligations already have been met (and have been removed from $\lambda(\sigma).inlist$). This worklist is filled with nodes in two ways. That is, the first node without any obligation is obviously the root note, so that we have $l(q_0)$ as first item of Ψ (line 3) and initially fill Ω with q_0's children (lines 5–7) after treating them as described above (line 6). The second option is that, whenever we remove in line 11 an obligation from $\lambda(\sigma)$ when considering some $\delta \neq l(q_0)$ s.t. $\lambda(\delta)$ is $\lambda(\sigma)$'s parent, we search whether the node is already in Ω and add it if this is not the case (lines 13–15).

Now let us show that this algorithm is complete and sound. That is (1) that it can always derive a sequence Ψ (a total order) from some acyclic ordering graph O, and (2) that a derived sequence Ψ is indeed a total order for DT.

Theorem 2. *For some acyclic ordering graph O, the algorithm as of Fig. 6 terminates and derives a sequence Ψ of variables $\psi_i \in \Sigma$.*

Proof (Sketch). Due to line 4 and the fact that we only append $\sigma \in \Sigma$ ($l : Q \rightarrow \Sigma$) to Ψ in line 17, this leaves us to show that the algorithm terminates correctly if O is a DAG. Given the algorithm's structure, the crucial lines in this respect are lines 9 and 10. That is, line 2 is no problem if O is a DAG, but we have to show that Ω becomes empty at some point such that we leave the while loop, and that we can indeed pop some q_σ in line 10 for avoiding a deadlock.

Let us start with the latter s.t. Ω is non-empty. Now let us assume that Ω contains some q_σ s.t. $|q_\sigma.inlist| > 0$ with $q_\delta \in q_\sigma.inlist$. Due to T and lines 10 to 15, this means that either q_δ is in Ω, or one of its ancestors $\lambda(var(\pi_i^k))$ in path Π^k in DT s.t. $i < j$ for $\delta = l(\pi_j^k)$. That is, since we initialized Ω with all children of q_0, due to lines 10 to 15 the only way for none of them to be in Ω would be that all obligations of q_δ were already fulfilled and q_δ was already chosen in line 10 and added to Ψ. But then q_δ would not be in $q_\sigma.inlist$ (see also the argument below). Assuming $\lambda(var(\pi_i^k))$ to be in Ω then means that either we could choose this node if its *inlist* is empty, or via its inlist we could again find some node in Ω as described above. Since O is acyclic and $|Q| = |\Sigma|$ is finite, the number of times we have to do this until finding some node in Ω s.t. its inlist is empty is limited. It directly follows that if $|\Omega| > 0$, then there is also always a node q_σ in Ω s.t. $|q_\sigma.inlist| = 0$ that we can choose in line 10.

Now let us show that Ω becomes empty eventually, which directly follows from the fact that $|Q|$ is finite and that we have that some $q_\sigma \in Q$ is added to Ω only once. That is, if q_0 is a parent of q_σ, then we add it to Ω in line 7. If not, then, when the first of q_σ's parents is chosen in line 10, we add q_σ to Ω in line 14. When in Ω, q_σ is not added a second time due to line 13. After q_σ was chosen in line 10 (and consequently removed from Ω) it will never be added again. That is, all of σ's obligations regarding variables that have to appear prior to σ have been met s.t. $\lambda(\sigma).inlist$ became empty—there is no further incoming edge that has not been considered so far and could add q_σ to Ω via lines 11 to 14. Since $|Q|$ is finite and there is always a node to choose in line 10, thus Ω becomes empty at some point s.t. the algorithm terminates successfully if O is acyclic.

Corollary 2. *Each $\sigma \in \Sigma$ appears exactly once in Ψ as of Theorem 2.*

The validity of the corollary is easy to see via Corollary 1, the definitions of T and Q, and the fact that some $q \in Q$ is added and removed from Ω (s.t. q's label is appended to Ψ) exactly once (for the latter see the proof of Theorem 2). That is, every q aside q_0 (but whose label is initially appended to Ψ in line 4) has some incoming edge(s) and if O is a DAG it is finally added to Ω (lines 7 or 14) when the first of its parents is selected (lines 5 or 10) as well as finally selected itself in line 10 (s.t. $l(q)$ is appended to Ψ in line 17) since the algorithm terminates (for both see the proof of Theorem 2). From Corollary 1 it then directly follows that each $\sigma \in \Sigma$ appears exactly once in Ψ.

Theorem 3. *The sequence Ψ returned by the algorithm as of Fig. 6 for some acyclic ordering graph O is a total order. This means that for every path Π in O's DT we have for any $0 \le i, j < |\Pi|$ s.t. $i \ne j$ that $k < m$ if $i < j$ or $k > m$ if $i > j$ for $\psi_k = \lambda(\pi_i)$ and $\psi_m = \lambda(\pi_j)$.*

Proof (Sketch). This directly follows from Corollary 2 and the proof of Theorem 2. That is, since q_σ is removed from Ω and appended to Σ only if all the obligations about variables that have to be present in Ω prior to σ (as encoded "recursively" in $\lambda(\sigma).inlist$), it is ensured that there is no path in DT that has some variable α being considered before σ s.t. α is not in Ψ when adding σ. Due to Corollary 2, we furthermore have that every $\sigma \in \Sigma$ is present in Ψ and appears exactly once. Thus Ψ is a total order as desired.

3.3 Reducing the Learned Decision Tree *DT* to an ROBDD

If we successfully retrieved a total variable order from DT, we use an algorithm depicted by Bryant in [4] to reduce our *ordered* decision tree to an ROBDD. The idea behind his algorithm is to implement the following three rules [5]:

1. **Remove duplicate leaf nodes:** Eliminate all but one DT's leaf nodes with the same label and redirect all edges from the eliminated nodes to the corresponding remaining equivalent one.
2. **Remove duplicate nodes representing variables:** If two nodes $n_1, n_2 \in N$ have the same label, the outgoing edges $e_0(n_1)$ and $e_0(n_2)$ point to equivalent nodes, and also the outgoing edges $e_1(n_1)$ and $e_1(n_2)$ point to equivalent nodes, then eliminate n_1 and redirect all its incoming edges to n_2.
3. **Remove redundant tests:** If a node n's outgoing edges $e_0(n)$ and $e_1(n)$ lead to the same node n', eliminate n and redirect its incoming edges to n'.

Figure 7 illustrates the application of these three reduction rules on an example decision tree with three variables. From left to right, we first applied rule 1, such that we only have two leaf nodes, one for each $b \in \mathbb{B}$. Then we merge redundant nodes (rule 2) leaving us with only two nodes labeled with x_3 instead of four. In the last step, we remove two nodes with redundant/meaningless tests for x_2 and x_3 arriving at the ROBDD on the right. If none of the three reduction rules is applicable anymore, then the result is an ROBDD.

3.4 Creating an ROBDD for the SUT's Specification

For creating an ROBDD from a Boolean function f, we use the algorithm presented in [2]. The underlying scheme is based on the *if-then-else normal form (INF)*, where a Boolean function is built entirely via the if-then-else operator, e.g., the if-then-else operator $x \to y_0, y_1$ is defined by $x \to y_0, y_1 = (x \wedge y_0) \vee (\neg x \wedge y_1)$. From f's INF we create an ROBDD by applying Shannon expansion [17], where the total variable order Ψ obtained from DT is used

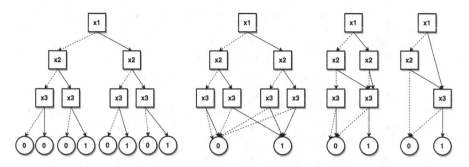

Fig. 7. Reduction of ordered decision tree to ROBDD, from left to right [5].

to replace the variables by constants in $\mathbb{B}$. Please note that any variable v present in TS but not appearing in DT or Ψ (v is of no consequence) should be appended to Ψ for this construction (but should be absent from the ROBDD in the end).

When replacing the variables by Boolean constants, the Shannon cofactors emerge. Each cofactor can be viewed as an outgoing edge of a node in the ROBDD where the replaced variable represents the node. While creating the ROBDD, equivalent nodes are replaced such that after finalizing the ROBDD none of the reduction rules introduced in Sect. 3.3 can be applied.

Since the size of the ROBDD depends heavily on the variable order used, and finding a variable order that minimizes an ROBDD's size is a co-NP-complete problem [4], we extract a variable order from DT via entropy-based learning, rather than trying to come up with an ideal order for the SUT's ROBDD to be used then also for the test suite T's ROBDD.

4   Experimental Results

For evaluating our approach, we investigated its performance for 20 examples taken from [24] representing formal specifications (as shown in Fig. 8) for TCAS II, an aircraft collision avoidance system. For these 20 Boolean specifications with 5 to 14 Boolean input variables, we generated corresponding Boolean functions and exhaustive test suites featuring all possible input combinations.

The results reported in Table 2 were obtained by generating 100 different random test suites T s.t. we could classify T for each example. Since we cannot yet classify T if its ordering graph has some cycle, we sometimes had to create more than the 100, where the corresponding number of discarded ones is given in Table 1 (there were next to none classifiable duplicates that we had to discard). Each T was derived by randomly selecting test cases t from an example's exhaustive test suite s.t. $t \in T$ with a probability of 0.5.

For each of an example's 100 test suites, we calculated the mutation score, i.e., the proportion of mutants that T was able to *kill*. If some T showed different behavior for a mutant f' compared to f, then T was able to kill the mutant. For generating the mutants f' we replaced f's binary operators with alternatives, where the number of resulting mutants ($\#f'$) is given in Table 1.

1. (¬(a ∧ b)) ∧ (d ∧ (¬e) ∧ (¬f) ∨ (¬d) ∧ e ∧ (¬f) ∨ (¬d) ∧ (¬e) ∧ (¬f)) ∧ (a ∧ c ∧ (d ∨ e) ∧ h ∨ a ∧ (d ∨ e) ∧ (¬h) ∨ b ∧ (e ∨ f))
2. (a ∧ ((c ∨ d ∨ e) ∧ g ∨ a ∧ f ∨ c ∧ (f ∨ g ∨ h ∨ i)) ∨ (a ∨ b) ∧ (c ∨ d ∨ e) ∧ i) ∧ (¬(a ∧ b)) ∧ (¬(c ∧ d)) ∧ (¬(c ∧ e)) ∧ (¬(d ∧ e)) ∧ (¬(f ∧ g)) ∧ (¬(f ∧ h)) ∧ (¬(f ∧ i)) ∧ (¬(g ∧ h)) ∧ (¬(h ∧ i))
3. (a ∧ ((¬d) ∨ (¬e) ∨ d ∧ e ∧ (¬((¬f) ∧ g ∧ h ∧ (¬i) ∨ (¬g) ∧ h ∧ i)) ∧ (¬((¬f) ∧ g ∧ l ∧ k ∨ (¬g) ∧ (¬i) ∧ k))) ∨ (¬((¬f) ∧ g ∧ h ∧ (¬i) ∨ (¬g) ∧ h ∧ i)) ∧ (¬((¬f) ∧ g ∧ l ∧ k ∨ (¬g) ∧ (¬i) ∧ k)) ∧ (b ∨ c ∧ (¬m) ∨ f)) ∧ (a ∧ (¬b) ∧ (¬c) ∨ (¬a) ∧ b ∧ (¬c) ∨ (¬a) ∧ (¬b) ∧ c)
4. a ∧ ((¬b) ∨ (¬c)) ∧ (d ∨ e)
5. a ∧ ((¬b) ∨ (¬c) ∨ b ∧ c ∧ (¬((¬f) ∧ g ∧ h ∧ (¬i) ∨ (¬g) ∧ h ∧ i)) ∧ (¬((¬f) ∧ g ∧ l ∧ k ∨ (¬g) ∧ (¬i) ∧ k))) ∨ f
6. ((¬a) ∧ b ∨ a ∧ (¬b)) ∧ (¬(c ∧ d)) ∧ (f ∧ (¬g) ∧ (¬h) ∨ (¬f) ∧ g ∧ (¬h) ∨ (¬f) ∧ (¬g) ∧ (¬h)) ∧ (¬(j ∧ k)) ∧ ((a ∧ c ∨ b ∧ d) ∧ e ∧ (f ∨ (i ∧ (g ∧ j ∨ h ∧ k))))
7. ((¬a) ∧ b ∨ a ∧ (¬b)) ∧ (¬(c ∧ d)) ∧ (¬(g ∧ h)) ∧ (¬(j ∧ k)) ∧ ((a ∧ c ∨ b ∧ d) ∧ e ∧((¬i) ∨ (¬g) ∧ k ∨ (¬j) ∧ ((¬h) ∨ (¬k))))
8. ((¬a) ∧ b ∨ a ∧ (¬b)) ∧ (¬(c ∧ d)) ∧ (¬(g ∧ h)) ∧ ((a ∧ c ∨ b ∧ d) ∧ e ∧ (f ∧ g ∨ (¬f) ∧ h))
9. (¬(c ∧ d)) ∧ ((¬e) ∧ f ∧ (¬g) ∧ (¬a) ∧ (b ∧ c ∨ (¬b) ∧ d))
10. a ∧ (¬b) ∧ (¬c) ∧ d ∧ (¬e) ∧ f ∧ (g ∨ (¬g) ∧ (h ∨ i)) ∧ (¬(j ∧ k ∨ (¬j) ∧ l ∨ m))
11. a ∧ (¬b) ∧ (¬c) ∧ ((¬(f ∧ (g ∨ (¬g) ∧ (h ∨ i)))) ∨ f ∧ (g ∨ (¬g) ∧ (h ∨ i)) ∧ (¬d) ∧ (¬e)) ∧ (¬(j ∧ k ∨ (¬j) ∧ l ∧ (¬m)))
12. a ∧ (¬b) ∧ (¬c) ∧ f ∧ (g ∨ (¬g) ∧ (h ∨ i)) ∧ ((¬e) ∧ (¬n) ∨ d) ∨ (¬n) ∧ (j ∧ k ∨ (¬j) ∧ l ∧ (¬m))
13. a ∨ b ∨ c ∨ (¬c) ∧ (¬d) ∧ e ∧ f ∧ (¬g) ∧ (¬h) ∨ i ∧ (j ∨ k) ∧ (¬l)
14. a ∧ (¬b) ∧ (¬c) ∧ f ∧ (g ∨ (¬g) ∧ (h ∨ i)) ∧ ((¬e) ∧ (¬n) ∨ d) ∨ (¬n) ∧ (j ∧ k ∨ (¬j) ∧ l ∧ (¬m))
15. a ∧ ((c ∨ d ∨ e) ∧ g ∨ a ∧ f ∨ c ∧ (f ∨ g ∨ h ∨ i)) ∨ (a ∨ b) ∧ (c ∨ d ∨ e) ∧ i
16. a ∧ ((¬d) ∨ (¬e) ∨ d ∧ e ∧ (¬((¬f) ∧ g ∧ h ∧ (¬i) ∨ (¬g) ∧ h ∧ i)) ∧ (¬((¬f) ∧ g ∧ l ∧ k ∨ (¬g) ∧ (¬i) ∧ k))) ∨ (¬((¬f) ∧ g ∧ h ∧ (¬i) ∨ (¬g) ∧ h ∧ i)) ∧ (¬((¬f) ∧ g ∧ l ∧ k ∨ (¬g) ∧ (¬i) ∧ k)) ∧ (b ∨ c ∧ (¬m) ∨ f)
17. (a ∧ c ∨ b ∧ d) ∧ e ∧ (f ∨ (i ∧ (g ∧ j ∨ h ∧ k)))
18. (a ∧ c ∨ b ∧ d) ∧ e ∧ ((¬i) ∨ (¬g) ∧ (¬k) ∨ (¬j) ∧ ((¬h) ∨ (¬k)))
19. (a ∧ c ∨ b ∧ d) ∧ e ∧ (f ∧ g ∨ (¬f) ∧ h)
20. (¬e) ∧ f ∧ (¬g) ∧ (¬a) ∧ (b ∧ c ∨ (¬b) ∧ d)

Fig. 8. The 20 TCAS II examples taken from [24].

Table 1. Number of detected cycles while creating 100 random test suites and the number of mutants $\#f'$ for each example.

Example	1	2	3	4	5	6	7	8	9	10
Cycles	155	197	444289	0	18	72	898	6	0	144
$\#f'$	22	34	45	4	19	27	20	16	9	14
Example	11	12	13	14	15	16	17	18	19	20
Cycles	75391	340002	192	43	47	641685	8588	2216	54	0
$\#f'$	18	16	12	11	16	36	10	10	8	7

Considering our classification into effective and ineffective test suites (sets T_+ and T_-), and comparing it to the maximum mutation score (1.0 for all examples), we would get only a few "false" positives ($MS(T \in T_+)$) like for example 8, where one of the two $T \in T_+$ killed only 14 out of 16 mutants (we found those two remaining mutants to be equivalent after closer inspection). For the total 37 Ts classified to be effective for some example, this means that only for one T the corresponding $MS(T)$ was less than the maximum achievable mutation score. Since T_+ was underrepresented in the random test suites (as we expected), we generated for each of the six examples 1/6/9/10/15/20 another 100 test suites s.t. we could classify 50 as effective and 50 as ineffective and report their performance in Table 3. Note that for examples 2, 3, 12, 14, and 16 we could not derive 50 effective test suites, likely a downside of us currently requiring O to be acyclic. Out of those 300 *effective* Ts only one for example 15 did not have $MS(T) = 1.00 (= max.)$ but killed 16 out of 17 generated mutants only ($MS(T) = 0.94$). If we consider the ratio between T_+ and T_- from Table 2 we can also say that our approach is quite conservative in handing out its quality

Table 2. Performance for 100 random T classified as effective T_+ or ineffective T_-.

Sample		$|T_i|$	$|T \in T_i|$ min.	avg.	max.	$MS(T \in T_i)$ min.	avg.	max.	Sample		$|T_i|$	$|T \in T_i|$ min.	avg.	max.	$MS(T \in T_i)$ min.	avg.	max.
1	T_+	1	63	63	63	1.00	1.00	1.00	11	T_+	0	–	–	–	–	–	–
	T_-	99	49	62	78	0.64	0.96	1.00		T_-	100	3973	4099	4219	1.00	1.00	1.00
2	T_+	0	–	–	–	–	–	–	12	T_+	0	–	–	–	–	–	–
	T_-	100	213	250	289	0.74	0.87	1.00		T_-	100	749	805	875	0.94	0.99	1.00
3	T_+	0	–	–	–	–	–	–	13	T_+	0	–	–	–	–	–	–
	T_-	100	331	398	444	0.75	0.93	1.00		T_-	100	1987	2045	2132	1.00	1.00	1.00
4	T_+	5	18	22	24	1.00	1.00	1.00	14	T_+	0	–	–	–	–	–	–
	T_-	95	9	15	21	0.75	0.99	1.00		T_-	100	44	63	77	1.00	1.00	1.00
5	T_+	1	265	265	265	1.00	1.00	1.00	15	T_+	22	234	259	278	1.00	1.00	1.00
	T_-	99	226	252	288	0.95	0.98	1.00		T_-	78	231	254	282	0.88	0.99	1.00
6	T_+	1	1031	1031	1031	1.00	1.00	1.00	16	T_+	0	–	–	–	–	–	–
	T_-	99	966	1000	1075	0.70	0.94	1.00		T_-	100	164	192	235	0.69	0.94	1.00
7	T_+	0	–	–	–	–	–	–	17	T_+	0	–	–	–	–	–	–
	T_-	100	475	498	553	0.85	0.97	1.00		T_-	100	968	1019	1067	1.00	1.00	1.00
8	T_+	2	125	127	129	0.88	0.94	1.00	18	T_+	1	504	504	504	1.00	1.00	1.00
	T_-	98	102	125	158	0.69	0.95	1.00		T_-	99	473	510	547	1.00	1.00	1.00
9	T_+	1	71	71	71	1.00	1.00	1.00	19	T_+	0	–	–	–	–	–	–
	T_-	99	50	63	73	0.55	0.92	1.00		T_-	100	103	124	·143	1.00	1.00	1.00
10	T_+	1	4211	4211	4211	1.00	1.00	1.00	20	T_+	2	61	69	77	1.00	1.00	1.00
	T_-	99	3978	4090	4219	0.86	0.99	1.00		T_-	98	47	63	78	0.85	0.98	1.00

label. Keeping in mind that T does not provide the entire truth table, thus the *learned* classification is certainly attractive from those two points of view, at least considering our first experiments. Since we saw in our experiments also that some Ts with an ideal mutation score of 1.0 were classified as ineffective ($T \in T_-$), there is the immediate question whether the computed mutation scores were holistic enough, and what would be an ideal benchmark for comparing our classification (since it could also have been more precise than the mutants).

In terms of encoding efficiency, we see in Table 3 that the average size (amount of decision nodes) in the ROBBD R derived for some T was below $2 * \#v$, and most of the times ranged between $\#v$ and $\#v + \frac{\#v}{2}$. Even the maximum size for any R was below $2.5 * \#v$. Thus it seems that our information gain based

Table 3. The experimental results for 6 of the 20 example specifications.

ex.	#v	$\varnothing|R|$	$max.|R|$	$MS(T \in T_+) = 1$	$MS(T \in T_-) = 1$	$\varnothing |T \in T_+|$	$\varnothing |T \in T_-|$
1	7	11.06	15	50	22	68.56	63.42
6	11	17.04	26	50	39	1847.38	1848.18
9	7	9.36	12	50	30	67.56	65.18
10	13	14.34	17	50	48	5467.16	5457.62
15	9	11.05	15	49	40	259.06	252.78
20	7	7.8	14	50	32	31.18	25.84

learning of DT gives a compact ROBDD R with a size far below the worst case $2^{\#v} - 1$ [1].

The run-time for our classification can vary quite a bit with the example. For examples 10 and 20, it took us about 117 s and about 0.5 s to classify all 100 test suites as of Table 3, which we find to be quite attractive.

5   Related Research

In [23], Weyuker introduces a method to assess test data adequacy through program inference. Weyuker defines the relation that if a program is adequately tested, then it is correct, but a correct program does not imply that it has been adequately tested. For assessing adequacy, Weyuker uses inference adequacy, where a test suite is adequate if and only if the test suite contains sufficient data to infer the computations defined in the program under test and its specifications. Weyuker infers programs in a subset of Lisp, but we learn a decision tree from the test data. Inference adequacy also depends on the determination of equivalence, but equivalence of a specification, a program, and an inferred program is in general undecidable. Therefore Weyuker uses approximations to make the inference adequacy criterion usable. Since T gives an incomplete truth table, our learned decision tree DT also is some sort of approximation. In [21] Walkinshaw introduces a test suite adequacy assessment method based on inductive inference, which does not require exact inference, but uses the Probably Approximately Correct (PAC) [20] framework for approximations. To determine equivalence of the inferred model of the test suite and the program under test's specifications we transfer both into ROBDDs where equivalence is decidable.

A family of different strategies, including MAX-A and MAX-B, for automatically generating test cases for Boolean expressions in disjunctive normal form (DNF) is given in [24], where they investigate also the fault detection effectiveness of the different strategies. For our evaluation we used their examples, but in contrast to evaluating test case generation (TCG), our approach classifies any given test suite T. In [6], Chen et al. describe how to generate test suites that satisfy the MUMCUT strategy for testing Boolean expressions in DNF. The MUMCUT strategy guarantees to detect seven fault types found in Boolean expressions. Also in that paper, the examples from [24] were used to evaluate their approach. In contrast to MAX-A, MAX-B, and MUMCUT, for our approach it is not necessary for the program under test's specifications to appear in a certain normal form.

A strategy to assess the effectiveness of a test suite for decisions (i.e. Boolean expressions) is the modified condition/decision coverage (MCDC) criterion [7] which requires that each condition within a decision is shown by execution to independently affect the outcome of the decision. Showing that each condition independently affects the decision's outcome requires either that the test case generation was directed to satisfy the MCDC criterion, or to execute the program with the inputs from the test suite and check which conditions affect the outcome. Our classification approach does not require the execution of the program under test. MCDC requires for n input variables a test suite at least of size $n + 1$. We saw the requirement reflected also in our experiments when considering T_+. Since the size of a BDD is very sensitive to its variable order, Friedman and Supowit showed in [9] an algorithm for finding an optimal one which is in $O(n^2 3^n)$. Grumberg et al. propose in [10] an approach in which the variable ordering algorithm for creating BDDs gains experience from training models and uses the learned knowledge for finding good orders. In our work, we use entropy and information gain measures for the concrete example and a specific local situation for establishing the variable order.

In contrast to the work about learning automata [13, 16, 18, 22] which is based on active learning while executing the program under test, our approach is passive which means that executing the program under test to classify the test suite effectiveness is not necessary.

6 Conclusion

In this paper, we proposed a new approach at classifying a test suite T's effectiveness in identifying a program's functional faults. To this end, we tailored a special learning algorithm from C4.5 in order to learn a representative decision tree DT from T. If possible, we showed how to isolate a total variable order Ψ from DT via a derived ordering graph, so that we then use Ψ when deriving a corresponding reduced ordered binary decision diagram also for the SUT's specification. If we were able to retrieve an order Ψ, we reduce also DT to an ROBDD in order to check the two ROBDDs for equivalence.

Our argument is that if they are equivalent, we can assume that a program satisfying T implements the desired functionality as described by the specification (in the form of Boolean functions). In our initial experiments as reported in this paper, we computed the mutation score for random test suites and compared it to our classification. Even if we assume only the maximum mutation score to be the benchmark for our effectiveness classification (without some error margin), there were only very few "false positives", i.e. 2 out of 337 effective Ts. That we classified also some test suites with a perfect mutation score to be ineffective raises the question whether our mutations, and the mutation score in general, is holistic enough as benchmark for our classification, or if our effectiveness label was more precise than the considered mutations. A corresponding investigation with more examples from multiple domains and further mutation operators [11, 12, 14] will be subject to future work.

Aside conducting more experiments and evaluating further benchmark options, future research will also target the question of whether there would be more attractive representations like multi-terminal binary decision diagrams [8] (compared to an ROBDD) for our cause. Currently we are working on finding a suitable approximation metric that relaxes exact equality. Also the implementation of a reordering algorithm is on our agenda, so that we can use our approach also if the initial ordering graph is not acyclic.

Acknowledgement. Parts of this work were accomplished at the VIRTUAL VEHI-CLE Research Center in Graz, Austria. The authors would like to acknowledge the financial support of the European Commission under FP-7 agreement number 608770 (project "edas"), of the COMET K2 - Competence Centers for Excellent Technologies Programme of the Austrian Federal Ministry for Transport, Innovation and Technology (bmvit), the Austrian Federal Ministry of Science, Research and Economy (bmwfw), the Austrian Research Promotion Agency (FFG), the Province of Styria and the Styrian Business Promotion Agency (SFG). They would furthermore like to express their thanks to their supporting industrial and scientific project partners, namely AVL List and to the Graz University of Technology.

References

1. Akers, S.B.: Binary decision diagrams. IEEE Trans. Comput. **27**(6), 509–516 (1978)
2. Andersen, H.R.: An Introduction to Binary Decision Diagrams. Lecture notes, available online. IT University of Copenhagen (1997)
3. Brandis, M.M., Mössenböck, H.: Single-pass generation of static assignment form for structured languages. ACM TOPLAS **16**(6), 1684–1698 (1994)
4. Bryant, E.R.: Graph-based algorithms for Boolean function manipulation. IEEE Trans. Comput. **35**(8), 677–691 (1986)
5. Bryant, R.E.: Symbolic Boolean manipulation with ordered binary-decision diagrams. ACM Comput. Surv. **24**(3), 293–318 (1992)
6. Chen, T., Lau, M., Yu, Y.: MUMCUT: a fault-based strategy for testing Boolean specifications. In: Proceedings of the Sixth Asia Pacific Software Engineering Conference (APSEC), pp. 606–613 (1999)
7. Chilenski, J., Miller, S.P.: Applicability of modified condition/decision coverage to software testing. Softw. Eng. J. **9**(5), 193–200 (1994)
8. Clarke, E.M., Fujita, M., Zhao, X.: Multi-terminal binary decision diagrams and hybrid decision diagrams. In: Sasao, T., Fujita, M. (eds.) Representations of Discrete Functions, pp. 93–108. Springer, New York (1996)
9. Friedman, S.J., Supowit, K.J.: Finding the optimal variable ordering for binary decision diagrams. In: Proceedings of the 24th ACM/IEEE Design Automation Conference (DAC), pp. 348–356 (1987)
10. Grumberg, O., Livne, S., Markovitch, S.: Learning to order BDD variables in verification. J. Artif. Intell. Res. **18**(1), 83–116 (2003)
11. Henard, C., Papadakis, M., Traon, Y.L.: MutaLog: a tool for mutating logic formulas. In: Proceedings of the 7th IEEE International Conference onSoftware Testing, Verification, and Validation Workshops, ICSTW, pp. 399–404. IEEE Computer Society, Washington, DC (2014)
12. Lau, M.F., Yu, Y.T.: An extended fault class hierarchy for specification-based testing. ACM Trans. Softw. Eng. Methodol. **14**(3), 247–276 (2005)
13. Meinke, K., Sindhu, M.A.: Incremental learning-based testing for reactive systems. In: Gogolla, M., Wolff, B. (eds.) TAP 2011. LNCS, vol. 6706, pp. 134–151. Springer, Heidelberg (2011)
14. Paul, T.K., Lau, M.F.: Redefinition of fault classes in logic expressions. In: Proceedings of the 12th International Conference on Quality Software, pp. 144–153. QSIC, IEEE Computer Society, Washington, DC (2012)
15. Quinlan, J.R.: C4.5: Programs for Machine Learning. Morgan Kaufmann Publishers Inc., San Francisco (1993)

16. Shahbaz, M., Groz, R.: Inferring Mealy machines. In: Cavalcanti, A., Dams, D.R. (eds.) FM 2009. LNCS, vol. 5850, pp. 207–222. Springer, Heidelberg (2009)
17. Shannon, C.: The synthesis of two-terminal switching circuits. Bell Syst. Tech. J. **28**(1), 59–98 (1949)
18. Steffen, B., Howar, F., Merten, M.: Introduction to active automata learning from a practical perspective. In: Bernardo, M., Issarny, V. (eds.) SFM 2011. LNCS, vol. 6659, pp. 256–296. Springer, Heidelberg (2011)
19. Tarjan, R.: Depth-first search and linear graph algorithms. In: 12th Annual Symposium on Switching and Automata Theory, pp. 114–121 (1971)
20. Valiant, L.G.: A theory of the learnable. Commun. ACM **27**(11), 1134–1142 (1984)
21. Walkinshaw, N.: The practical assessment of test sets with inductive inference techniques. In: Proceedings of the 5th International Academic and Industrial Conference on Testing - Practice and Research Techniques (TAIC PART), pp. 165–172 (2010)
22. Walkinshaw, N., Taylor, R., Derrick, J.: Inferring extended finite state machine models from software executions. Empir. Softw. Eng. **21**(3), 811–853 (2016)
23. Weyuker, E.J.: Assessing test data adequacy through program inference. ACM Trans. Program. Lang. Syst. **5**(4), 641–655 (1983)
24. Weyuker, E.J., Goradia, T., Singh, A.: Automatically generating test data from a Boolean specification. IEEE Trans. Softw. Eng. **20**(5), 353–363 (1994)

Lightweight Symbolic Verification of Graph Transformation Systems with Off-the-Shelf Hardware Model Checkers

Sebastian Gabmeyer[1(✉)] and Martina Seidl[2]

[1] Security Engineering Group, TU Darmstadt, Darmstadt, Germany
gabmeyer@seceng.informatik.tu-darmstadt.de
[2] Institute for Formal Models and Verification, JKU Linz, Linz, Austria
martina.seidl@jku.at

Abstract. We present a novel symbolic bounded model checking approach to test reachability properties of model-driven software implementations. Given a concrete initial state of a software system, a type graph, and a set of graph transformations, which describe the system's structure and its behavior, the system is tested against a reachability property that is expressed in terms of a graph constraint. Without any user intervention, our approach exploits state-of-the-art model checking technologies successfully used in hardware industry. The efficiency of our approach is demonstrated in two case studies.

1 Introduction

The growing demand for more sophisticated functionality considerably increases the complexity of state-of-the-art software and the complexity of today's software development [1,10,18]. With the rise in complexity, more defects tend to get introduced into the code [27]. To counter this challenge, graphical and textual modeling languages, like the Unified Modeling Language (UML) [20], began to permeate the modern software development process. The motivation of lifting models to first-class development artifacts is twofold: first, models abstract away irrelevant details and, second, they express ideas and solutions in the language of the problem domain offering a focused view to the developers.

In the context of the model-driven engineering (MDE) paradigm, *model transformations* play a pivotal role [8,23] when rewriting the models, e.g., to generate executable code or to perform refactorings, or when specifying the behavior of models. Unfortunately, software development based on models and model transformations is not immune to defects. In fact, errors introduced at the modeling layer might propagate to the executable code and might be hard to detect. Baurry et al. [3] emphasize that model transformations show characteristics that lead to challenging barriers to systematic testing. One particular problem encountered when testing is the complexity of the resulting output models whose correctness cannot be easily validated. A natural solution is a constructive approach where first the models are generated by executing the model transformation and then checking constraints the output model has to satisfy. If the

B.K. Aichernig and C.A. Furia (Eds.): TAP 2016, LNCS 9762, pp. 94–111, 2016.
DOI: 10.1007/978-3-319-41135-4_6

model transformation contains errors, however, this approach does not provide any debugging support, because the intermediate models are not considered and hence the defect becomes hard to trace. Also, the testing is usually non-exhaustive and model transformations are often applied nondeterministically. Again, as a consequence, defects might be overseen. A solution is the lightweight, i.e., depth-bounded, integration of verification approaches like model checking into the testing process. In model checking, a specification is tested against the system and, in case a violation is found, an error trace is returned. Model checking is successfully used to verify hardware systems; for software, however, there are still many challenges that have to be overcome. Models and model transformations miss many of the features that make software model checking difficult and, thus, model checking is a promising technique to overcome the barriers of testing model transformations.

In this paper, we propose a lightweight verification approach based on symbolic model checking for testing the correctness of graph transformations. It is "lightweight" in the sense that it only allows to verify systems up to a user-defined object count. Among the multitude of available model transformation languages, we choose graph transformations [11,21], which offer a formal and concise language to describe modifications on graphs and, hence, on models. Graph transformations can be shown to be Turing complete [17] and, therefore, they are as expressive as any other conventional programming language. Any software system may thus formally be described by a graph transformation system (GTS). The testing and verification of correctness properties of graph transformation systems has been previously explored and implemented in previous works, most notably by CHECKVML [22] and GROOVE [16]. Both of these approaches represent states as graphs and enumerate the set of all reachable states before evaluating a property to valid or producing a counterexample trace. With MOCOCL [6] we too presented a model checker that enumerates the states on the fly leading to better performance when short counterexamples exist.

In contrast to previous works, we present a symbolic model checking approach in this paper that uses logical formulas to represent the state space. For the symbolic encoding of graph transformation systems we employ relational logic because of (a) the high resemblance between sentences of relational logic, on the one hand, and graphs and graph transformations on the other hand, and (b) the tool support available to convert bounded, first-order relational logic into propositional logic [26]. We thus map the execution semantics of graph transformation systems to bounded, first-order relational logic. On this basis we construct a relational transition system (RTS) that is then automatically checked by state-of-the-art hardware model checkers. A similar yet preliminary relational encoding of graph transformations in ALLOY [14] has been presented by [2]. Our approach, in contrast, performs the encoding fully automatic, needs no manual interaction with ALLOY during the verification, and is extensible to accommodate the translation of amalgamated/parallel graph transformations [4] and arithmetic integer expression in attribute values. Both of these extensions have been implemented but are saved for future work as they go beyond the scope of this paper.

This paper is structured as follows. We start with a presentation of our running example in Sect. 2. Then we introduce the required preliminaries in Sect. 3. In Sect. 4 we provide a high-level overview of our proposed approach. In Sect. 5 we outline the relational semantics of graph transformations in depth and discuss the symbolic encoding. Then we present the results of two case studies in Sect. 6. Section 7 concludes with an outlook on future work.

2   Running Example

In the Dining Philosophers (DP) problem's setup [9,12] a group of philosophers sits around a table with a plate in front of each of them and a fork on each side of the plate. Philosophers transition through a sequence of three states: *thinking*, *hungry*, and *eating*. Once they finish eating they go back into think-

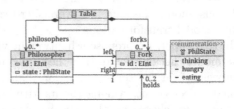

Fig. 1. Metamodel of DP

ing. Each philosopher requires two forks to start eating. These forks, however, are shared with the philosophers sitting to the philosopher's left and right.

The static structure of the DP problem's graph transformation system is given in terms of the metamodel shown in Fig. 1. The behavior of each philosopher is defined by four graph transformations depicted in Fig. 2. The *Get Hungry* transformation rewrites the philosopher's `state` attribute to transition from

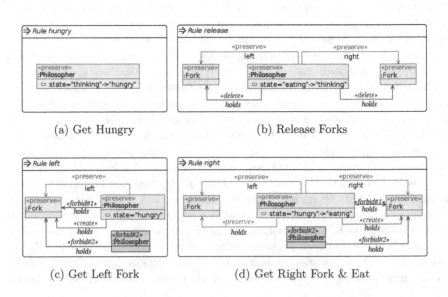

(a) Get Hungry   (b) Release Forks

(c) Get Left Fork   (d) Get Right Fork & Eat

Fig. 2. Graph transformations for the dining philosophers in HENSHIN

state *thinking* to state *hungry*. A hungry philosopher needs to eat and attempts to acquire a left fork first; this is achieved by applying the *Get Left Fork* transformation that establishes a `hold` reference between a *hungry* philosopher and her `left` fork. The negative application conditions (NAC), *forbid#1* and *forbid#2*, ensure that a `holds` reference my only be established to those forks not held by the philosopher herself (*forbid#1*) or any other philosopher (*forbid#2*). Once a philosopher holds the left fork, the *Get Right Fork &Eat* transformation picks up the appropriate right fork and changes the philosopher's `state` from *hungry* to *eating*. Again, the NACs *forbid#1* and *forbid#2* prohibit forks from being picked up if held by a philosopher. If a philosopher is done eating, the *Release Forks* transformation puts back the forks on the table and switches the philosopher's `state` to *thinking* again.

3 Preliminaries

Graph Transformations. Graphs and graph transformations are a popular choice to formally describe models and model transformations. For this purpose the theory of graph transformations has been extended to support rewriting of attributed, typed graphs with inheritance and containment (part-of) relations [5]. In the following, we summarize the concepts relevant for this work. For details see [11,21]. A *graph* $G = (V_G, E_G)$ consists of a set V_G of nodes, a set E_G of edges. Further, we define a source and a target function, $src : E_G \to V_G$ and $tgt : E_G \to V_G$, that map edges to their source and target vertices. A *morphism* $m : G \to H$ is a structure preserving mapping between graphs G and H. A double pushout graph transformation $p : L \leftarrow K \to R$, with injective morphisms $l : K \to L$ and $r : K \to R$, describes how the left-hand side (LHS) graph L is transformed into the right-hand side (RHS) graph R via an interface graph K. A graph transformation $p : L \leftarrow K \to R$ is *applied* to a *host graph* G if there exists an injective morphism $m : L \to G$, called a *match*, that maps the LHS graph L into the host graph G. This match must not violate the *dangling edge condition*, which demands that all neighbors of a node that is marked for deletion are deleted by p as well. A match must also satisfy certain application conditions contained in the LHS that describe either forbidden patterns, so-called *negative application conditions* (NAC), or desired patterns, so-called *positive application conditions* (PAC). The application of transformation p at match m rewrites graph G to the *result graph* H. A transformation p preserves those nodes and edges that are both in the domain of morphisms l and r, while it deletes those nodes and edges in L that are not in the co-domain of l and creates those nodes and edges in R that are not in the co-domain of r.

Relational Logic. Bounded, first-order relational logic[1] extends propositional logic with relational *variables* of a given arity, a finite *universe* of objects, and *quantifiers*. Each relational variable is assigned an upper bound and, optionally,

---

[1] Our presentation of the logic follows the one presented for ALLOY [13] and KODKOD [26] that in turn are based on Tarski's exposition of the relational calculus [24].

problem := univ relation* formula

univ := {obj[, obj]*}

relation := rel:arity[(lower,)? upper]

varDecl := rel : expr

lower := constant

upper := constant

constant := {tuple*}

tuple := ⟨obj[, obj]*⟩

arity := N

obj := ID

rel := ID

expr := rel | unary | binary | comprehension

unary := expr unop

unop := $^+$ | $^{-1}$

binary := expr binop expr

binop := ∪ | ∩ | \ | . | ×

comprehension := {varDecl | formula}

formula := atomic | composite | quantified

atomic := expr ⊆ expr

composite := ¬formula | formula logop formula

logop := ∧ | ∨

quantified := quantifier varDecl | formula

quantifier := ∀ | ∃

(a) Syntax

P: problem → binding → boolean
R: relation → binding → boolean
M: formula → binding → boolean
E: expr → binding → constant
binding: rel → constant

$P[\![U\ r_1 \ldots r_n\ F]\!]b = R[\![r_1]\!]b \wedge \cdots \wedge R[\![r_n]\!]b \wedge M[\![F]\!]b$

$R[\![r\ :\ [L]]\!]b = R[\![r\ :\ [L,L]]\!]b$
$R[\![r\ :\ [L,U]]\!]b = L \subseteq b(r) \subseteq U$

$M[\![p \subseteq q]\!]b = E[\![p]\!]b \subseteq E[\![q]\!]b$
$M[\![\neg F]\!]b = \neg M[\![F]\!]b$
$M[\![F\ op\ G]\!]b = M[\![F]\!]b\ op\ M[\![G]\!]b$ where $op = \{\wedge, \vee\}$
$M[\![\forall v : p\ |\ F]\!]b = \bigwedge_{x \in E[\![p]\!]b} M[\![F]\!](b \oplus [v \mapsto x])$
$M[\![\exists v : p\ |\ F]\!]b = \bigvee_{x \in E[\![p]\!]b} M[\![F]\!](b \oplus [v \mapsto x])$

$E[\![p\ op\ q]\!]b = E[\![p]\!]b\ op\ E[\![q]\!]b$ where $op = \{\cup, \cap, \backslash\}$
$E[\![p\ .\ q]\!]b = \{\langle p_1, \ldots, p_{n-1}, q_2, \ldots, q_m \rangle\ |$
$\qquad \langle p_1, \ldots, p_n \rangle \in E[\![p]\!]b \wedge \langle q_1, \ldots, q_m \rangle \in E[\![q]\!]b$
$\qquad \wedge p_n = q_1\}$
$E[\![p \times q]\!]b = \{\langle p_1, \ldots, p_n, q_1, \ldots, q_n \rangle\ |$
$\qquad \langle p_1, \ldots, p_n \rangle \in E[\![p]\!]b \wedge \langle q_1, \ldots, q_n \rangle \in E[\![q]\!]b\}$
$E[\![p^{-1}]\!]b = \{\langle p_2, p_1 \rangle\ |\ \langle p_1, p_2 \rangle \in E[\![p]\!]b\}$
$E[\![p^+]\!]b = \{\langle x, y \rangle\ |\ \exists p_1, \ldots, p_n |$
$\qquad \langle x, p_1 \rangle, \langle p_1, p_2 \rangle, \ldots, \langle p_n, y \rangle \in E[\![p]\!]b\}$
$E[\![\{v : p\ |\ F\}]\!]b = \{x \in E[\![p]\!]b\ |\ M[\![F]\!](b \oplus [v \mapsto x])\}$
$E[\![r]\!]b = b(r)$

(b) Semantics

Fig. 3. Syntax and semantics of relational logic [26]

a lower bound. Upper and lower bounds are specified as sets of tuples constructed from the set of objects in the universe. Syntax and semantics are provided in Fig. 3. A bounded, first-order relational problem P is a tuple $(U, Rel, F, ar, \sqcap, \sqcup)$ consisting of

1. a finite *universe* of discourse U, i.e., a set of uninterpreted *objects*,
2. a set Rel of relational variables,
3. a first-order relational formula F,
4. a map $ar : Rel \to \mathbb{N}$ that assigns an arity to each relational variable $r \in Rel$,
5. maps $\sqcap : Rel \to \mathcal{P}(U^n)$ and $\sqcup : Rel \to \mathcal{P}(U^n)$ that define n-ary lower and upper bounds for relations.

A relational *constant* is a set of n-ary tuples including the empty set. The set of relational *expressions* is recursively defined as the smallest set consisting of the empty set and the set of all atoms, i.e., the universe U, the relations $r \in Rel$, and all expressions resulting from applying either (i) a unary operator like *transitive closure* ($^+$) or *transposition* ($^{-1}$) to another expression or (ii) a binary operator, *union* (∪), *intersection* (∩), *join* (.), *difference* (\), or *product* (×), to the former and another expression (see Fig. 3). The evaluation of an expression yields a set of tuples over U. An atomic *relational formula* is a sentence constructed over two relational *expressions* connected by the subset ⊆ operator. Formulas can be quantified and composed into composite formulas using the usual logical connectives, *and* (∧), *or* (∨), and *not* (¬). A *model* of a relational problem is an assignment, i.e., a *binding*, of tuples to relational variables such that (1) the assigned tuples lie within the lower and upper bounds of the relational variable and (2) the formula evaluates to true. Note that this treatment of relational logic is untyped; admissible bindings to relational variables are solely defined by their lower and their upper bounds. Further note, that the logic also supports reasoning over bit-vectors of fixed-size n that represent integer values in the range $(-2^{n-1}, 2^{n-1} - 1)$.

A *relational transition system* (RTS) extends a relational problem by a set *Rel'* of next state relational variables. Moreover, an RTS replaces the lower bound $\sqcap$ with an initial binding ι.

Definition 1. *A bounded, first-order relational transition system S is a tuple $(U, Rel, Rel', T, ar, \iota, \sqcup)$ that consists of*

1. *a finite universe of discourse U,*
2. *a set Rel of unary and binary relational variables,*
3. *a set $Rel' = \{r' | r \in Rel\}$ of next state relational variables,*
4. *a transition relation T, i.e., a conjunction of first-order relational formulas over $Rel \cup Rel'$,*
5. *a map $ar : Rel \cup Rel' \to \mathbb{N}$ that assigns an arity to each relational variable $r \in Rel \cup Rel'$,*
6. *an initial state map $\iota : Rel \to \mathcal{P}(U^n)$ that assigns to each relational variables its initial binding,*
7. *an upper bound map $\sqcup : (Rel \cup Rel') \to \mathcal{P}(U^n)$.*

A *state* in an RTS is a binding b of a set of tuples to each relational variable $r \in Rel$. A *trace* is a finite sequence of states $b_0 b_1 \dots b_n$ with $\iota = b_0$ such that $P[\![U \ r_1 \dots r_n r'_1 \dots r'_n \ T]\!] b_0 \cup b'_1 \wedge \dots \wedge P[\![U \ r_1 \dots r_n r'_1 \dots r'_n \ T]\!] b_{n-1} \cup b'_n$ is satisfied. Here, b'_i denotes the binding for the next state relational variables in *Rel'*. Denote by ρ a relational formula that defines a *reachability* property for an RTS, then a trace $b_0 b_1 \dots b_n$ is called a *witness* of ρ if $P[\![U \ r_1 \dots r_n r'_1 \dots r'_n \ \rho]\!] b_n$ evaluates to *true*.

4 Architecture

Our symbolic model checking approach tests a model-driven implementation of a software system against a reachability property up to a certain bound. Here, a model-driven implementation of a system consists of

(a) an EMF[2] *model* $\mathbb{M}$ that describes the static structure of the system and
(b) a set $\mathcal{R}$ of *graph transformations* that describes the system's execution behavior.

For the verification our tool expects in addition the following inputs specified by a verification engineer:

---

[2] Eclipse Modeling Framework (EMF): eclipse.org/modeling/emf/.

(c) an instance model M_ι of $\mathbb{M}$ that describes the *initial state* of the system,

(d) a graph constraint that describes the *reachability property*, and

(e) an *object bound map* $\Gamma : V_T \to \mathbb{N}$ that defines the maximal number of objects per class in instances of $\mathbb{M}$.

Internally, the EMF model $\mathbb{M}$ is represented as an attributed type graph $G_T = (V_T, E_T)$ with inheritance and containment edges [5], whose vertices V_T represent the classes and whose edges E_T represent the references and the attributes of the system. Attribute types and values are restricted to integers *Int*, Boolean *Bool*, and user-defined enumerations *Enum*. The initial state M_ι is a typed graph $G_M = (V_M, E_M)$ with a type morphism $type : G_M \to G_T$ that maps "objects" $obj_C \in V_M$ to their types, i.e., classes, $C \in V_T$. A reachability property is provided the verification engineer and modeled as a graph constraint [11], which describes a desired or an undesired pattern that is matched against an instance of $\mathbb{M}$. Next observe that the semantics of bounded, first-order relational logic is defined by propositional logic [25]. By applying these semantic definitions to the previously constructed RTS we construct a sequential circuit, or more specifically, an *and-inverter graph* (AIG), which is, roughly speaking, a Boolean circuit that uses only AND and NOT gates. We store the resulting AIG—together with the reachability properties that we want to verify—in the AIGER file format, which is the standardized input format of all model checkers that compete in the Hardware Model Checking Competition. By storing the (depth-bounded) GTS in an AIGER file, we are not limited to a specific model checker and we can directly exploit the most recent developments in hardware model checking like the successful IC3 algorithm [7].

In the following we give a high-level description of the workflow that generates in three steps from a model-driven implementation, first, a symbolic, relational transition system, second, a propositional formula by instantiating the first-order quantifiers in the transition relation of the RTS, and third, an and-inverter graph by rewriting the propositional formula (see Fig. 4). In particular, the `emf2fol` converter first constructs the universe U from the object bound map Γ. It then generates unary and binary relational variables for each class, and attribute and reference in $\mathbb{M}$, respectively. Next, it assigns appropriate upper bounds, i.e., sets of atoms from U, to each relational variable. Finally, it extracts the initial state of the RTS from M_ι. The `gt2fol` converter generates from the set of graph transformations the transition relation T as a conjunction of existentially quantified relational logic formulas and from the graph constraint the reachability property ρ. Note that due to the use of double pushout graph transformations, which are free of side effects, we can straightforwardly derive all relational frame conditions for the RTS (cf. [19]).

Next, the `fol2bool` converter uses the KODKOD API to instantiate[3] the bounded, first-order relational formulas of the transition relation and the reachability property into Boolean functions, i.e., propositional formulas. The resulting Boolean functions are rewritten into an AIG by the `bool2aig` converter and stored in the AIGER format. Next, a model checker `mc` is used to verify the

---

[3] Note that we do not use KODKOD's model finding capabilities but only use it to translate relational logic formulas into propositional formulas.

AIG. In case the model checker determines that a desired or undesired state is reachable it reports the result to the user together with a witness that may be used to re-construct a trace of the RTS. Otherwise, it returns *"unreachable."*

5   Relational Semantics of Graph Transformation Systems

In the following, we constructively specify the relational semantics of a GTS, that is, we define a mapping between components of the GTS and the components of a bounded, first-order relational transition system (RTS). The mapping that we explain in this section is implemented in the `emf2fol` and the `gt2fol` converters (see Fig. 4).

Relational Variables, Universe, Bounds, and Initial State. First, the `emf2fol` component reads in the type graph $\mathbb{M} = (V_T, E_T)$. The universe U, which consists of a set of (uninterpreted) objects, is derived by `emf2fol` from the object bound map $\Gamma : V_T \to \mathbb{N}$ and is defined as $U = \{(obj_{C,i}) \mid C \in V_T, 0 < i \le \Gamma(C)\}$ where C denotes an element in the of classes V_T from the type graph $\mathbb{M}$ and $obj_{C,i}$ an instance, i.e., an object, of class C.

Next, `emf2fol` uses the function $relgen : V_T \cup E_T \to Rel$ to generate for each class C in V_T a unary relational variable C and likewise for each enumeration E in *Enum* a unary relational variable E. For each attribute $attr \in E_T$ the translation generates a binary relational variable $\mathsf{C\_attr}$ and for each reference $ref \in E_T$ from a source class C to a target class D it creates a binary relational variable $\mathsf{C\_ref}$. Moreover, relational variables Int and Bool are generated for the primitive types *Int* and *Bool* if necessary.

The upper bound map $\sqcup : Rel \to \mathcal{P}(U^n)$ is derived as follows. Given a unary relational variable $\mathsf{C} = relgen(C), C \in V_T$ the upper bound is defined by $\sqcup(\mathsf{C}) = \{(c_i) \mid 0 < i \le \Gamma(C)\}$. The upper bound of a relational variable for an attribute $\mathsf{C\_attr}$ is constructed from the product of the upper bounds of class C and the domain of the attribute, i.e., $\sqcup(\mathsf{C\_attr}) = \sqcup(\mathsf{C}) \times \sqcup(\mathbb{D})$, where

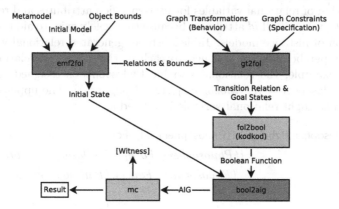

Fig. 4. Workflow of our symbolic model checking approach (external tools are displayed in light gray)

$\mathbb{D} \in \{\mathsf{Int}, \mathsf{Bool}, \mathsf{E}_1, \ldots, \mathsf{E}_n\}$. Likewise, the upper bound of a relational variable derived from a reference is constructed from the product of the source and the target class's upper bounds, i.e., $\sqcup(\mathsf{C\_ref}) = \sqcup(\mathsf{C}) \times \sqcup(\mathsf{D})$ with source class C and target class D. If a class C has subclasses, the union of all its subclasses' instances is added to C's upper bound. This reflects the *is-a* relationship between instances of a subtype and its supertype. Formally, let $Sub(C)$ denote the set of all subclasses of class C. The upper bound of C is then defined as above plus the union of all upper bounds of its subclasses, i.e., $\sqcup(C) = \{(c_i) \mid 0 < i \leq \Gamma(C)\} \cup \bigcup_{S \in Sub(C)} \sqcup(S)$.

Finally, the initial state map $\iota : Rel \to \mathcal{P}(U^n)$, which defines a relational variable's initial binding, is derived from the initial model M_ι. Let $atom : V_{M_\iota} \cup E_{M_\iota} \to U$ be a function that maps an object $v \in V_{M_\iota}$, an object reference or an attribute $e \in E_{M_\iota}$ to an object in U, then ι is defined as follows.

$$
\iota(r) = \begin{cases}
\{atom(v) \mid v \in V_{M_\iota}, type(v) = C\} & \text{if } \exists\, C \in V_T.\ relgen(C) = \mathsf{r} \\[4pt]
\{(atom(v), atom(a)) \mid a \in E_{M_\iota}, \\
\quad type(a) = attr, src_{M_\iota}(a) = v\} & \text{if } \exists\, attr \in E_T.\ relgen(attr) = \mathsf{r} \\[4pt]
\{(atom(v), atom(e)) \mid e \in E_{M_\iota}, \\
\quad type(e) = ref, src_{M_\iota}(e) = v\} & \text{if } \exists\, ref \in E_T.\ relgen(ref) = \mathsf{r}
\end{cases}
$$

Example. For the Dining Philosophers problem (see Sect. 2) emf2fol derives the universe $U = \{Table_1, Philosopher_1, Philosopher_2, Fork_1, Fork_2, -2, -1, 0, 1\}$ from the object bound map $\Gamma = \{(Table, 1), (Philosopher, 2), (Fork, 2)\}$ and the 2-bit integer values are allocated for the PhilState enumeration.[4] Next, the emf2fol component generates unary relational variables Table, Philosopher, Fork, and PhilState. As enumerations are mapped onto integers, emf2fol automatically infers the necessary bitwidth of 2 to represent the three literals *thinking*, *hungry*, and *eating* of enumeration *PhilState*, which are mapped to -2, -1, and 0, respectively. Further, binary relational variables are generated for each attribute and reference, e.g., for reference *forks* in class *Table* the relational variable Table_forks is generated. Note that it is possible to instruct emf2fol to omit the generation of relational variables for user-specified attributes and references. For example, we omit all *id* attributes because they solely exist to aid the manual construction of instance models. Table 1 lists all generated relational variables.

Next, upper bounds are assigned to each of the generated relational variables. For example, the relational variable Philosopher is assigned the upper bound $\sqcup(\mathsf{Philosopher} = \{(Philosopher_1), (Philosopher_2)\}$. The upper bound of the Philosopher_right relational variable is defined as

$$
\begin{aligned}
\sqcup(\mathsf{Philosopher\_right}) &= \sqcup(\mathsf{Philosopher}) \times \sqcup(\mathsf{Fork}) \\
&= \{(Philosopher_1, Fork_1), (Philosopher_1, Fork_2) \\
&\quad\ (Philosopher_2, Fork_1), (Philosopher_2, Fork_2)\}.
\end{aligned}
$$

---

[4] Note that internally integers are stored using the two's complement representation; hence, with n-bits the integer values in the range $[-2^{n-1}, 2^{n-1} - 1]$ can be represented.

Table 1. Generated variables and bounds for the Dining Philosophers problem

Class	Variable	Upper Bound
Table	Table	$\{(Table_1)\}$
philosophers	Table_philosophers	$\{(Table_1, Philosopher_1), (Table_1, Philosopher_2)\}$
forks	Table_forks	$\{(Table_1, Fork_1), (Table_1, Fork_2)\}$
Philosopher	Philosopher	$\{(Philosopher_1), (Philosopher_2)\}$
right	Philosopher_right	$\{(Philosopher_1, Fork_1), (Philosopher_1, Fork_2), (Philosopher_2, Fork_1),$ $(Philosopher_2, Fork_2)\}$
left	Philosopher_left	$\{(Philosopher_1, Fork_1), \ldots, (Philosopher_2, Fork_2)\}$
holds	Philosopher_holds	$\{(Philosopher_1, Fork_1), \ldots, (Philosopher_2, Fork_2)\}$
state	Philosopher_state	$\{(Philosopher_1, -2), \ldots, (Philosopher_1, 0), (Philosopher_2, -2), \ldots,$ $(Philosopher_2, 0)\}$
Fork	Fork	$\{(Fork_1), (Fork_2)\}$
PhilState	PhilState	$\{(-2), (-1), (0)\}$
Int	Int	$\{(-2), (-1), (0), (1)\}$

Table 1 also lists the upper bounds derived for the Dining Philosophers problem. The initial state map for two dining philosophers is defined as follows:

$$\iota = \{(\mathsf{Table}, \{(Table_1)\}), (\mathsf{Philosopher}, \{(Philosopher_1), (Philosopher_2)\}),$$
$$(\mathsf{Fork}, \{(Fork_1), (Fork_2)\}), (\mathsf{Table\_philosophers}, \{(Table_1, Philosopher_1),$$
$$(Table_1, Philosopher_2)\}), (\mathsf{Table\_forks}, \{(Table_1, Fork_1), (Table_1, Fork_2)\}),$$
$$(\mathsf{Philosopher\_state}, \{(Philosopher_1, -2), (Philosopher_2, -2)\}), \ldots\}.$$

Graph Transformations. The `gt2fol` component translates graph transformations into a symbolic transition relation T. Formally, `gt2fol` translates a set Π of graph transformation into a conjunction of first-order, relational formula as follows. Given sets Rel and Rel' of current and next state relational variables derived by *relgen* as described above, from each (double pushout) graph transformation $p_i : Lhs_i \leftarrow K_i \rightarrow Rhs_i$ in $\Pi = \{p_1, \ldots, p_n\}$, with negative and positive application conditions Nac_i and Pac_i, respectively, the transition relation T

$$T := \bigwedge_i (Pre(Lhs_i, Pac_i, Nac_i, Rhs_i) \implies Post(Lhs_i, Rhs_i)) \wedge \qquad (1)$$

$$\neg \left(\bigvee_i Pre(Lhs_i, Pac_i, Nac_i, Rhs_i) \right) \implies Rel \doteq Rel'$$

is derived where $Pre : G \times G \times G \times G \rightarrow \mathbb{F}$ is a function that generates from a quadruple of graphs a conjunction $f \in \mathbb{F}$ of relational formulas that mimic the match conditions of the transformation's LHS. Here, $\mathbb{F}$ denotes the set of all relational formulas. Function $Post : G \times G \rightarrow \mathbb{F}$, on the other hand, generates a conjunction of relational formulas from the LHS and RHS that mimic the deletions in the LHS and the additions/modifications on the RHS. Intuitively, Formula 1 states, that whenever one of the graph transformations is applicable, then perform the necessary modifications on the graph; otherwise, if none of the transformations is applicable, do not perform any changes. Here, $Rel \doteq Rel'$ is defined as $r_1 = r_1' \wedge r_2 = r_2' \wedge \cdots \wedge r_n = r_n'$ with $r_i \in Rel$ and $r_i' \in Rel'$.

Function *Pre* generates the following relational formulas, i.e., constraints, from the transformation's LHS. For each object obj_C of class C in the LHS we allocate a fresh, relational variable c and add a constraint $\exists c : C$ that binds c to tuples in C. If obj_C of class C has a reference *ref* to a target object obj_D of class D, with relational variables c, d allocated for obj_C and obj_D, and relation C_ref generated for reference *ref*, then the condition $(c, d) \subseteq$ C_ref is derived.

If an attribute *attr* of obj_C is assigned an expression e, then *Pre* generates formula $(c, expr(e)) \in$ C_attr where $expr : Int \cup Bool \cup Enum \to Rexpr$ converts an integer, Boolean, or enumeration expression into a corresponding relational expression. This expression describes an additional constraint that a matching subgraph must satisfy. Thus, we generate a condition that requires the attribute value of the object that is bound to c to evaluate to the same value as $expr(e)$. For an overview of the conditions generated by *Pre* see Table 2.

Table 2. Relational formulas generated by function *Pre*

	LHS/RHS element	Formula
Preserve/Delete	Object $c \in C$	$\exists c : C$
	Reference *ref* with $src(ref) = c \in C$, $tgt(ref) = d \in D$	$(c, d) \subseteq$ C_ref
	Attribute *attr* with $src(attr) = c \in C$, expression e	$(c, expr(e)) \subseteq$ C_attr
Forbid	Object $c \in C$	$\neg \exists c : C$
	Reference *ref*	*same as above*
	Attribute *attr*	*same as above*
Create	Object $c \in C$	$\exists c : C' \wedge c \nsubseteq C$
	Reference *ref*	—
	Attribute *attr*	—

If the graph transformation contains PAC patterns, they are translated into formulas of relational logic like the LHS pattern because they, too, demand the existence of nodes, edges, or matching attribute expressions in the matching host graph. Thus, the translation of LHS and PAC patterns follow the same procedure as described above.

Negative application conditions, in contrast to LHS and PAC patterns, describe forbidden patterns that must not be satisfied by any matching subgraph. As such we generate equivalent relational formulas as for the LHS, but negate them such that the formula $\neg \exists n : N$ is generated assuming that the relational variable n was allocated for a node in the NAC graph of type N. Note that none of the conditions generated for references and attributes in the NAC graph need to be negated and are thus equivalent to those generated for the LHS graph.

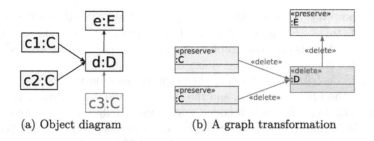

(a) Object diagram   (b) A graph transformation

Fig. 5. Dangling edge example

Finally, the injectivity[5] and the dangling edge conditions, also generated by *Pre*, are necessary to faithfully translate the graph modifying instructions into relational logic. The injectivity condition ensures that all elements of the LHS, the NACs, and the PACs are mapped to exactly one element in a matching host graph, which is enforced by binding each existentially quantified relational variable to a distinct object of the universe. The generated *injectivity* condition performs a pairwise test of inequality on all variables bound by the same expression. For example, given variables c1, c2, both of which are bound by C, the condition ¬(c1 = c2) is generated to ensure that c1 and c2 are assigned to two different objects. The second condition ensures that no *dangling edges* are left behind after deleting nodes from the graph. This implies that all possible references to and from a node that is scheduled for deletion need to be deleted explicitly. We translate this requirement into a condition that checks whether the set of all possible references from and to an object that is scheduled for deletion coincides with the set of actually deleted references. For example, in Fig. 5b object obj_D, an instance of class D, is deleted together with references coming from two objects, $obj_{C,1}$ and $obj_{C,2}$, and one reference to object obj_E. Class D may have references coming from objects of class C and references to object of class E. In the following we assume that the translation generates unary relational variables C, D, and E for classes C, D, and E, binary relational variables C_toD and D_toE, and allocates existentially quantified variables c1, c2, d, and e (see Fig. 5a). The formula C_toD − {(c1, d), (c2, d)} = ∅ resembles the dangling edge condition for reference between objects of class C and class D. It consists of the following components:

- The relational variable C_toD is bound to the set of all tuples (obj_C, obj_D) with $obj_c \in \sqcup(\textsf{C})$ and $obj_d \in \sqcup(\textsf{D})$ having a *toD* reference;
- the expression C_toD represents the set of all *possible* references between class C and class D;
- the set {(c1, d), (c2, d)} represents the *actually deleted* objects.

Thus, the formula above checks whether the set of all actually deleted references, i.e., (c1, d) and (c2, d), coincides with the set of all existing references between C

---

[5] Currently, we only support injective graph pattern matching.

and D. If, however, a third reference had pointed from c3 to d (see Fig. 5a), the expression C_toD $- \{(c1, d), (c2, d)\}$ would evaluate to $\{(c3, d)\}$ and thus violate $\{(c3, d)\} = \emptyset$. In this case the graph transformation must not be applied as the dangling edge condition would be violated.

The RHS describes the effects of the graph transformation; once a matching subgraph of the LHS, the NACs, and the PACs is found it is rewritten according to the RHS that specifies which nodes, edges, and attributes are created and/or deleted. The function *Post* generates relational formulas over *Rel* and *Rel'* that mimic the modifications of the transformation's RHS as follows. If the transformation creates an object obj_C of class C, two conditions are created, one by *Pre* and one by *Post*. First, function *Pre* checks for the non-existence of an object bound to relational variable c in the current state with $\exists c : C' \wedge c \nsubseteq C$, i.e., the formula asserts that the object bound to c is *inactive* in the current state relational variable C. Second, function *Post* generates a condition that adds the new object (bound to c) to relational variable C such that the next state relational variable C' is set to $C' = C + c$. The procedure for the deletion of an object bound to c is similar except that (i) *Pre* checks for the existence of an object that is scheduled for deletion, i.e. $\exists c : C$ and (ii) *Post* updates the next state relational variable C' to reflect the removal of the object (bound to c), i.e., $C' = C - c$. Addition and deletion of (multiple) objects to and from a relational variable can be combined, i.e., $C' = C + \{c_1, \ldots, c_m\} - \{c_{m+1}, \ldots, c_n\}$. Note that the addition and deletion of references and attributes proceeds analogous to the addition and deletion of objects. For example, *Post* generates for the deletion of a reference *ref* from an object bound to c pointing to an object bound to d the formula C_ref' $=$ C_ref $- (c, d)$. The formulas generated by *Post* are summarized in Table 3. In addition, the *Post* function also generates conditions for those relational variables that do not change, as otherwise arbitrary tuples could be assigned to these relational variables.

Table 3. Relational formulas generated by function *Post*

LHS/RHS element	Formula
Object $c \in C$	$C' = C - c$
Reference *ref* with $src(ref) = c \in C$, $tgt(ref) = d \in D$	C_ref' $=$ C_ref $- (c, d)$
Attribute *attr* with $src(attr) = c \in C$, expression e	C_attr' $=$ C_attr $- (c, expr(e))$
Object $c \in C$	$C' = C + c$
Reference *ref* with $src(ref) = c \in C$, $tgt(ref) = d \in D$	C_ref' $=$ C_ref $+ (c, d)$
Attribute *attr* with $src(attr) = c \in C$, expression e	C_attr' $=$ C_attr $+ (c, expr(e))$

The first three rows are labeled **Delete** and the last three rows are labeled **Create**.

$$\underbrace{\exists \textbf{a1} : \textbf{A}, \exists \textbf{a2} : \textbf{A}', \exists \textbf{b} : \textbf{B}, \exists \textbf{c} : \textbf{C},}_{\text{LHS,RHS, and PAC nodes}} \underbrace{\neg \exists \textbf{d} : \textbf{D}}_{\text{NAC}} \mid$$

$$\underbrace{match(\textbf{a1}, \textbf{a2}, \textbf{b}, \textbf{c}, \textbf{d})}_{\text{match constraints}} \wedge \underbrace{inj(\textbf{a1}, \textbf{b}, \textbf{c}, \textbf{d})}_{\substack{\text{injectivity} \\ \text{constraints}}} \wedge \underbrace{dec(\textbf{a1}, \textbf{b}, \textbf{c})}_{\substack{\text{dangling} \\ \text{edge} \\ \text{constraints}}} \Longrightarrow$$

$$\underbrace{\textbf{A}' = \textbf{A} - \textbf{a1} + \textbf{a2} \wedge \textbf{B}' = \textbf{B} - \textbf{b}}_{\text{modification constraints}} \wedge \underbrace{\textbf{C}' = \textbf{C} \wedge \textbf{D}' = \textbf{D} \wedge \textbf{E}' = \textbf{E}}_{\text{non-modification constraints}}$$

Fig. 6. Scheme of a relational formula produced from a graph transformation

$$\underbrace{\exists \textbf{a} : \textbf{A}, \exists \textbf{b} : \textbf{B}, \exists \textbf{c} : \textbf{C},}_{\text{LHS and PAC nodes}} \underbrace{\neg \exists \textbf{d} : \textbf{D}}_{\text{NAC}} \mid$$

$$\underbrace{match(\textbf{a}, \textbf{b}, \textbf{c}, \textbf{d})}_{\text{match constraints}} \wedge \underbrace{inj(\textbf{a1}, \textbf{b}, \textbf{c}, \textbf{d})}_{\substack{\text{injectivity} \\ \text{constraints}}}$$

Fig. 7. Scheme of a relational formula produced from a graph constraint

The encoding outlined in Tables 2 and 3 translates a graph transformation $p \in \mathcal{R}$ over Rel, which is fixed w.l.o.g to $Rel = \{\textsf{A}, \textsf{B}, \textsf{C}, \textsf{D}, \textsf{E}\}$ for the following explanations, into a relational formula following the scheme outlined in Fig. 6. Here, function $match$ returns constraints that mimic the transformation's LHS and controls the creation of new nodes, while functions inj and dec generate injectivity constraints and dangling edge conditions, respectively.

Graph Constraints. Reachability properties are modeled by graph constraints that the verification engineer supplies. In contrast to graph transformations, a graph constraint does not alter a matching host graph; it may thus be used to describe a desired or an undesired pattern in a graph, i.e., a good or a bad state of the system. Thus, graph constraints are graph transformations with identical left-hand and right-hand sides. Formally, a graph constraint is translated into a relational formula $\rho := Pre_\rho[Lhs, Pac, Nac]$, where function $Pre_\rho : G \times G \times G \to \mathbb{F}$ translates the triple LHS, PAC, and NAC into a conjunction of relational formulas. For this purpose, the encoding presented in Table 2 are re-used to translate a graph constraint into a relational formula. The scheme of the relational formula generated from a graph constraint is depicted in Fig. 7. It coincides with that of a graph transformation (see Fig. 6) in all but two aspects: (1) the absence of the implication, i.e., there is no RHS, and (2) the dangling edge condition, which is omitted because a graph constraint may not delete elements.

6 Case Studies

In two case studies, we compare our tool GRYPHON with the state-of-the-art tool GROOVE [16]. First, we consider the Dining Philosophers problem of Sect. 2

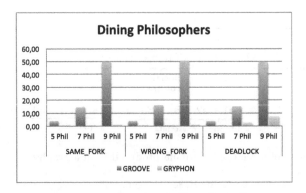

Fig. 8. Runtime comparison (sec) of GROOVE and GRYPHON on the dining philosopher benchmark

and second, we showcase the railway interlocking scenario inspired by [15]. The experiments were run on an Intel™Core i5 M580 2.67 GHz CPU with 8 GB of RAM running Gentoo 2.2 (Linux kernel 3.14.14). For the benchmarks we use the Oracle™ Java™ SE 7 Runtime Environment (build 1.7.0_71-b14), the Henshin API[6] in version 0.0.1, the IC3 based model checker iimc[7] in version 2.0, and GROOVE[8] in version 5.5.2 (build: 20150324114640). The heap size was set to 6 GB and the timeout was set to 720 s. The runtimes of each benchmark were averaged over 10 consecutive runs.

Case Study 1: Dining Philosophers. For this benchmark with our tool, we modeled the Dining Philosophers problem as described in Sect. 2. In a similar manner, we modeled the metamodel, i.e., the type graph, used for the implementation of the graph transformation in GROOVE. Then we formulated the following three invariants: (i) *No two philosophers hold the same fork* (SAME_FORK), (ii) *if a philosopher holds a fork, its either her left or her right fork* (LEFT_RIGHT), and (iii) *the philosophers do not deadlock* (DEADLOCK).

For the benchmarks we use initial models with five, seven, and nine thinking philosophers. We consider the test case, where none of them holds a fork at the beginning. Figure 8 compares the runtimes of our tool with the runtimes of GROOVE. Interestingly, for GROOVE we observed a deviation of up to one third of its average runtime. Note that for neither of the tools, we experienced time or memory timeouts. The latter is especially remarkable for GROOVE as it performs an explicit search of the state space. GRYPHON could solve all benchmarks of this case study in less than 10 s.

Case Study 2: Interlocking Railway Systems. The second set of benchmarks targets an interlocking railway systems [15]. A railway system is described by a

---

[6] Available from https://www.eclipse.org/henshin/install.php.

[7] Available from http://ecee.colorado.edu/wpmu/iimc/download/.

[8] Available from https://sourceforge.net/projects/groove/files/groove/5.5.2/.

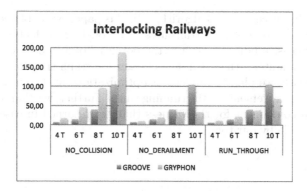

Fig. 9. Runtime comparison (sec) of GROOVE and GRYPHON for the interlocking railway benchmark with 4, 6, 8, and 10 trains (T)

scheme plan that consists of a *track plan*, a *control table*, and a set of *release tables*. The topology of the railway network is captured by the *track plan*, which displays tracks and their lengths, entry and exit tracks, and points. A *route* consists of a set of tracks, the first of which may be entered if the guarding signal shows proceed. Each row in the control table is associated with a route and specifies the tracks that need to be *cleared* in order for a train to pass the signal guarding the route. If the route passes a point, the control table specifies the required *position* of the point. A point is locked either in *normal* position, leading the train straight ahead, or in *reverse* position, in which case the train is routed to another line. A train must obtain a *lock* on a point prior to passing it and is required to release it after traversing the point. The *release table* associated with a point specifies the track, where a train must release the acquired lock.

The verification of the railway system then centers around three safety properties: (i) *collision freedom* prohibits two trains occupying the same track; (ii) *no-derailment* demands that a point does not change position while being occupied by a train; (iii) *run-through* requires a point to be set in position as specified by the control table for the specific route when a train is about to enter the point.

For the evaluation, we define four different initial states that instantiate the implementation with four, six, eight, and ten trains. The results are shown in Fig. 9. On the NO_COLLISION property, GROOVE is faster by a factor of two to three. For the other two properties, GROOVE is (slightly) faster for the benchmarks on 4 and 6 trains, but with 8 and 10 trains, the symbolic approach outperforms the explicit approach on average.

7 Conclusion

We presented a novel model checking approach for the verification of graph transformations as used in model-driven engineering. Our approach is completely automatic and allows modelers to benefit from the very efficient hardware model checkers, e.g. the successful IC3 algorithm. In this paper, we explained the internal realization of our tool that translates the modeling artifacts to sequential circuits. In two case studies we showed the potential of our tool by comparing it with GROOVE, a state-of-the-art model checker for graph transformations.

In future work, we plan to implement optimizations in the encoding and we expect further improvements in the running times. Further, we plan to implement a visualization component for the witness that are returned in case a property is shown reachable by our tool.

References

1. Baier, C., Katoen, J.-P.: Principles of Model Checking. MIT Press, Cambridge (2008)
2. Baresi, L., Spoletini, P.: On the use of alloy to analyze graph transformation systems. In: Corradini, A., Ehrig, H., Montanari, U., Ribeiro, L., Rozenberg, G. (eds.) ICGT 2006. LNCS, vol. 4178, pp. 306–320. Springer, Heidelberg (2006)
3. Baudry, B., Ghosh, S., Fleurey, F., France, R.B., Le Traon, Y., Mottu, J.-M.: Barriers to systematic model transformation testing. Commun. ACM 53(6), 139–143 (2010)
4. Biermann, E., Ermel, C., Taentzer, G.: Lifting parallel graph transformation concepts to model transformation based on the eclipse modeling framework. Electron. Commun. ECEASST 26 (2010)
5. Biermann, E., Ermel, C., Taentzer, G.: Formal foundation of consistent EMF model transformations by algebraic graph transformation. Softw. Syst. Model. 11(2), 227–250 (2012)
6. Bill, R., Gabmeyer, S., Kaufmann, P., Seidl, M.: Model checking of CTL-extended OCL specifications. In: Combemale, B., Pearce, D.J., Barais, O., Vinju, J.J. (eds.) SLE 2014. LNCS, vol. 8706, pp. 221–240. Springer, Heidelberg (2014)
7. Bradley, A.R.: SAT-based model checking without unrolling. In: Jhala, R., Schmidt, D. (eds.) VMCAI 2011. LNCS, vol. 6538, pp. 70–87. Springer, Heidelberg (2011)
8. Czarnecki, K., Helsen, S.: Feature-based survey of model transformation approaches. IBM Syst. J. 45(3), 621–645 (2006)
9. Dijkstra, E.W.: Cooperating sequential processes, ewd 123. https://www.cs.utexas.edu/users/EWD/transcriptions/EWD01xx/EWD123.html
10. Dijkstra, E.W.: The humble programmer. Commun. ACM 15(10), 859–866 (1972)
11. Ehrig, H., Ehrig, K., Prange, U., Taentzer, G.: Fundamentals of Algebraic Graph Transformation. Monographs in Theoretical Computer Science. An EATCS Series. Springer, Heidelberg (2006)
12. Hoare, C.A.R.: Communicating Sequential Processes. Prentice-Hall International, Upper saddle River (1985)
13. Jackson, D.: Automating first-order relational logic. In: Proceedings of the 8th ACM SIGSOFT International Symposium on Foundations of Software Engineering, pp. 130–139. ACM (2000)
14. Jackson, D.: Alloy: a lightweight object modelling notation. ACM Trans. Softw. Eng. Methodol. 11(2), 256–290 (2002)
15. James, P., Moller, F., Nguyen, H.N., Roggenbach, M., Schneider, S.A., Treharne, H.: On modelling and verifying railway interlockings. Tracking Train Lengths Sci. Comput. Program. 96, 315–336 (2014)

16. Kastenberg, H., Rensink, A.: Model checking dynamic states in GROOVE. In: Valmari, A. (ed.) SPIN 2006. LNCS, vol. 3925, pp. 299–305. Springer, Heidelberg (2006)
17. McBurney, D.L., Sleep, M.R.: Graph rewriting as a computational model. In: Yonezawa, A., Ito, T. (eds.) Concurrency: Theory, Language, And Architecture. LNCS, vol. 491, pp. 235–256. Springer, Heidelberg (1989)
18. Naur, P., Randell, B. (eds.) Software Engineering: Report of a Conference Sponsored by the NATO Science Committee, Garmisch, Germany, 7–11 October 1968, Brussels, Scientific Affairs Division, NATO. NATO (1969)
19. Niemann, P., Hilken, F., Gogolla, M., Wille, R.: Assisted generation of frame conditions for formal models. In: Proceedings of the 2015 Design, Automation & Test in Europe Conference & Exhibition, DATE 2015, San Jose, CA, USA, pp. 309–312. EDA Consortium (2015)
20. Object Management Group OMG. OMG Unified Modeling Language (OMG UML), Infrastructure V2.4.1, August 2011. http://www.omg.org/spec/UML/2.4.1/
21. Rozenberg, G. (ed.): Handbook of Graph Grammars and Computing by Graph Transformations. Foundations, vol. 1. World Scientific, Singapore (1997)
22. Schmidt, A., Varró, D.: CheckVML: a tool for model checking visual modeling languages. In: Stevens, P., Whittle, J., Booch, G. (eds.) UML 2003. LNCS, vol. 2863, pp. 92–95. Springer, Heidelberg (2003)
23. Sendall, S., Kozaczynski, W.: Model transformation: the heart and soul of model-driven software development. IEEE Softw. **20**(5), 42–45 (2003)
24. Tarski, A.: On the calculus of relations. J. Symb. Log. **6**(3), 73–89 (1941)
25. Torlak, E.: A Constraint Solver for Software Engineering: Finding Models and Cores of Large Relational Specifications. Ph.D. Thesis, Massachusetts Institute of Technology, 2009. AAI0821754
26. Torlak, E., Jackson, D.: Kodkod: a relational model finder. In: Grumberg, O., Huth, M. (eds.) TACAS 2007. LNCS, vol. 4424, pp. 632–647. Springer, Heidelberg (2007)
27. Zeller, A.: Why Programs Fail: A Guide to Systematic Debugging, 2nd edn. Morgan Kaufmann Publishers Inc., San Francisco (2009)

Testing-Based Formal Verification for Theorems and Its Application in Software Specification Verification

Shaoying Liu$^{(\boxtimes)}$

Department of Computer Science, Hosei University, Tokyo, Japan
sliu@hosei.ac.jp

Abstract. Verifying a specification for software can be converted into theorem proving. In this paper, we describe a testing-based formal verification (TBFV) method for automatically testing theorems. The advantage of the method over conventional theorem proving is that it can quickly detect faults if the theorem is not valid and quickly provide us with confidence in the validity of the theorem if it is valid. We discuss the principle and algorithms for test case generation in TBFV and present an example to illustrate how TBFV can be applied in checking designs. We also present a prototype supporting tool we have developed and a controlled experiment for evaluating the performance of TBFV. The result shows that TBFV is effective and efficient to find faults in certain setting.

1 Introduction

Before undertaking the implementation of a software system, it is important to ensure that the corresponding specification is consistent and valid in order to prevent faults in the specification from slipping into the implementation. The ideal approach to fulfilling this goal is perhaps to formally verify the relevant consistency and validity properties. A property can be expressed as a theorem, therefore, verifying a property becomes proving a theorem.

A theorem is usually expressed as a sequent $H_1, H_2, ..., H_r \vdash C$. To check whether conclusion C can be deduced from the hypotheses $H_1, H_2, ..., H_r$, a formal proof needs to be conducted. But unfortunately, formal proof is usually unable to be fully automated, although some machine theorem prover, such as ACL2 [1] and PVS [2], may help automate part of the proof process. Since such a proof is inevitably tedious and rather difficult to carry out in practice, it may not be suitable for realistic software verification during the development process, considering various theoretical and practical constraints [3].

Furthermore, since it is rare in practice for a software specification not to contain faults just after it is written, formal proof of its properties will have little chance to succeed. One may argue that even if a formal proof cannot be successful, conducting the proof may help humans detect faults. Our experience

This work was supported by JSPS KAKENHI Grant Number 26240008.

B.K. Aichernig and C.A. Furia (Eds.): TAP 2016, LNCS 9762, pp. 112–129, 2016.
DOI: 10.1007/978-3-319-41135-4_7

suggests that this may be true, but the challenge is that the cost, complexity and difficulty of such a proof are too high to afford for most practitioners and companies (except a few rare cases). We believe that one possible solution to this challenge is automatic fault detection by means of rigorous testing. Although testing is unable to guarantee the validity of theorems like proof, it can help uncover and remove faults and build sufficient confidence in the validity in practice. This view has been justified by the fact that almost all of the software systems in use are not formally proved; the developers' confidence in their quality is ensured only by testing (both static and dynamic testing).

In this paper, we put forward a testing-based formal verification (TBFV) method for this goal. By formal verification in the context of "testing-based" here, we do not mean formal proof. Instead, we mean a rigorous analysis following well-defined rules in general (e.g., test coverage rules). TBFV is characterized by generating test cases (i.e., values for the free variables in the theorem) to evaluate the hypotheses and the conclusion in the manner consistent with the principle of formal proof. When the hypotheses evaluate to true with a test case, if the conclusion evaluates to false with the same test case, it will indicate the invalidity of the theorem; in other words, it finds faults in the theorem. As discussed in Sect. 7, this technique is highly effective to detect faults in faulty properties. The challenge is how to determine the validity of the theorem if it is truly valid. In Sect. 5, we discuss this issue and propose a condition under which the analyst (or designer) should have a sufficient confidence in the validity of the theorem.

Compared with formal proof, TBFV has two major advantages. One is that it can be fully automated, which allows practitioners to avoid the complexity and cost problems in formal proof. This advantage has and will continue to make the technique attractive in practice according to our experiences with industry in both Japan and China. Another advantage is that it can identify faults quickly for faulty properties, as indicated by our experiment presented in Sect. 7.

The rest of the paper is organized as follows. Sections 2 to 5 discuss the principle of the TBFV method, handling of quantifiers, test case generation algorithms, and building confidence in theorems. Sections 6 to 9 present an example, an experiment for evaluating TBFV, and a prototype supporting tool. Finally, Sect. 10 concludes the paper and points out future research directions.

2   Principle of TBFV

In this section, we elaborate on the principle underlying the TBFV method and identify important issues to be addressed in the subsequent sections.

Let sequent $H_1, H_2, ..., H_r \vdash C$ denote a theorem in first order predicate logic. To verify the validity of the theorem using TBFV, we take the following steps:

Step 1: Convert the conjunction of the hypotheses $H_1 \wedge H_2 \wedge \cdots \wedge H_r$ into a disjunctive normal form and make the following sequent:

$P_1 \vee P_2 \vee \cdots \vee P_n \vdash C$, where each P_i $(i = 1...n)$ is a conjunction of atomic predicates (e.g., relations) or their negations.

Step 2: Generate a test set T_i (a set of test cases) from each P_i (i.e., every test case in T_i satisfies P_i) for the sequent $P_i \vdash C$, which is called a *sub-theorem*.

A detailed explanation for this theory is given below.

Step 3: Analyze the test result for $P_i \vdash C$ to determine whether any fault is found, or a sufficient confidence in the validity of the sub-theorem can be established.

To apply TBFV, quantifiers in the hypotheses, if any, must be removed properly. This will ensure that the hypotheses can be automatically transformed into a disjunctive normal form in **Step 1** with a standard algorithm. According to the first order predicate calculus, to prove $P_1 \vee P_2 \vee \cdots \vee P_n \vdash C$, we must prove every $P_i \vdash C$ $(i = 1, 2, ..., n)$. To this end, as mentioned in **Step 2**, a test set T_i must be generated in which every test case satisfies P_i, and then used to evaluate C. If there exists any test case t in T_i such that $C(t)$ evaluates to false, it proves that $P_i \vdash C$ is not valid. In other words, the presence of faults is confirmed. But if no test case in T_i leads to such a result, we must decide whether T_i is adequate to establish a confidence in the sub-theorem for the verifier (the person who is carrying out the verification), as required in **Step 3**. If not, additional tests must be carried out until the confidence is built.

Three issues involved in these steps are particularly important for the effectiveness of TBFV. The first is how a quantifier can be removed properly. Another issue is how a test set should be generated based on the conjunctive clause P_i in **Step 2**. The last issue is how the invalidity or validity of each sub-theorem $P_i \vdash C$ and the corresponding theorem $P_1 \vee P_2 \vee \cdots \vee P_n \vdash C$ can be determined in **Step 3**. These issues are discussed in turn from the next section.

3   Treatment of Quantifiers

In principle, every quantified predicate expression in the hypothesis P_i of $P_i \vdash C$ is converted into a boolean function, which is treated as an atomic predicate, in order to allow for the application of the standard algorithm to convert non-quantified predicate expressions into disjunctive normal forms. Specifically, let a universally quantified expression be $\forall x \in X \cdot P(x)$. Then, we convert it into a boolean function, say $f(X')$, which is defined as follows:

$$f(X': 2^X) \triangleq \bigwedge_{x \in X'} P(x)$$

where the name f must not occur in $P(x)$ and X' is the input variable of f denoting a subset of X (where 2^X represents the power set of X). Given a specific X', if every element x in X' satisfies $P(x)$, f will yield *true*; otherwise, it will yield *false*. When $X' = X$, $\forall x \in X \cdot P(x)$ is equivalent to $f(X')$; otherwise, $(\forall x \in X \cdot P(x)) \Rightarrow f(X')$.

Similarly, let an existentially quantified expression be $\exists_{x \in X} \cdot P(x)$. Then, we convert it into a boolean function, say $g(X')$, which is defined as follows:

$$g(X': 2^X) \triangleq \bigvee_{x \in X'} P(x)$$

where the name g must not occur in $P(x)$ and X' is the input variable of g denoting a subset of X. Given a specific X', if some x in X' satisfies $P(x)$, g will yield $true$; otherwise, it will yield $false$. When $X' = X$, $\exists_{x \in X} \cdot P(x)$ is equivalent to $g(X')$; otherwise, $g(X') \Rightarrow (\exists_{x \in X} \cdot P(x))$.

This treatment will help us to choose an appropriate subset X' of the domain X as a test case to evaluate the quantified expression. In the case of universally quantified expression, this treatment will not affect the judgement of finding faults in a test using TBFV. That is, if the boolean function f helps confirm the presence of faults, the corresponding quantified expression will also be able to do so. However, in the case of the existentially quantified expression, the same relationship between it and the boolean function g may not be established, but if using g confirms the presence of faults, it will be able to provide a warning message about the possibility of fault presence in the original sub-theorem.

4   Test Set Generation

To test whether $P_i \vdash C$ is valid or not, it is necessary to generate a test set such that each test case of the set satisfies P_i. Since P_i is supposed to be a conjunction of atomic predicates or their negation, say $P_i = Q_i^1 \wedge Q_i^2 \wedge \cdots \wedge Q_i^m$, generating a test set for P_i is equivalent to generating a test set to satisfy $Q_i^1 \wedge Q_i^2 \wedge \cdots \wedge Q_i^m$. There might be a situation where conclusion C contains more free variables than the hypothesis P_i. For example, all of the free variables in P_i are x_1, x_2, and x_3, but C contains the free variables x_1, x_2, x_3, and y. In this case, a test case should not only contain values for x_1, x_2, and x_3, but also contain a value for y. The values for x_1, x_2, and x_3 must be produced under the constraint of P_i, but the value for y should be chosen randomly from its type because for any value of y, x_1, x_2, and x_3 must satisfy C if the sub-theorem is valid.

We first discuss how to automatically generate a test case for atomic predicates and then for their conjunctions.

4.1   Test Case Generation for Atomic Predicates

Let $Q_i^j(x_1, x_2, ..., x_q)$ $(j = 1, ..., m)$ be an atomic predicate occurring in $Q_i^1 \wedge Q_i^2 \wedge \cdots \wedge Q_i^m$. The variables x_1, x_2, ..., x_q are free variables but may be part of all the free variables x_1, x_2, ..., x_w used in the conjunction, where $w \geq q$. A variable can denote either a numeric value or a value of compound type (e.g., set, sequence, map, or composite type) that is available in many of the model-based formal notations, such as VDM-SL, Z, and SOFL [4], although their syntax may differ slightly. We start discussing the case of atomic expressions with only numeric variables, and then extend to expressions with variables of compound types.

4.1.1   Numeric Variables

An atomic predicate can be divided into the following three kinds, depending on the pattern of expressions involving free variables.

(a) Only one free variable x_1 (i.e., $q = 1$) is involved and $Q_i^j(x_1)$ has the format $x_1 \ominus E$, where $\ominus \in \{=, >, <, >=, <=, <>\}$ is a relational operator and E a constant. The operator $>=$ means "greater than or equal to", $<=$ means "less than or equal to"; $<>$ means inequality; and the others are commonly used operators.

(b) Only one free variable x_1 is involved and $Q_i^j(x_1)$ has the format $E_1 \ominus E_2$, where E_1 and E_2 are both terms (or arithmetic expressions) and both contain the free variable x_1.

(c) More than one free variable is involved and $Q_i^j(x_1, x_2, ..., x_q)$ has the format $E_1 \ominus E_2$, where E_1 and E_2 are both terms possibly involving all the free variables $x_1, x_2, ..., x_q$.

Generating a test case to satisfy $x_1 \ominus E$ in case (a) is rather simple. A collection of test case generation algorithms for this kind of expression is given in Table 1, where σ is a positive integer, which can be produced randomly, and ":=" denotes the assignment operator. For example, when operator $\ominus$ is ">=", "<>" or ">", a test case for variable x_1 can be produced by the assignment $x_1 := E + \sigma$, whilst the remaining input variables $x_2, x_3, ..., x_q$ are assigned any value from their type, respectively. Note that each of the algorithms in the table can be used independently.

Table 1. Algorithms for case (a)

No. of algorithms	$\ominus$	Algorithms of test case generation for x_1	Algorithms of test case generation for the remaining input variables ($i = 2, ..., q$)
(1)	$=$	$x_1 := E$	$x_i := any \in Type(x_i)$
(2)	$>=, <>$ or $>$	$x_1 := E + \sigma$	$x_i := any \in Type(x_i)$
(3)	$<=$ or $<$	$x_1 := E - \sigma$	$x_i := any \in Type(x_i)$

Generating a test case to satisfy $E_1 \ominus E_2$ in case (b) becomes a little more complicated: it first needs to transform the format $E_1 \ominus E_2$ to the format $x_1 \ominus E$, and then to apply the algorithms for case (a).

Generating a test case to satisfy $E_1 \ominus E_2$ in case (c) requires more actions:

(1) Randomly assigning values from appropriate types to the variables $x_2, ..., x_q$ to transform the format into the format $E_1 \ominus E_2$ in case (b).

(2) Applying the algorithms for case (b) to the derived format $E_1 \ominus E_2$.

4.1.2   Compound Variables

The above algorithms cannot handle operators defined in compound data types. Since the essential idea for handling operations of compound variables for all kinds of compound types is similar, we only choose the *set type* in SOFL as an example to discuss the algorithms for test case generation.

Let $q = 1$ and $Q_i^j(x_1, x_2, ..., x_q)$ be $E(x_1)$, where x_1 is a variable denoting a single set of elements, $E(x_1)$ is a term involving x_1 and an operator defined on set types, such as *inset* (membership), *notin* (non-membership), *card* (cardinality), *union* (union of sets), *inter* (intersection of sets), *diff* (difference between sets), *subset* (subset), *psubset* (proper subset), and *power* (power set). Then, a set of algorithms for generating a test case from each kind of atomic predicate is shown in Table 2, in which E_1 and E_2 denote two set values (i.e., two specific sets), $get(E_1)$ represents an element obtained from set E_1 (a nondeterministic operator), and w is a natural number.

Table 2. Algorithms for test case generation from set type expressions

No. of algorithms	Expression $E(x_1)$	Algorithms of test case generation the for x_1	Randomly selecting values for rest input variables ($i = 2, ..., q$)
(1)	x_1 *inset* E_1	$x_1 := get(E_1)$	$x_i \in Type(x_i)$
(2)	x_1 *notin* E_1	$x_1 := get(Type(x_1) \setminus E_1)$	$x_i \in Type(x_i)$
(3)	$card(x_1) = u$	$x_1 := \{a_1, a_2, ..., a_u\}$, where $x_1 : set\ of\ T$, and $a_k \in T$, $k = 1, 2, ..., u$	$x_i \in Type(x_i)$
(4)	$union(x_1, E_1) = E_2$	$x_1 := E_2 \setminus E_1$	$x_i \in Type(x_i)$
(5)	$inter(x_1, E_1) = E_2$	$x_1 := E_2$, where $E_2 \subseteq E_1$	$x_i \in Type(x_i)$
(6)	$diff(x_1, E_1) = E_2$	$x_1 := E_1$ *union* E_2	$x_i \in Type(x_i)$
(7)	$subset(x_1, E_1)$	$x_1 := E_1$	$x_i \in Type(x_i)$
(8)	$psubset(x_1, E_1)$	$x_1 := E_1 \setminus \{get(E_1)\}$	$x_i \in Type(x_i)$
(9)	$x_1 = E_1$	$x_1 := E1$	$x_i \in Type(x_i)$
(10)	$x_1 <> E_1$	$x_1 := \{get(Type(x_1))\} \setminus E_1$	$x_i \in Type(x_i)$
(11)	$power(x_1) = E_1$	$x_1 := getLargest(E_1)$	$x_i \in Type(x_i)$

In this table, x_1 in Algorithms (1) and (2) denotes an *element* of a set (e.g., E_1), while in the rest of algorithms it denotes a set whose type is *set of T* where T is the element type already defined. Algorithm (1) shows that a test case for x_1 can be generated by assigning any value from E_1 (as indicated by the assignment $x_1 := get(E_1)$). Algorithm (3) indicates that a test case for set x_1 to satisfy the condition $card(x_1) = u$ is to randomly select u elements from its element type T. Algorithm (4) states that a test case for set x_1 to satisfy the condition $union(x_1, E_1) = E_2$ (the union of x_1 and E_1 is equal to E_2) is to assign the difference set between E_2 and E_1 (i.e., $x_1 := E_2 \setminus E_1$). The other algorithms in the table can be similarly interpreted, we therefore do not elaborate on them for brevity.

Note that the algorithms in the table are suitable for dealing with expressions involving only one input variable x_1. However, if more than one input variable is involved, a similar measure to that of dealing with numeric terms can be taken. That is, first randomly select values $v_2, ..., v_q$ for variables $x_2, ..., x_q$ to convert the expression into one satisfying the condition required, and then apply the corresponding algorithms in Table 2 to generate a satisfactory value for x_1. Thus, a full test case for the predicate can be generated.

4.2   Generation for Conjunctions

We can now focus on the more challenging issue of generating test cases from the conjunction $Q_i^1 \wedge Q_i^2 \wedge \cdots \wedge Q_i^m$. A primitive way as proposed in our previous publication [5] is to generate a test case satisfying one of the atomic predicates, say Q_i^j ($j = 1, ..., m$), and then use the same test case to evaluate the rest atomic predicates in the conjunction. If it also satisfies all of the rest atomic predicates, a qualified test case for the conjunction is found; otherwise, another attempt to generate a new test case must be made to repeat the same process. However, our experience suggests that this algorithm may not be efficient in many situations. Existing SAT solvers, such as RISS [6], may be used for test data generation for a conjunction, but since the SAT solver only deals with propositional logic, its capability is limited for our formal notation that adopts first-order predicate logic. Existing SMT solvers, such as Yices [7] and Z3 [8], may be a better possibility for the solution due to their capability of dealing with predicate logic, but they are difficult to be adopted in our work for two major reasons. One is that they do not cope with many operators both syntactically and semantically that are defined in various types of our SOFL language with which a theorem is written. This poses an obstacle to the generation of test data satisfying the required criteria and predicates that involve those operators. Another reason is the difficulty in incorporating the SMT solver into our supporting tool for the TBFV approach presented in this paper. In fact, our work on TBFV is part of our ongoing Agile Formal Engineering Method project that aims to build tool supports for both specification and its verification based on our SOFL language that has been using by industry in Japan and other countries. Therefore, we must build an independent tool support with the capability of dealing with all of the syntaxes in SOFL.

   In this section, we propose a new and more efficient algorithm for generating test cases for conjunctions below than our previous algorithm. The essential idea of the algorithm is first to form an *ordered partition* of the atomic predicate set $\{Q_i^1, Q_i^2, ..., Q_i^m\}$ according to *variable dependency*, and then properly apply the primitive algorithm mentioned above to generate a qualified test case for the conjunction if it is satisfiable. Before introducing the details of the algorithm, we first need to introduce several notations and concepts to be used in the algorithm below.

Notations:

- $Var(E)$ denotes the set of free variables occurring in predicate E.
- $[1..n]$ denotes the set of integers $\{1, 2, \ldots, n\}$.
- $\{Q_i^1, Q_i^2, ..., Q_i^m\}$ denotes all of the atomic predicates in the conjunction $Q_i^1 \wedge Q_i^2 \wedge \cdots \wedge Q_i^m$.

Definition 1. *Let E_1 and E_2 be two predicate expressions. If E_2 contains more free variables than E_1, i.e., $Var(E_1) \subset Var(E_2)$, E_2 is said to be dependent on E_1 and the dependency relation is represented as $E_1 \sqsubseteq E_2$.*

For example, predicate $x + y > 0$ is dependent on $x > 0$; that is, $x > 0 \sqsubseteq x + y > 0$.

Definition 2. *Let $\{R_1, R_2, ..., R_u\}$ be a set of predicate sets. If it satisfies the following two conditions*
  (1) $\forall_{i \in [1..u-1]} \forall_{E_1 \in R_i, E_2 \in R_{i+1}} \cdot E_1 \sqsubseteq E_2$
  (2) $\forall_{i \in [1..u]} \forall_{E_1, E_2 \in R_i} \cdot \neg(E_1 \sqsubseteq E_2)$,
  we say $\{R_1, R_2, ..., R_u\}$ is an ordered set of predicate sets on $\sqsubseteq$.

For instance, $\{\{x > 0, y > 1\}, \{x + y > 10\}, \{x * y + z > 1, x + y * z < 100\}\}$ is an ordered set of predicates on $\sqsubseteq$, while $\{\{x > 0, x * y > 1\}, \{x + y > 10\},$ $\{x * y + z > 1, x + y * z < 100\}\}$ is not an ordered set because there exists a predicate $x * y > 1$ in the first predicate set on which the predicate $x + y > 10$ in the second predicate set is not dependent (violating condition (1)). It is also because the two predicates in the first predicate set satisfies the dependent relation, i.e., $x > 0 \sqsubseteq x * y > 1$, which violates condition (2) in the definition.

Definition 3. *Let R be a predicate set and t be a test case. If t satisfies every predicate in R, we say t satisfies R.*

Suppose $R = \{x > 0, x + y < 10\}$ and a test case $t = \{(x, 5), (y, 3)\}$. Then, obviously t satisfies R by definition because t satisfies both $x > 0$ and $x + y < 10$.

On the basis of these symbols and concepts, we give an algorithm for generating a test case from the conjunction below.

Algorithm 4.2.1. /*Java-based pseudocode*/

No. 1 Construct a partition $\{R_1, R_2, ..., R_u\}$ for the set $\{Q_i^1, Q_i^2, ..., Q_i^m\}$
($1 \leq u \leq m$) such that $\{R_1, R_2, ..., R_u\}$ is an ordered set of predicate sets on $\sqsubseteq$;

No. 2 $t_0 := \{\}$; $i := 1$; $flag := 0$; /*initializing variable t_0 representing the initial test case*/

No. 3 *while* ($i \leq u \,\|\, flag \leq NoOfFailure$) {

  $A := ObtainInstantiatedPredicates(R_i, t_{i-1})$; /*A is an array of predicates*/

  $t_i := GenerateTestCase(A)$; /*$t_i$ is a new test case generated based on the predicates in A*/
    if ($t_i = \{\}$)
        $\{i := i - 1;\ flag := flag + 1;\}$
    else $\{i := i + 1;\}$
    }

No.4 *if* ($flag > NoOfFailure$) {Display a test case generation failure message} *else* {Display a test case generation success message and t_i is the generated test case}

No. 5 End.

The essential idea of the algorithm is to generate a test case that satisfies all of the predicates in R_i ($1 \leq i \leq u$) and then utilize the values in the test case in generating a more complete test case for R_{i+1}. Repeat this process until R_u is reached and a qualified test case is produced. However, if the generation fails for R_i, it will go one step back to retry generating a test case for R_{i-1} and then repeat the same process. But if the number of failings to generate the qualified test case satisfying all R_1, R_2, ..., R_u reaches the pre-defined number denoted by *NoOfFailure* (e.g., 100), a failure message will be issued as the result of the algorithm.

In the algorithm, the *function ObtainInstantiatedPredicates(R_i, t_{i-1})* obtains an array A whose elements are the atomic predicates resulting from substituting the value of every variable in test case t_{i-1} for the same variable in the atomic predicates in R_i. For instance, suppose

    $R_i = \{x * y + z > 1, x + y * z < 100\}$, containing two predicates and
    $R_{i-1} = \{x + y > 10\}$, and the test case for R_{i-1} is
    t_{i-1} = $\{(x, 8), (y, 9)\}$. Then, we get A from *ObtainInstantiated*
    Predicates(R_i, t_{i-1}) as follows:
    $A = \{8 * 9 + z > 1, 8 + 9 * z < 100\}$.

To generate a test case for R_i based on A, we need to apply the function *GenerateTestCase*(A). The test case generated from this function is actually a more complete one than t_{i-1} that satisfies all of the atomic predicates in A. Assume that array A has n atomic predicates as its elements, we give an algorithm used to implement the function *GenerateTestCase*(A) below.

Algorithm 4.2.2. /* Java-based pseudocode*/

```
satisfyingConjunction := false;
    for (int i := 0; i < A.length(); i++){
    t_c := GenerateTestCasefromFirstPredicate(A(0));
    j := 0;
while (j < A.length() && Satisfy(A(j), t_c)){
    j := j + 1;
    }
if (j < A.length())
    {A := Rotate(A); }
    else {satisfyingConjunction := true;
       break; }
    }
    if (satisfyingConjunction == false) {
    t_c = {};
    }
    return t_c;
```

The essential idea of this algorithm is first to generate a test case satisfying the first atomic predicate of A (i.e., $A(0)$) and then to test whether it satisfies all of the other atomic predicates in A. If yes, a successful test case is generated; otherwise, repeat the same process for the other atomic predicates in A until all of the atomic predicates of A is exhausted. In this algorithm, the function $GenerateTestCasefromFirstPredicate(A(0))$ produces a test case as the result that satisfies the first atomic predicate in A. $Satisfy\ (A(j), t_c)$ yields true if test case t_c satisfies $A(j)$; otherwise it yields false. $Rotate(A)$ yields a permutation of A by moving the first element of A to the last position and all of the other elements are shifted to one position on the left in A. For the sake of space, examples are omitted.

5   Building Confidence

From the discussions above, we can clearly see the benefit of the TBFV method in determining the invalidity of the sub-theorem $P_i \vdash C$ (also with the same merit for the whole theorem). However, if the sub-theorem is valid, using TBFV to prove its validity is a challenge. In theory, testing-based approach generally lacks the power of proving the sub-theorem for the obvious reason. In this case, what we can expect is to achieve a sufficient confidence of the theorem. The question is what test cases and how many of them should be tried to establish the confidence. Apparently, it is extremely difficult to give a unique answer for this question. We propose a criterion for generating adequate test cases based on the idea of equivalent domain partition for black-box testing [9] next.

Criterion 5.1. Let x_1, x_2, ..., x_q be all of the free variables occurring in P_i. Then, the test set T for verifying $P_i \vdash C$ should contain all of the tuples (each tuple is a test case) in the following product set:

$$valueSpace(x_1) \times valueSpace(x_2) \times \cdots \times valueSpace(x_q)$$

where $valueSpace(x_i)$ $(i = 1, ..., q)$ denotes a set of the following three values in the type of x_i:

(1) *Great value*,
(2) *special value* or *boundary value*, and
(3) *small value*.

The notions of great value, special or boundary value, and small value for each data type can be defined differently. For example, for the integer *int* type, a great value can be a sufficiently big positive integer; a small value can be a sufficiently small negative integer; and a special value can be zero. But for a set type (e.g., *set of int*), a great value can be a large set of integers; a small value can be a small set of integers; and a boundary value is the empty set $\{\}$. The decision on the specific value of each kind in practice can be made by the verifier, or by the supporting tool that implements a pre-defined criterion.

As far as the number of necessary test cases is concerned, it is really difficult to say and to decide. It should depends on the criticality of the corresponding property and the software system under verification. Considering the time and cost constraints in practice, our experience suggests that if a fairly large number of test cases (e.g., 200) are used but still no fault is found, it should be reasonable enough to be confident of the theorem and the validity of the corresponding property, although this may never be 100 % correct. Of course, this number can be flexible for different systems and situations in practice.

6   Example

For the sake of space, we only take the *feasibility* property of the operation *charging card with cash* in the *Suica Card System* described in Sect. 7 for example to show how the TBFV method can be applied. The feasibility of the operation requires that for every input satisfying the pre-condition, there must exists an output that satisfies the post-condition. Specifically, the property is given as follows:

$(\forall_{x \in NonPositiveInt} \cdot x < amount1 \wedge x \leq {}^\sim buffer) \wedge amount1 \in int \wedge {}^\sim buffer \in int \wedge {}^\sim buffer < 50000 \vdash$

${}^\sim buffer + amount1 > 50000 \wedge$

$\exists_{overlimit_msg1 \in string} \cdot overlimit_msg1 = $ "*Amount is over the limit.*"

$\vee$

${}^\sim buffer + amount1 < 50000 \wedge$

$\exists_{buffer \in int} \cdot buffer = {}^\sim buffer + amount1$

In this property, $NonPositiveInt$ denotes the set containing zero and all the negative integers, the decorated variable ${}^\sim buffer$ denotes the value of the state variable *buffer* of the Suica Card before the operation whilst *buffer* represents the value after the operation, and *string* is a built-in type containing all of possible strings.

To generate test cases for the hypothesis, we first need to remove the universal quantifier as suggested in Sect. 3 by selecting a subset of $NonPositiveInt$. We use $SubNonPositiveInt$ to represent the subset and let $SubNonPositiveInt = \{-1, 0\}$, considering the nature of the values in $NonPositiveInt$ and the body of the quantified expression. We then convert the hypothesis into the following predicate:

$(-1 < amount1 \wedge -1 \leq {}^\sim buffer) \wedge (0 < amount1 \wedge 0 \leq {}^\sim buffer) \wedge$

$amount1 \in int \wedge {}^\sim buffer \in int \wedge {}^\sim buffer < 50000 .$

This predicate can be further simplified but we omit the discussion for the sake of space. Based on this predicate, we generate three test cases for all of the two free variables $amount1$ and ${}^\sim buffer$ as shown in Table 3. It is apparent that only test case 3 makes the hypothesis true but make the conclusion false because there is no case of ${}^\sim buffer + amount1 = 50000$ is defined in the conclusion, which is a fault.

Table 3. Example test cases

Variables	Test case 1	Test case 2	Test case 3
$amount1$	150000	0	35000
$\tilde{}buffer$	0	49999	15000

7 Experiment

7.1 Background

We have applied our TBFV technique to verify 52 properties that are derived from a *mutant formal specification* in SOFL for the *Suica Card System* (SCS) of the East Japan Railway Company. The original formal specification defines the following services in 6 modules: *registering a card, buying tickets, charging card with cash, charging from bank account, entering station, exiting station,* and *updating commutation ticket.* The derived properties include *feasibility, integration properties,* and *some relevant algebraic properties* whose detailed definitions are presented in our previous publication [10].

Our experiment was designed to concentrate only on one important thing that is the *fault detection rate* using TBFV, which is defined as follows:

Fault detection rate = the number of the faults found / the total number of faults injected

The reason is simple. Before understanding how good the performance of our TBFV method is in comparison with other verification techniques (e.g., formal proof, specification review), we first need to know how effective the TBFV technique is in finding faults. An experiment for comparison requires more resources, training, and material preparations, therefore we plan to conduct it in the future.

For the purpose of our experiment in this paper, we created the mutant formal specification by injecting 231 faults in the original specification. The faults are roughly divided into two categories: *consistency-related fault* and *validity-related fault*. A consistency-related fault is a defect that results in the violation of some consistency properties mentioned above. A validity-related fault is a defect that does not violate any consistency-related properties but is undesirable with respect to the user's requirements. A simple example is that the operator "+" (plus) should be "−" (minus) in the expression $card.buffer=$ $\tilde{}card.buffer$ $+ ticket.price$ that defines the updating of the *buffer* of the Suica *card* after a train ticket with the *price* is purchased.

An experienced researcher in our lab was asked to inject the faults based on the consideration of fault distribution (evenly injecting faults throughout the specification rather than concentrating on some parts) and to derive the 52 properties from the formal specification. The faults were created mainly by applying some mutation operators normally used for mutation testing [11]. The mutation operators include *operator replacement, insertion,* and *deletion* at arithmetic,

Table 4. The summary of the experiment result

Processes	Pro-perties	Faults injected	Faults Found	Fault detection rate	Test cases
Buy_With_Card	5	29 (C: 24, V: 5)	28 (C: 24, V: 4)	96.6 % (C: 100 %, V: 80 %)	12
Buy_With_Card_Cash	10	47 (C: 40, V: 7)	46 (C: 39, V: 7)	97.9 % (C: 97.5 %, V: 100 %)	22
Charge_ With_Cash	5	23 (C: 17, V: 6)	22 (C: 17, V: 5)	95.7 % (C: 100 %, V: 83.3 %)	12
Charge_From_Bank	10	44 (C: 36, V: 8)	43 (C: 36, V: 7)	97.7 % (C: 100 %, V: 87.5 %)	25
Entering_Station	5	16 (C: 15, V: 1)	16 (C: 15, V: 1)	100 % (C: 100 %, V: 100 %)	12
Exiting_Station	5	25 (C: 21, V: 4)	24 (C: 21, V: 3)	96 % (C: 100 %, V: 75 %)	14
Register_Card	6	29 (C: 23, V: 6)	28 (C: 23, V: 5)	96.6 % (C: 100 %, V: 83.3 %)	15
Update_Commute_ Ticket	6	18 (C: 14, V: 4)	18 (C: 14, V: 4)	100 % (C: 100 %, V: 100 %)	13
All processes	52	231 (C: 190, V: 41)	225 (C: 189, V: 36)	97.4 % (C: 99.5 %, V: 87.8 %)	125

condition, or logical expression levels, and violation of informal requirements. The experiment was carried out manually by three experienced graduate students. They followed the instructions of our TBFV technique to generate test cases, evaluate each property, and analyze the evaluation result to determine whether and what faults are found. The identified faults are all finally confirmed by the person who carried out the fault injection into the specification.

7.2   Experiment Result

Table 4 shows the details of the experiment. The column named **Processes** lists up all of the processes used in the experiment. The column named **Properties** gives the numbers of the properties derived from each corresponding process. The columns named **Inserted faults**, **Detected faults**, and **Test cases** give the number of the injected faults, the faults detected by using TBFV, and the test case produced, respectively. In the columns of **Inserted faults** and **Detected faults**, each number of faults (e.g., 29) is actually divided into two parts: C: No1, V: No2, where No1 denotes the number of the consistency-related faults and No2 represents the number of the validity-related faults. Thus, 29 (C: 24, V: 5) for example, means that the total 29 faults are constituted by 24 consistency-related faults and 5 validity-related faults.

The result of the experiment demonstrates that our TBFV is effective in the sense that it uses a small number of test cases to find all or most of the injected faults. The average fault detection rate for all of the 52 properties derived from all of the 8 process specifications is 97.4 % in which the average consistency-related fault detection rate is 99.5 % and the validity-related fault detection rate is 87.8 %.

7.3   Experience and Lessons

Our experience in the experiment indicates three positive aspects of the TBFV method. One is the simplicity in use. Another aspect is the high effectiveness and efficiency of the TBFV technique because all or most of the injected faults could be found with a small number of test cases. Although this result is limited due to the relatively small scale of the experiment, the result indicates a high potential of the technique. The final positive point is that the technique can be applied without any need to understand formal proof. This will likely create a high possibility for practitioners to adopt the technique with little psychological barriers.

We have also learned two important lessons. One is that the TBFV technique can only tell us whether there exist any faults in the target property or not, but it may not necessarily directly tell us what are the faults. In fact, the majority of the injected faults were found in the process of test case generation, which takes up approximately 86 % of the total faults we found in the experiment. The reason is that generating test cases inevitably requires the verifier to exam every aspect of the property, which often leads to the discovery of faults. Another lesson learned is concerned with verifying a sub-theorem such as $P_i \vdash C$ where P_i is a contradiction. The difficulty lies in the lack of a theoretical instruction on when the test case generation based on P_i should be given up. Although such a situation may be easily found out by humans, it is likely to pose a threat when test cases are generated automatically with a tool.

8   Supporting Tool

A prototype software tool called *TBFV-Tool* to support our TBFV method has been developed by our research group, but its improvement is still undergoing. In this paper, we only briefly report the desired functionality in the tool.

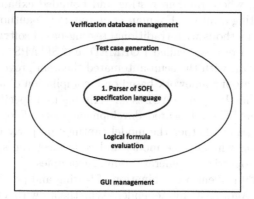

Fig. 1. Structure of the supporting tool TBFV-Tool

Figure 1 shows the structure of the tool. The core of the tool is a parser of the SOFL specification language [4] using which logical expressions in a theorem can be written. SOFL stands for *Structured Object-Oriented Formal Language*, and its grammar for writing logical expressions inherits from VDM-SL but with many improvements for comprehensibility. In the examples of this paper, we try not to show the SOFL syntax in order to save the space for explaining it. Instead, we use the commonly used first order predicate logic in the examples. The second layer of the tool includes two functional modules: test case generation and logical formula evaluation. The former is responsible for automatically generating test cases from logical formulas whilst the latter performs evaluation of logical formulas with the generated test cases. The uttermost outside layer has two functional modules: verification database management and GUI management. The former manages all of the documents in relation to the verification of the theorem whilst the latter deals with GUI pages for human and machine interaction, including building all of the necessary frames and areas for displaying all of the necessary information. The implementation of the entire tool is still ongoing and its details will be reported somewhere else after its completion.

9   Related Work

The idea of our TBFV method is shared by some of existing studies, but they are mostly concerned with how testing is used to facilitate theorem proving while our aim is to avoid theorem proving by only using testing to detect faults and enhance confidence in the validity of theorems.

Chamarthi and Manolios present a method in [12] for rigorously analyzing designs and their specifications using an interactive theorem prover called ACL2s [1]. The main idea is to use the deductive verification engine of ACL2s to decompose properties into subgoals that are either proven to be true or tested to find counterexamples. In this work, deduction and testing are used in an interleaved, synergistic fashion, where random testing and bounded exhaustive testing are adopted as the testing strategy. Eakman *et al.* report the authors' experience in integrating formal methods with traditional testing-based software development process through two projects called FORMED and SITAPS, respectively. The former combines UML with the semi-automated theorem prover ACL2s and the latter developed a proof framework based on a compilation of a domain specific language (DSL) called Ivory into ACL2s for verifying user specified and compiler generated assertions. The advocated development methodology includes modelling in a DSL, testing whether the model captures properly the properties of specification, testing whether the model and code meet the specification, and formally proving properties or generate counter-examples.

Dybjer *et al.* [13] present a combination of testing and proving by extending the proof assistant Agda/Alfa for dependent type theory with a tool QuickCheck for random testing of functional programs. Testing is used for debugging programs and specifications before a proof is attempted. It can also be used repeatedly during proof for testing suitable subgoals. Paraskevopoulou *et al.* have ported the QuickCheck framework to Coq [14], a formal proof management system, with a result of constructing a prototype Coq plugin called QuickChick [15]. The purpose of QuickChick is to support formal proof with testing and to verify the correctness of the testing code written manually, but it does not try to automatically generate test data satisfying properties. Instead, it provides ways for the users to construct property-based generators, thus giving experienced users more control over how the data is generated. Bulwahn describes a new QuickCheck for Isabelle/HOL that detects faulty specifications and invalid conjectures using not only random testing but also bounded exhaustive testing and symbolic testing [16]. The work reported in [17] also discusses how testing can be used to improve formal proof for programs, but the technique relies on domain partition of the induction variable used in a loop to be proved. Chamarthi *et al.* present an idea of using random testing to find countexamples to conjectures for theorem proving [18]. A similar technique is also adopted by Owre in his work on integrating testing with formal proof using PVS [19].

For test case generation based on pre-post style formal specifications, an early work on partitioning the conjunction of pre-condition, post-condition, and invariant to generate test cases for a VDM operation was reported by Dick and Faivre [20]. The similar principles are applied by Legeard *et al.* for test case generation from B or Z notation [21], and has been adapted in many test case generation tools, some of which use interactive theorem prover [22]. TestEra [23] is a testing tool that accepts representation constraints and generates non-isomorphic test data by using a solution enumeration technique to use propositional constraint solver or SAT engine [24]. Aichernig and Salas took the mutation testing view to propose a fault-based approach to test case generation for pre- and post-condition specifications in OCL [25,26]. The essential idea is first to mutate the pre- and post-conditions and then try to generate test cases from the specification that help find the anticipated errors.

10 Conclusion

We have proposed the TBFV method for verifying software specification properties in realistic software development. The method is characterized by using testing to replace formal proof in theorem proving where each theorem can be used to represent a system property. A group of algorithms for test case generation from formal logical expressions are described, and various important issues, such as building confidence by testing, effectiveness evaluation by experiment, and tool support, are discussed. Although theoretically the TBFV method may not replace formal proof in verifying the validity of theorems, it can bring practical benefits with high confidence, such as saving time and cost, for industrial software development due to its operational simplicity and automation.

Our future research will continue to concentrate on developing more effective test case generation methods, improving the capability of the current supporting tool, and applying the method in more software projects.

Acknowledgment. I would like to thank my students Mo Li, Hayato Ikeda, and Ye Yan for their contributions in developing the supporting tool for the TBFV method proposed in this paper. Hayato Ikeda's work on the tool is particularly appreciated.

References

1. Dillinger, P.C., Manolios, P., Vroon, D., Moore, J.S.: The ACL2 Sedan. In: Proceedings of 7th Workshop on User Interfaces for Theorem Provers (UITP 2006). Electronic Notes in Theoretical Computer Science, pp. 3–18. Elsevier, 15 May 2007
2. Owre, S., Rushby, J., Shankar, N., Henke, F.V.: Formal verification for fault-tolerant architetures: prolegomena to the design of PVS. IEEE Trans. Softw. Eng. **21**(2), 107–125 (1995)
3. Leavens, T., Rustand, K., Leino, M., Muller, P.: Specification and verification challenges for sequential object-oriented programs. Formal Aspects Comput. **19**, 159–189 (2007)
4. Liu, S.: Formal Engineering for Industrial Software Development Using the SOFL Method. Springer, Heidelberg (2004). ISBN: 3-540-20602-7
5. Liu, S., Nakajima, S.: A decompositional approach to automatic test case generation based on formal specifications. In: 4th IEEE International Conference on Secure Software Integration and Reliability Improvement (SSIRI 2010), Singapore, 9–11 June 2010, pp. 147–155 (2010)
6. Manthey, N.: Solver Description of RISS 2.0 and PRISS 2.0, KRR Teport 12–02, Knowledge Representation and Reasoning, Technical University Dresden (2012)
7. Dutertre, B.: Yices 2.2. In: Biere, A., Bloem, R. (eds.) CAV 2014. LNCS, vol. 8559, pp. 737–744. Springer, Heidelberg (2014)
8. de Moura, L., Bjørner, N.S.: Z3: an efficient SMT solver. In: Ramakrishnan, C.R., Rehof, J. (eds.) TACAS 2008. LNCS, vol. 4963, pp. 337–340. Springer, Heidelberg (2008)
9. Beizer, B.: Black-Box Testing. Wiley, New York (1995)
10. Liu, S., McDermid, J.A., Chen, Y.: A rigorous method for inspection of model-based formal specifications. IEEE Trans. Reliab. **59**(4), 667–684 (2010)
11. Kuhn, D.R.: Fault classes and error detection capability of specification-based testing. ACM Trans. Softw. Eng. Methodol. **8**(4), 411–424 (1999)
12. Chamarthi, H.R., Manolios, P.: Automated specification analysis using an interactive theorem prover. In: Formal Methods in Computer-Aided Design (FMCAD 2011), 30 October–2 November 2011, pp. 46–53. IEEE Press (2011)
13. Dybjer, P., Haiyan, Q., Takeyama, M.: Combining testing and proving in dependent type theory. In: Basin, D., Wolff, B. (eds.) TPHOLs 2003. LNCS, vol. 2758, pp. 188–203. Springer, Heidelberg (2003)
14. Bertot, Y., Castern, P.: Interactive Theorem Proving and Program Development: Coq'Art: The Calculus of Inductive Constructions. Springer, Heidelberg (2013)
15. Paraskevopoulou, Z., Hirtcu, C., Denes, M., Lamproulos, L., Pierce, B.C.: Foundational property-based testing. In: Urban, C., Zhang, X. (eds.) ITP. LNCS, vol. 9236, pp. 325–343. Springer, Heidelberg (2015)
16. Bulwahn, L.: The new quickcheck for isabelle. In: Hawblitzel, C., Miller, D. (eds.) CPP 2012. LNCS, vol. 7679, pp. 92–108. Springer, Heidelberg (2012)
17. Hähnle, R., Wallenburg, A.: Using a software testing technique to improve theorem proving. In: Petrenko, A., Ulrich, A. (eds.) FATES 2003. LNCS, vol. 2931, pp. 30–41. Springer, Heidelberg (2004)
18. Chamarthi, H.R., Dillinger, P.C., Kaufmann, M.: Integrating testing and interactive theorem proving. In: Proceedings of 10th International Workshop on the ACL2 Theorem Prover and Its Applications (EPTCS 70), 3–4 November 2011, pp. 4–19 (2011)

19. Owre, S.: Random testing in PVS. In: Workshop on Automated Formal Methods (AFM) (2006)
20. Dick, J., Faivre, A.: Automating the generation and sequencing of test cases from model-based specifications. In: Larsen, P.G., Wing, J.M. (eds.) FME 1993. LNCS, vol. 670, pp. 268–284. Springer, Heidelberg (1993)
21. Legeard, B., Peureux, F., Utting, M.: Automated boundary testing from Z and B. In: Eriksson, L.-H., Lindsay, P.A. (eds.) FME 2002. LNCS, vol. 2391, pp. 21–40. Springer, Heidelberg (2002)
22. Helke, S., Neustupny, T., Santen, T.: Automating test case generation from Z specifications with Isabelle. In: Till, D., Bowen, J.P., Hinchey, M.G. (eds.) ZUM 1997. LNCS, vol. 1212, pp. 52–71. Springer, Heidelberg (1997)
23. Khurshid, S., Marinov, D.: TestEra: specification-based testing of Java programs using SAT. Autom. Softw. Eng. **11**(4), 403–434 (2004)
24. Khurshid, S., Marinov, D., Shlyakhter, I., Jackson, D.: A case for efficient solution enumeration. In: Giunchiglia, E., Tacchella, A. (eds.) SAT 2003. LNCS, vol. 2919, pp. 272–286. Springer, Heidelberg (2004)
25. Aichernig, B.K., Salas, P.A.P.: Test case generation by OCL mutation and constraint solving. In: Cai, K.-Y., Ohnishi, A. (eds.) Proceedings of Fifth International Conference on Quality Software (QSIC 2005), Melbourne, Australia, 19–21 September 2005, pp. 64–71. IEEE CS Press (2005)
26. Aichernig, B.K.: Model-based mutation testing of reactive systems. In: Liu, Z., Woodcock, J., Zhu, H. (eds.) Theories of Programming and Formal Methods. LNCS, vol. 8051, pp. 23–36. Springer, Heidelberg (2013)

Your Proof Fails? Testing Helps to Find the Reason

Guillaume Petiot[1], Nikolai Kosmatov[1(✉)], Bernard Botella[1], Alain Giorgetti[2], and Jacques Julliand[2]

[1] CEA, LIST, Software Reliability Laboratory, PC 174, 91191 Gif-sur-Yvette, France
{guillaume.petiot,nikolai.kosmatov,bernard.botella}@cea.fr
[2] FEMTO-ST/DISC, University of Franche-Comté, 25030 Besançon Cedex, France
{alain.giorgetti,jacques.julliand}@femto-st.fr

Abstract. Applying deductive verification to formally prove that a program respects its formal specification is a very complex and time-consuming task due in particular to the lack of feedback in case of proof failures. Along with a non-compliance between the code and its specification (due to an error in at least one of them), possible reasons of a proof failure include a missing or too weak specification for a called function or a loop, and lack of time or simply incapacity of the prover to finish a particular proof. This work proposes a complete methodology where test generation helps to identify the reason of a proof failure and to exhibit a counterexample clearly illustrating the issue. We define the categories of proof failures, introduce two subcategories of contract weaknesses (single and global ones), and examine their properties. We describe how to transform a formally specified C program into C code suitable for testing, and illustrate the benefits of the method on comprehensive examples. The method has been implemented in STADY, a plugin of the software analysis platform FRAMA-C. Initial experiments show that detecting non-compliances and contract weaknesses allows to precisely diagnose most proof failures.

1 Introduction

Among formal verification techniques, *deductive verification* consists in establishing a rigorous mathematical proof that a given program meets its specification. When no confusion is possible, one also says that deductive verification consists in "proving a program". It requires that the program comes with a formal specification, usually given in special comments called *annotations,* including function contracts (with pre- and postconditions) and loop contracts (with loop variants and invariants). The *weakest precondition calculus* proposed by Dijkstra [19] reduces any deductive verification problem to establishing the validity of first-order formulas called *verification conditions*.

In modular deductive verification of a function f calling another function g, the roles of the pre- and postconditions of f and of the callee g are dual. The precondition of f is assumed and its postcondition must be proved, while at

© Springer International Publishing Switzerland 2016
B.K. Aichernig and C.A. Furia (Eds.): TAP 2016, LNCS 9762, pp. 130–150, 2016.
DOI: 10.1007/978-3-319-41135-4_8

any call to g in f, the precondition of g must be proved before the call and its postcondition is assumed after the call. The situation for a function f with one call to g is presented in Fig. 1. An arrow in this figure informally indicates that its initial point provides a hypothesis for a proof of its final point. For instance, the precondition Pre_f of f and the postcondition $Post_g$ of g provide hypotheses for a proof of the postcondition $Post_f$ of f. The called function g is proved separately.

To reflect the fact that some contracts become hypotheses during deductive verification of f we use the term *subcontracts for f* to designate contracts of called functions and loops in f.

Motivation. One of the most important difficulties in deductive verification is the manual processing of proof failures by the verification engineer since proof failures may have several causes. Indeed, a failure to prove Pre_g in Fig. 1

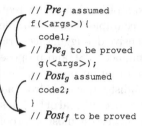

```
// Pref assumed
f(<args>){
    code1;
    // Preg to be proved
    g(<args>);
    // Postg assumed
    code2;
}
// Postf to be proved
```

Fig. 1. Proof of f that calls g

may be due to a *non-compliance* of the code to the specification: either an error in the code code1, or a wrong formalization of the requirements in the specification Pre_f or Pre_g itself. The verification can also remain inconclusive because of a *prover incapacity* to finish a particular proof within allocated time. In many cases, it is extremely difficult for the verification engineer to decide how to proceed: either suspect a non-compliance and look for an error in the code or check the specification, or suspect a prover incapacity, give up automatic proof and try to achieve an interactive proof with a proof assistant (like COQ [41]).

A failure to prove the postcondition $Post_f$ (cf. Fig. 1) is even more complex to analyze: along with a prover incapacity or a non-compliance due to errors in the pieces of code code1 and code2 or to an incorrect specification Pre_f or $Post_f$, the failure can also result from a *too weak* postcondition $Post_g$ of g, that does not fully express the intended behavior of g. Notice that in this last case, the proof of g can still be successful. However, the current automated tools for program proving do not provide a sufficiently precise indication on the reason of the proof failure. Some advanced tools produce a counterexample extracted from the underlying solver that cannot precisely indicate if the verification engineer should look for a non-compliance, or strengthen subcontracts (and which one of them), or consider adding additional lemmas or using interactive proof. So the verification engineer must basically consider all possible reasons one after another, and maybe initiate a very costly interactive proof. For a loop, the situation is similar, and offers an additional challenge: to prove the invariant preservation, whose failure can be due to several reasons as well.

The motivation of this work is twofold. First, we want to provide the verification engineer with a more precise feedback indicating the reason of each proof failure. Second, we look for a counterexample that either confirms the non-compliance and demonstrates that the unproven predicate can indeed fail on a test datum, or confirms a subcontract weakness showing on a test datum which subcontract is insufficient.

Approach and Goals. The diagnosis of proof failures based on a counterexample generated by a prover can be imprecise since from the prover's point of view, the code of callees and loops in f is replaced by the corresponding subcontracts. To make this diagnosis more precise, one should take into account their code as well as their contracts. A recent study [42] proposed to use function inlining and loop unrolling (cf. Sect. 6). We propose an alternative approach: to use advanced test generation techniques in order to diagnose proof failures and produce counterexamples. Their usage requires a translation of the annotated C program into an executable C code suitable for testing. Previous work suggested several comprehensive debugging scenarios relying on test generation only in the case of non-compliances [38], and proposed a rule-based formalization of annotation translation for that purpose [37]. The cases of subcontract weakness remained undetected and indistinguishable from a prover incapacity.

The overall goal of the present work is to provide a complete methodology for a more precise diagnosis of proof failures in all cases, to implement it and to evaluate it in practice. The proposed method is composed of two steps. The first step looks for a non-compliance. If none is found, the second step looks for a subcontract weakness. We propose a new classification of subcontract weaknesses into *single* (due to a single too weak subcontract) and *global* (possibly related to several subcontracts), and investigate their relative properties. Another goal is to make this method automatic and suitable for a non-expert verification engineer.

The contributions of this paper include:

- a classification of proof failures into three categories: *non-compliance* (NC), *subcontract weakness* (SW) and *prover incapacity*,
- a definition and comparative analysis of *global* and *single* subcontract weaknesses,
- a new program transformation for diagnosis of subcontract weaknesses,
- a complete testing-based methodology for diagnosis of proof failures and generation of counterexamples, suggesting possible actions for each category, illustrated on several comprehensive examples,
- an implementation of the proposed solution in a tool called STADY[1], and
- experiments showing its capability to diagnose proof failures.

Paper Outline. Section 2 presents the tools used in this work and an illustrative example. Section 3 defines the categories of proof failures and counterexamples, and presents program transformations for their identification. The complete methodology for the diagnosis of proof failures is presented in Sect. 4. Our implementation and experiments are described in Sect. 5. Finally, Sects. 6 and 7 present some related work and a conclusion.

2   FRAMA-C Toolset and Illustrating Example

This work is realized in the context of FRAMA-C [31], a platform dedicated to analysis of C code that includes various analyzers in separate plugins. The WP

---

[1] See also http://gpetiot.github.io/stady.html.

plugin performs weakest precondition calculus for deductive verification of C programs. Various automatic SMT solvers can be used to prove the verification conditions generated by WP. In this work we use ALT-ERGO 0.99.1 and CVC3 2.4.1. To express properties over C programs, FRAMA-C offers the behavioral specification language ACSL [4,31]. Any analyzer can both add ACSL annotations to be verified by other ones, and notify other plugins about its own analysis results by changing an annotation status.

For combinations with dynamic analysis, FRAMA-C also supports E-ACSL [18,40], a rich executable subset of ACSL suitable for *runtime assertion checking*. E-ACSL can express function contracts (pre/postconditions, guarded behaviors, completeness and disjointness of behaviors), assertions and loop contracts (variants and invariants). It supports quantifications over bounded intervals of integers, mathematical integers and memory-related constructs (e.g. on validity and initialization). It comes with an instrumentation-based translating plugin, called E-ACSL2C [30,33], that allows to evaluate annotations at runtime and report failures. The C code generated by E-ACSL2C is inadequate[2] for test generation, which creates the need for a dedicated translation tool.

For test generation, this work relies on PATHCRAWLER [6,32,43], a Dynamic Symbolic Execution (DSE) testing tool. It is based on a specific constraint solver, COLIBRI, that implements advanced features such as floating-point and modular integer arithmetic. PATHCRAWLER provides coverage strategies like *all-paths* (all feasible paths) and *k-path* (feasible paths with at most k consecutive loop iterations). It is *sound*, meaning that each test case activates the test objective for which it was generated. This is verified by concrete execution. PATHCRAWLER is also *complete* in the following sense: if the tool manages to explore all feasible paths of the program, then the absence of a test for some test objective means that the test objective is infeasible (i.e. impossible to activate), since the tool does not approximate path constraints [6, Sect. 3.1].

Example. To illustrate various kinds of proof failures, let us consider the example of C program in Fig. 2 coming from [23]. It implements an algorithm proposed in [3, p. 325] that sequentially generates *Restricted Growth Functions* (RGF). A function $a : \{0, \ldots, n-1\} \rightarrow \{0, \ldots, n-1\}$ is an *RGF of size* $n > 0$ if $a(0) = 0$ and $a(k) \le a(k-1) + 1$ for any $1 \le k \le n-1$ (that is, the growth of $a(k)$ w.r.t. the previous step is at most 1). It is defined by the ACSL predicate is_rgf on lines 1–2 of Fig. 2, where the RGF a is represented by the C array of its values. For convenience of the reader, some ACSL notations are replaced by mathematical symbols (e.g. keywords \exists, \forall and integer are respectively denoted by $\exists$, $\forall$ and $\mathbb{Z}$).

Figure 2 shows a main function f and an auxiliary function g. The precondition of f states that a is a valid array of size n>0 (lines 22–23) and must be an RGF (line 24). The postcondition states that the function is only allowed to modify the

---

[2] E-ACSL2C relies on complex external libraries (e.g. to handle memory-related annotations and unbounded integer arithmetic of E-ACSL) and does not assume the precondition of the function under verification, whereas the translation for test generation can efficiently rely on the underlying test generator or constraint solver for these purposes [37].

```
1  /*@ predicate is_rgf(int *a, Z n) =          23        requires \valid(a+(0..n-1));
2      a[0] == 0 ∧ ∀ Z i; 1 ≤ i < n ⇒           24        requires is_rgf(a,n);
          (0 ≤ a[i] ≤ a[i-1]+1); */              25        assigns a[1..n-1];
3                                                 26        ensures is_rgf(a,n);
4  /*@ lemma max_rgf: ∀ int* a; ∀ Z n;          27        ensures \result == 1 ⇒
5      is_rgf(a, n) ⇒ (∀ Z i; 0 ≤ i < n ⇒      28            ∃ Z j; 0 ≤ j < n ∧
          a[i] ≤ i); */                          29            (\at(a[j],Pre) < a[j] ∧
6                                                 30                ∀ Z k; 0 ≤ k < j ⇒
7  /*@ requires n > 0;                           31                    \at(a[k],Pre) == a[k]); */
8      requires \valid(a+(0..n-1));              31 int f(int a[], int n) {
9      requires 1 ≤ i ≤ n-1;                     32   int i,k;
10     requires is_rgf(a,i+1);                   33   /*@ loop invariant 0 ≤ i ≤ n-1;
11     assigns a[i+1..n-1];                      34       loop assigns i;
12     ensures is_rgf(a,n); */                   35       loop variant i; */
13 void g(int a[], int n, int i) {               36   for (i = n-1; i ≥ 1; i--)
14   int k;                                      37   if (a[i] ≤ a[i-1]) { break; }
15   /*@ loop invariant i+1 ≤ k ≤ n;            38   if (i == 0) { return 0; } // Last RGF.
16       loop invariant is_rgf(a,k);             39   //@ assert a[i]+1 ≤ 2147483647;
17       loop assigns k, a[i+1..n-1];            40   a[i] = a[i] + 1;
18       loop variant n-k; */                    41   g(a,n,i);
19   for (k = i+1; k < n; k++) a[k] = 0;         42   /*@ assert ∀ Z l; 0 ≤ l < i ⇒
20 }                                                       \at(a[l],Pre) == a[l]; */
21                                                43   return 1;
22 /*@ requires n > 0;                           44 }
```

Fig. 2. Successor function for restricted growth functions (RGF)

values of array a except the first one a[0] (line 25), and that the generated array a is still an RGF (line 26). Moreover, this (simplified) contract also states that if the function returns 1 then the first modified value in RGF a has increased (lines 27–30). Here \at(a[j],Pre) denotes the value of a[j] in the Pre state, i.e. before the function is executed.

We focus now on the body of the function f in Fig. 2. The loop on lines 36–37 goes through the array from right to left to find the rightmost non-increasing element, that is, the maximal array index i such that a[i] ≤a[i-1]. If such an index i is found, the function increments a[i] (line 40) and fills out the rest of the array with zeros (call to g, line 41). The loop contract (lines 33–35) specifies the interval of values of the loop variable, the variable that the loop can modify as well as a loop variant that is used to ensure the termination of the loop. The loop variant expression must be non-negative whenever an iteration starts, and must strictly decrease after each iteration.

The function g is used to fill the array with zeros to the right of index i. In addition to size and validity constraints (lines 7–8), its precondition requires that the elements of a up to index i form an RGF (lines 9–10). The function is allowed to modify the elements of a starting from the index i+1 (line 11) and generates an RGF (line 12). The loop invariants indicate the value interval of the loop variable k (line 15), and state that the property is_rgf is satisfied up to k (line 16). This invariant allows a deductive verification tool to deduce the postcondition. The annotation loop assigns (line 17) says that the only values the loop can change are k and the elements of a starting from the index i+1. The term n-k is a variant of the loop (line 18).

The ACSL lemma on lines 4–5 states that if an array is an RGF, then each of its elements is at most equal to its index. Its proof requires induction and cannot be performed by WP, which uses it to ensure the absence of overflow at line 40 (stated on line 39).

The functions of Fig. 2 can be fully proved using WP. Suppose now this example contains one of the following four mistakes: the verification engineer *either* forgets to specify the precondition on line 24, *or* writes the wrong assignment a[i]=a[i]+2; on line 40, *or* puts a too general clause **loop assigns** i,a[1..n-1]; on line 34, *or* forgets to provide the lemma on lines 4–5. In each of these four cases, the proof fails (for the precondition of g on line 41 and/or the assertion on line 39) *for different reasons*. In fact, the code and specification are not compliant only in the first two cases, while the third failure is due to a too weak subcontract, and the last one comes from a prover incapacity. This work proposes a complete testing-based methodology to automatically distinguish the three reasons and suggest suitable actions in each case.

3   Categories of Proof Failures and Counterexamples

Let P be a C program annotated in E-ACSL, and f the function under verification in P. Function f is assumed to be recursion-free. It may call other functions, let g denote any of them. A *test datum V* for f is a vector of values for all input variables of f. The *program path* activated by a test datum V, denoted π_V, is the sequence of program statements executed by the program on the test datum V. We use the general term of a *contract* to designate the set of E-ACSL annotations describing a loop or a function. A function contract is composed of pre- and postconditions including E-ACSL clauses **requires, assigns** and **ensures** (cf. lines 22–30 in Fig. 2). A loop contract is composed of **loop invariant, loop variant** and **loop assigns** clauses (cf. lines 15–18 in Fig. 2).

In Sect. 3.1, we define non-compliance and briefly recall the detection technique published in [37]. Section 3.2 is part of the original contribution of this paper, which introduces new categories of proof failures and a new detection technique.

3.1   Non-compliance

Figure 3 illustrates the translation of an annotated program P into another C program, denoted P^{NC}, on which we can apply test generation to produce test data violating some annotations at runtime. In Fig. 3, f is the function under verification and g is a called function. This translation is formally presented in [37]. P^{NC} checks all annotations of P in the corresponding program locations and reports any failure. For instance, the postcondition $Post_f$ of f is evaluated by the following code inserted at the end of the function f in P^{NC}:

$$\text{\textbf{int} post\_f; } Spec2Code(Post_f, \text{ post\_f}); \text{ fassert(post\_f);} \tag{†}$$

For an E-ACSL predicate P, we denote by $Spec2Code(P, b)$ the generated C code that evaluates the predicate P and assigns its validity status to the Boolean variable b (see [37] for details). The function call fassert(b) checks the condition b and

```
1 /*@ requires P1;
2     ensures P2; */
3 Type_g g(...) {
4    code1;
5 }
6 /*@ requires P5;
7     ensures P6; */
8 Type_f f(...) {
9    code2;
10   g(...);
11   //@ loop invariant P3;
12   while(b) {
13      code3;
14   }
15   code4;
16   //@ assert P4;
17   code5;
18 }
```

$\rightarrow$

```
1 Type_g g(...) {
2    int pre_g; Spec2Code(P1, pre_g);
3    fassert(pre_g);
4    code1;
5    int post_g; Spec2Code(P2,post_g);
6    fassert(post_g);
7 }
8 Type_f f(...) {
9    int pre_f; Spec2Code(P5, pre_f);
10   fassume(pre_f);
11   code2;
12   g(...);
13   int inv1; Spec2Code(P3, inv1);
14   fassert(inv1);
15   while(b) {
16      code3;
17      int inv2; Spec2Code(P3, inv2);
18      fassert(inv2);
19   }
20   code4;
21   int asrt; Spec2Code(P4, asrt);
22   fassert(asrt);
23   code5;
24   int post_f; Spec2Code(P6,post_f);
25   fassert(post_f);
26 }
```

Fig. 3. (a) An annotated code, vs. (b) its translation in P^{NC} for $\mathfrak{D}^{\mathrm{NC}}$

reports the failure and exits whenever b is false. Similarly, preconditions and post-conditions of a callee g are evaluated respectively before and after executing the function g. A loop invariant is checked before the loop (for being initially true) and after each loop iteration (for being preserved by the previous loop iteration). An assertion is checked at its location. To generate only test data that respect the precondition Pre_f of f, Pre_f is checked at the beginning of f by an inserted code similar to (†) except that fassert is replaced by fassume that assumes the given condition.

Definition 1 (Non-compliance). *We say that there is a* non-compliance *(NC) between code and specification in P if there exists a test datum V for f respecting its precondition, such that the execution of P^{NC} reports an annotation failure on V. In this case, we say that V is a* non-compliance counterexample *(NCCE).*

Test generation on the translated program P^{NC} can be used to generate NCCEs. We call this technique *Non-Compliance Detection*, denoted $\mathfrak{D}^{\mathrm{NC}}$. In this work we use the PATHCRAWLER test generator that will try to cover all program paths. Since the translation step added a branch for the false value of each annotation, PATHCRAWLER will try to cover at least one path where the annotation does not hold. (An optimization in PATHCRAWLER avoids covering the same fassert failure many times.) The $\mathfrak{D}^{\mathrm{NC}}$ step may have three outcomes. If an NCCE V has been found, it returns (nc, V, a) indicating the failing annotation a and recording the program path π_V activated by V on P^{NC}. Second, if it has managed to perform a complete exploration of all program paths without finding any NCCE, it returns no (cf. the discussion of completeness in Sect. 2). Otherwise, if only a partial exploration of program paths has been performed (due to a timeout, partial coverage criterion or any other limitation), it returns ? (unknown).

3.2   Subcontract Weakness and Prover Incapacity

Following the modular verification approach, we assume that the called functions have been verified before the caller f. To simplify the presentation, we also assume that the loops preserve their loop invariants, and focus on other proof failures occurring during the modular verification of f.

More formally, a *non-imbricated* loop (resp. function, assertion) in f is a loop (resp. function called, assertion) in f lying outside any loop of f. A *subcontract for* f is the contract of some non-imbricated loop or function in f. A *non-imbricated annotation* in f is either a non-imbricated assertion or an annotation in a subcontract for f. For instance, the function f of Fig. 2 has two subcontracts: the contract of the called function g and the contract of the loop on lines 33–37. The contract of the loop in g on lines 15–19 is not a subcontract for f, but is a subcontract for g.

We focus on non-imbricated annotations in f and assume that all subcontracts for f are respected: the called functions in f respect their contracts, and the loops in f preserve their loop invariants and respect all imbricated annotations. Let c_f denote the contract of f, $\mathcal{C}$ the set of non-imbricated subcontracts for f, and $\mathcal{A}$ the set of all non-imbricated annotations in f and annotations of c_f. In other words, $\mathcal{A}$ contains the annotations included in the contracts $\mathcal{C} \cup \{c_f\}$ as well as the non-imbricated assertions in f. We also assume that every subcontract of f contains a (loop) assigns clause. This is not restrictive since such a clause is necessary to prove any nontrivial code.

Subcontract Weakness. To apply testing for the contracts of called functions and loops in $\mathcal{C}$ instead of their code, we use a new program transformation of P producing another program P^{SW}. The code of all non-imbricated function calls and loops in f is replaced by the most general code respecting the corresponding subcontract as follows.

For the contract $c \in \mathcal{C}$ of a called function g in f, the program transformation (illustrated by Fig. 4) generates a new function g_sw with the same signature whose code simulates any possible behavior respecting the postcondition in c, and replaces all calls to g by a call to g_sw. First, g_sw allows any of the variables (or, more generally, left-values) listed in the **assigns** clause of c to change its value (line 2 in Fig. 4(b)). It can be done by assigning a non-deterministic value of the appropriate type using a dedicated function, denoted here by Nondet() (or simply by adding an array of fresh input variables and reading a different value for each use and each function invocation). If the return type of g is not **void**, another non-deterministic value is read for the returned value ret (line 3 in Fig. 4(b)). Finally, the validity of the postcondition is evaluated (taking into account these new non-deterministic values) and assumed in order to consider only executions respecting the postcondition, and the function returns (lines 4–5 in Fig. 4(b)).

Similarly, for the contract $c \in \mathcal{C}$ of a loop in f, the program transformation replaces the code of the loop by another code that simulates any possible behavior

```
1 /*@ assigns k1,...,kN;              1 Type_g g_sw(...){
2   @ ensures P; */                   2   k1=Nondet(); ... kN=Nondet();
3 Type_g g(...){ code1; }             3   Type_g ret = Nondet();
4                                      4   int post; Spec2Code(P, post);
5                              →       5   fassume(post); return ret;
6                                      6 } //respects contract of g
7                                      7 Type_g g(...){ code1; }
8 Type_f f(...){ code2;               8 Type_f f(...){ code2;
9   g(Args_g);                        9   g_sw(Args_g);
10  code3; }                          10  code3; }
```

Fig. 4. (a) A contract $c \in C$ of callee g in f, vs. (b) its translation for $\mathfrak{D}^{\mathrm{SW}}$

```
1 Type_f f(...){ code1;                  1 Type_f f(...){ code1;
2   /*@ loop assigns x1,...,xN;          2   x1=Nondet(); ... xN=Nondet();
3     @ loop invariant I; */  → 3   int inv1; Spec2Code(I, inv1);
4   while(b){ code2; }                    4   fassume(inv1 && !b); //respects loop contract
5   code3; }                              5   code3; }
```

Fig. 5. (a) A contract $c \in C$ of a loop in f, vs. (b) its translation for $\mathfrak{D}^{\mathrm{SW}}$

respecting c, that is, ensuring the "loop postcondition" $I \wedge \neg b$ after the loop, as shown in Fig. 5. In addition, the transformation treats in the same way as in P^{NC} all other annotations in $\mathcal{A}$: preconditions of called functions, initial loop invariant verifications and the pre- and postcondition of f (they are not shown in Figs. 4(b) and 5(b) but an example of such transformation is given in Fig. 3).

Definition 2 (Global subcontract weakness). *We say that P has a* global subcontract weakness *for f if there exists a test datum V for f respecting its precondition, such that the execution of P^{NC} does not report any annotation failure on V, while the execution of P^{SW} reports an annotation failure on V. In this case, we say that V is a* global subcontract weakness counterexample *(global SWCE) for the set of subcontracts C.*

Remark 1. Notice that we do not consider the same counterexample as an NCCE and an SWCE. Indeed, even if it is arguable that some counterexamples may illustrate both a subcontract weakness and a non-compliance, we consider that non-compliances usually come from a direct conflict between the code and the specification and should be addressed first, while subcontract weaknesses are often more subtle and will be easier to address when non-compliances are eliminated.

Again, test generation can be applied on P^{SW} to generate global SWCE candidates. When it finds a test datum V such that P^{SW} fails on V, we use runtime assertion checking: if P^{NC} fails on V, then V is classified as an NCCE, otherwise V is a global SWCE (cf. Remark 1). We call this technique *Global Subcontract Weakness Detection* for the set of all subcontracts, denoted $\mathfrak{D}^{\mathrm{SW}}_{\mathrm{global}}$. The $\mathfrak{D}^{\mathrm{SW}}_{\mathrm{global}}$ step may have four outcomes. It returns (nc, V, a) if an NCCE V has been found for the failing annotation a, and (sw, V, a, C) if V has been finally classified as an SWCE, where a is the failing annotation and C is the set of subcontracts. The program path π_V activated by V and leading to the failure (on P^{NC} or P^{SW}) is recorded as well. If $\mathfrak{D}_{\text{global}}^{\text{SW}}$ has managed to perform a complete exploration of all program paths without finding a global SWCE, it returns no. Otherwise, if only a partial exploration of program paths has been performed it returns ? (unknown).

A global SWCE does not explicitly indicate which single subcontract $c \in \mathcal{C}$ is too weak (cf. Remark 2 below). To do so, we propose another program transformation of P into an instrumented program P_c^{SW}. It is done by replacing only one non-imbricated function call or loop by the most general code respecting the postcondition of the corresponding subcontract c (as indicated in Figs. 4 and 5) and transforming other annotations in $\mathcal{A}$ in the same way as in P^{NC}.

Definition 3 (Single subcontract weakness). *Let c be a subcontract for f. We say that c is a too weak subcontract (or has a single subcontract weakness) for f if there exists a test datum V for f respecting its precondition, such that the execution of P^{NC} does not report any annotation failure on V, while the execution of P_c^{SW} reports an annotation failure on V. In this case, we say that V is a single subcontract weakness counterexample (single SWCE) for the subcontract c in f.*

For any subcontract $c \in \mathcal{C}$, test generation can be separately applied on P_c^{SW} to generate single SWCE candidates. If such a test datum V is generated, it is checked on P^{NC} to classify it as an NCCE or a single SWCE (cf. Remark 1). This technique, applied for all subcontracts one after another until a first counterexample V is found, is called *Single Contract Weakness Detection*, and denoted $\mathfrak{D}_{\text{single}}^{\text{SW}}$. The $\mathfrak{D}_{\text{single}}^{\text{SW}}$ step may have three outcomes. It returns (nc, V, a) if an NCCE V has been found for a failing annotation a, and $(\text{sw}, V, a, \{c\})$ if V has been finally classified as a single SWCE, where a is the failing annotation and c is the single too weak subcontract. The program path π_V activated by V and leading to the failure (on P^{NC} or P_c^{SW}) is recorded as well. Otherwise, it returns ? (unknown).

Global vs. Single Subcontract Weaknesses. Even after an exhaustive path testing, the absence of a single SWCE for any subcontract c cannot ensure the absence of a global SWCE, as detailed in the following remark.

Remark 2. A proof failure can be due to the weakness of several subcontracts, while no single one of them is too weak. In other words, the absence of single SWCEs does not imply the absence of global SWCEs. When a single SWCE exists, it can indicate a single too weak subcontract more precisely than a global SWCE.

```
1  int x;
2  /*@ ensures x ≥ \old(x)+1; assigns x;*/
3  void g1() { x=x+2; }
4  /*@ ensures x ≥ \old(x)+1; assigns x;*/
5  void g2() { x=x+2; }
6  /*@ ensures x ≥ \old(x)+1; assigns x;*/
7  void g3() { x=x+2; }
8  /*@ ensures x ≥ \old(x)+4; assigns x;*/
9  void f() { g1(); g2(); g3(); }
```

```
1  int x;
2  /*@ ensures x ≥ \old(x)+1; assigns x;*/
3  void g1() { x=x+1; }
4  /*@ ensures x ≥ \old(x)+1; assigns x;*/
5  void g2() { x=x+1; }
6  /*@ ensures x ≥ \old(x)+1; assigns x;*/
7  void g3() { x=x+2; }
8  /*@ ensures x ≥ \old(x)+4; assigns x;*/
9  void f() { g1(); g2(); g3(); }
```

(a) Absence of single SWCEs for any subcontract does not imply absence of global SWCEs

(b) Global SWCEs do not help to find precisely a too weak subcontract

Fig. 6. Two examples where the proof of f fails due to subcontract weaknesses

Indeed, consider the example in Fig. 6a, where the proof of the postcondition of f fails. If we apply $\mathfrak{D}_{single}^{SW}$ to any of the subcontracts, we always have x $\geq$ \old(x) +5 at the end of f (we add 1 to x by executing the translated subcontract, and add 2 twice by executing the other two functions' code), so the postcondition of f holds and no weakness is detected. If we run $\mathfrak{D}_{global}^{SW}$ to consider all subcontracts at once, we only get x$\geq$\old(x) +3 after executing the three subcontracts, and can exhibit a global SWCE.

On the other hand, running $\mathfrak{D}_{global}^{SW}$ produces a global SWCE that does not indicate which of the subcontracts is too weak, while $\mathfrak{D}_{single}^{SW}$ can sometimes be more precise. For Fig. 6b, since the three callees are replaced by their subcontracts for $\mathfrak{D}_{global}^{SW}$, it is impossible to find out which one is too weak. Counterexamples generated by a prover suffer from the same precision issue: taking into account all subcontracts instead of the corresponding code prevents from a precise identification of a single too weak subcontract. In this example $\mathfrak{D}_{single}^{SW}$ can be more precise, since only the replacement of the subcontract of g3 also leads to a single SWCE: we can have x $\geq$\old(x) +3 by executing g1, g2 and the subcontract of g3, exhibiting the contract weakness of g3. Thus, the proposed $\mathfrak{D}_{single}^{SW}$ technique can provide the verification engineer with a more precise diagnosis than counterexamples extracted from a prover.

We define a combined *subcontract weakness detection* technique, denoted $\mathfrak{D}^{SW}$, by applying $\mathfrak{D}_{single}^{SW}$ followed by $\mathfrak{D}_{global}^{SW}$ until the first counterexample is found. In other words, $\mathfrak{D}^{SW}$ looks first for single, then for global subcontract weaknesses. $\mathfrak{D}^{SW}$ may have the same four outcomes as $\mathfrak{D}_{global}^{SW}$. It allows us to be both precise (and indicate when possible a single subcontract being too weak), and complete (able to find global subcontract weaknesses even when there are no single ones).

Prover Incapacity. When neither a non-compliance nor a global subcontract weakness exists, we cannot demonstrate that it is impossible to prove the property.

Definition 4 (Prover incapacity). *We say that a proof failure in P is due to a prover incapacity if for every test datum V for f respecting its precondition, neither the execution of P^{NC} nor that of P^{SW} reports any annotation failure on V. In other words, there is no NCCE and no global SWCE for P.*

4   Diagnosis of Proof Failures Using Structural Testing

In this section, we present an overview of our method for diagnosis of proof failures using the detection techniques of Sect. 3, illustrate it on several examples and provide a comprehensive list of suggestions of actions for each category of proof failures.

The Method. The proposed method is illustrated by Fig. 7. Suppose that the proof of the annotated program P fails for some non-imbricated annotation $a \in \mathcal{A}$. The first step tries to find a non-compliance using $\mathfrak{D}^{NC}$. If such a non-compliance is found, it generates an NCCE (marked by ① in Fig. 7) and classifies the proof failure as a non-compliance. If the first step cannot generate a counterexample,

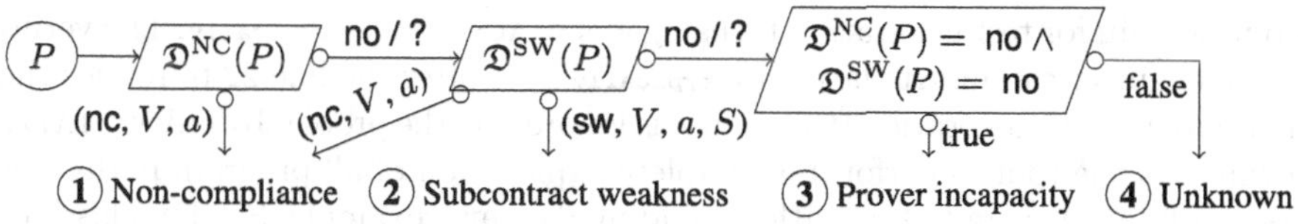

Fig. 7. Combined verification methodology in case of a proof failure on P

the $\mathfrak{D}^{SW}$ step combines $\mathfrak{D}^{SW}_{single}$ and $\mathfrak{D}^{SW}_{global}$ and tries to generate single SWCEs, then global SWCEs, until the first counterexample is generated. It can be classified either as a non-compliance ① (that is possible if path testing in $\mathfrak{D}^{NC}$ was not exhaustive, cf. Remark 1 and Definitions 2 and 3) or a subcontract weakness ②. If no counterexample has been found, the last step checks the outcomes. If both $\mathfrak{D}^{NC}$ and $\mathfrak{D}^{SW}$ have returned no, that is, both $\mathfrak{D}^{NC}$ and $\mathfrak{D}^{SW}_{global}$ have performed a complete path exploration without finding a counterexample, the proof failure is classified as a prover incapacity ③ (cf. Definition 4). Otherwise, it remains unclassified ④.

Figure 8 illustrates the method on several variants of the illustrating example. It details the lines modified in the program of Fig. 2 to obtain the new variant, the intermediate results of deductive verification, $\mathfrak{D}^{NC}$ and $\mathfrak{D}^{SW}$, and the final outcome. The final outcome includes the proof failure category and, if any, the generated counterexample V, the recorded path π_V, the reported failing annotation a and a set of too weak subcontracts S. This outcome can be extremely helpful for the verification engineer. Suppose we try to prove in WP a modified version of the function f of Fig. 2 where the precondition at line 24 is missing (cf. #1 in Fig. 8). The proof of the precondition on line 10 (for the call of g on line 41) fails without indicating a precise reason. The $\mathfrak{D}^{NC}$ step generates an NCCE (case ①) where is_rgf(a,n) is clearly false due to a[0] being non-zero, and indicates the failing annotation (coming from line 10). That helps the verification engineer to understand and fix the issue.

Let us suppose now that the clause on line 34 has been erroneously written as follows: `loop assigns i, a[1..n-1];` (cf. #2 in Fig. 8). The loop on lines 36–37 still preserves its invariant. The $\mathfrak{D}^{NC}$ step does not find any NCCE, as this modification did not introduce any non-compliance between the code and its specification. Thanks to the spec-to-code replacement shown in Fig. 5, $\mathfrak{D}^{SW}_{single}$ for the contract of this loop will detect a single subcontract weakness for the loop contract (case ②), leading to a failure of the precondition of g (on line 10) for the call on line 41. With this indication, the verification engineer will try to strengthen the loop contract and find the issue.

Suppose now the lemma on lines 4–5 is missing (cf. #4 in Fig. 8). The proof of the assertion at line 39 of Fig. 2 (stating the absence of overflow at line 40) fails without giving a precise reason, since the prover does not perform the induction and cannot deduce the right bounds on a[i]. Neither $\mathfrak{D}^{NC}$ nor $\mathfrak{D}^{SW}$ produces a counterexample, and as the initial program has too many paths, their outcomes are ? (unknown) (case ④). For such situations, we introduce the possibility to reduce the input domain for test generation by using a new ACSL clause `typically`. The verification engineer can insert the clause `typically` n<5; after the line 22 to reduce the array size for test generation (this clause is ignored by the proof). Running STADY now allows the tool to perform a complete exploration of all program paths (for n<5) both for $\mathfrak{D}^{NC}$ and $\mathfrak{D}^{SW}$ without finding a counterexample. STADY classifies the proof failure for the program with the reduced domain as a prover incapacity (case ③, cf. #3 in Fig. 8). That gives the verification engineer more confidence that the proof failure has the same reason on the initial program for bigger sizes n. She may now try an interactive proof or add additional lemmas or assertions, and does not waste her time looking for a bug or a subcontract weakness.

#	Modified lines		Intermediate outcome			Final outcome of STADY
	Line	New (added) clause	Proof (failing annot.)	$\mathfrak{D}^{NC}$	$\mathfrak{D}^{SW}$	
0	–	–	✓	–	–	Proved
1	24	(deleted)	? (1.39, 41, 26)	nc	–	$V = \langle$n=1; a[0]=-214739$\rangle$ is an NCCE
2	34	`loop assigns` `i,a[1..n-1];`	? (1.39, 41, 42, 26–30)	?	sw for 1.33–34	$V = \langle$ n=2; a[0]=0; a[1]=0; nondet$_{a[1]}$=97157; nondet$_i$=0 $\rangle$ is an SWCE
3	4–5 after 22	(deleted) `typically` n<5;(added)	? (1.39)	no	no	Prover incapacity (for the program with reduced domain)
4	4–5	(deleted)	? (1.39)	?	?	Unknown

Fig. 8. Method results for different versions of the illustrating example

Suggestions of Actions. Based on the possible outcomes of the method (illustrated in Fig. 7), we are able to suggest the most suitable actions to help the verification engineer with the verification task. A reported *non-compliance* (nc, V, a) means that there is an inconsistency between the precondition, the annotation a and the code of the path π_V leading to a. Thanks to the counterexample, the user will understand the issue by *tracing the values of variables along π_V*, or exploring them in a dubugger [35]. In FRAMA-C, the execution on V can be conveniently explored using VALUE or PATHCRAWLER [31]. If an NCCE is generated, there is *no need to try an automatic or interactive proof, or look for a subcontract weakness*—it will not help.

A reported *subcontract weakness* (sw, V, a, S) for a set of subcontracts S means that at least one of them has to be strengthened. By Definitions 2 and 3, the non-compliance is excluded here, that is, the execution of P^{NC} on V respects the annotation a. Thus the suggested action is to *strengthen the subcontract(s) of S*. In the case of a single subcontract weakness, S is a singleton so the suggestion is very precise and helpful to the user. Again, *trying interactive proof or writing additional assertions or lemmas will be useless* here since the property can obviously not be proved.

For a *prover incapacity,* the verification engineer may *add lemmas, assertions or hypotheses* that can help the theorem prover to succeed, or *try another theorem prover,* or *use a proof assistant* like COQ, even if it can be more complex and time-consuming.

Finally, when the verdict is *unknown,* i.e. test generation for $\mathfrak{D}^{NC}$ and/or $\mathfrak{D}^{SW}$ times out, the verification engineer may *strengthen the precondition* for test generation to reduce the input domain, or *extend the timeout* to give STADY more time to conclude.

5 Implementation and Experiments

Implementation. The proposed method for diagnosis of proof failures has been implemented as a FRAMA-C plugin, named STADY. It relies on other plugins: WP [31] for deductive verification and PATHCRAWLER [6] for structural test generation. STADY currently supports a significant subset of the E-ACSL specification language, including `requires`, `ensures`, `behavior`, `assumes`, `loop invariant`, `loop variant` and `assert` clauses. Quantified predicates `\exists` and `\forall` and builtin terms as `\sum` or `\numof` are translated as loops (recall that E-ACSL allows only finite intervals of quantification). Logic functions and named predicates are treated by inlining. The `\old` and `\at(-,Pre)` constructs are treated by saving the initial values of formal parameters and global variables at the beginning of the function. Validity checks of pointers are partially supported due to the current limitation of the underlying test generator: we can only check the validity of input pointers and global arrays. The `assigns` clauses are considered only during the $\mathfrak{D}^{SW}$ phase: we do not try to fix an incomplete `assigns` clause (with missing variables, leading to a non-compliance) because provers usually give a sufficiently clear feedback about that; but we do try to identify a too weak (i.e. too permissive) `assigns` clause since provers would report a failure elsewhere in this case. Inductive predicates, recursive functions and real numbers are not yet supported.

The research questions we address in our experiments are the following.

RQ1 Is STADY able to precisely diagnose most proof failures in C programs?
RQ2 What are the benefits of the $\mathfrak{D}^{SW}$ step (in particular, with respect to $\mathfrak{D}^{NC}$)?
RQ3 Is STADY able to generate NCCEs or SWCEs even with a partial testing coverage?
RQ4 Is STADY's execution time comparable to the time of an automatic proof?

| | #mut | Proof | | | | $\mathfrak{D}^{NC}$ | | | | $\mathfrak{D}^{SW}$ | | | | $\mathfrak{D}^{NC} + \mathfrak{D}^{SW}$ | | |
		#✓	%	$t^✓$	$t^?$	#✗	%	$t^✗$	$t^?$	#✗	%	$t^✗$	$t^?$	%	t	#?
Total	928	80 /928	8.6			776 /848	91.5			48 /72	66.7			97.2		24
Max			20.8	⩽ 4.4	⩽ 61.3		96.2	⩽ 9.4	⩽ 8.3		100.0	⩽ 6.4	⩽ 11.6	100.0	⩽ 19.9	
Mean			8	≈ 2.6	≈ 13.0		92.6	≈ 2.4	≈ 2.5		80.0	≈ 2.4	≈ 6.3	98.1	≈ 2.7	

Fig. 9. Summarized experiments of proof failure diagnosis for mutants with STADY

Experimental Protocol. The evaluation used 20 annotated programs from an independent benchmark [7], whose size varies from 35 to 100 lines of annotated C code. These programs manipulate arrays, they are fully specified in ACSL and their specification expresses non-trivial properties of C arrays. To evaluate the method presented in Sect. 4 and its implementation, we apply STADY on systematically generated altered versions[3] (or *mutants*) of correct C programs. Each mutant is obtained by performing a single modification (or *mutation*) on the initial program. The mutations include: a binary operator modification in the code or in the specification, a condition negation in the code, a relation modification in the specification, a predicate negation in the specification, a partial loop invariant or postcondition deletion in the specification. Such mutations model frequent errors in the code and specification (e.g. confusions between $+$ and $-$, $\leq$ and $<$, $\leq$ and $\geq$, a missing loop invariant, pre- or postcondition, etc.) that can lead to proof failures. In this study, we do not mutate the precondition of the function under verification, and restrict possible mutations on binary operators to avoid creating absurd expressions, in particular for pointer arithmetic.

The first step tries to prove each mutant using WP. In our experiments, each prover tries to prove each verification condition during at most 40 s. The proved mutants respect the specification and are classified as correct. Second, we apply the $\mathfrak{D}^{NC}$ method on the remaining mutants. It classifies proof failures for some mutants as non-compliances and indicates a failing annotation. The third step applies the $\mathfrak{D}^{SW}$ method on remaining mutants, classifies some of them as subcontract weaknesses and indicates a weak subcontract. If no counterexample has been found by the $\mathfrak{D}^{SW}$, the mutant remains unclassified. The results are summarized in Fig. 9. The columns present the number of generated mutants, and the results of each of the three steps: the number (#) and ratio (%) of classified mutants, maximal and average execution time of the step over classified mutants ($t^{\checkmark}$ or $t^{\times}$) and over non-classified mutants ($t^?$) at this step. The ratios are computed with respect to the number of unclassified mutants remaining after the previous step. The $\mathfrak{D}^{NC} + \mathfrak{D}^{SW}$ columns sum up selected results after both $\mathfrak{D}^{NC}$ and $\mathfrak{D}^{SW}$ steps: the average and maximal time (t) are shown globally over all mutants. The time is computed until the proof is finished or until the first counterexample is generated. The final number of remaining unclassified mutants (#?) is given in the last column.

Experimental Results. For the 20 considered programs, 928 mutants have been generated. 80 of them have been proved by WP. Among the 848 unproven mutants, $\mathfrak{D}^{NC}$ has detected a non-compliance induced by the mutation in 776 mutants (91.5 %), leaving 72 unclassified. Among them, $\mathfrak{D}^{SW}$ has been able to exhibit a counterexample (either an NCCE or an SWCE) for 48 of them (66.7 %), finally leaving 24 programs unclassified.

Regarding **RQ1**, STADY has found a precise reason of the proof failures and produced a counterexample in 824 of the 848 unproven mutants, i.e. classifying 97.2 %. Exploring the benefits of detecting a prover incapacity requires to manually reduce the input domain, to try additional lemmas or an interactive proof, so

---

[3] Available at: https://github.com/gpetiot/StaDy/tree/master/TAP_2016/benchmark.

it was not sufficiently investigated in this study (and probably requires another, non mutational approach).

Regarding **RQ2**, $\mathfrak{D}^{NC}$ alone diagnosed 776 of 848 unproven mutants (91.5 %). $\mathfrak{D}^{SW}$ diagnosed 48 of the 72 remaining mutants (66.7 %) bringing a significant complementary contribution to a better understanding of reasons of many proof failures.

To address **RQ3**, we set a timeout for any test generation session to 5 s (i.e. one session for the $\mathfrak{D}^{NC}$ step, and several sessions for $\mathfrak{D}^{SW}$ steps), and limit the number of explored program paths using the *k-path* criterion (cf. Sect. 2) with $k = 4$. Both the session timeout and *k-path* heavily limit the testing coverage but STADY still detects 97.2 % of faults in the generated programs. That demonstrates that the proposed method can efficiently classify proof failures and generate counterexamples even with a partial testing coverage and can therefore be used for programs where the total number of paths cannot be limited (e.g. by the `typically` clause).

Concerning **RQ4**, on the considered programs WP needs on average 2.6 s per mutant (at most 4.4 s) to prove a program, and spends 13.0 s on average (at most 61.3 s) when the proof fails. The total execution time of STADY is comparable: it needs on average 2.7 s per unproven mutant (at most 19.9 s).

Summary. The experiments show that the proposed method can automatically classify a significant number of proof failures within an analysis time comparable to the time of an automatic proof and for programs for which only a partial testing coverage is possible. The $\mathfrak{D}^{SW}$ technique offers an efficient complement to $\mathfrak{D}^{NC}$ for a more complete and more precise diagnosis of proof failures.

6   Related Work

Assisting program verification and generation of counterexamples have been addressed in different research work (e.g. [2,5,8,10,13,17,20,21,28,29,34,36,39]). We detail below a few projects most closely related to the present work.

Understanding Proof Failures. When SMT solvers fail on some verification conditions and provide a counter-model to explain that failure, the counter-model can be turned into a counterexample for the program under verification. This non-trivial task is designed in [29] and implemented for SPARK, a subset of Ada targeted for formal verification. This static analysis is complementary to our combination of static and dynamic analyses. It would be useful to adapt it to C/ACSL programs. For C programs, SMT models are already exploited, for instance by the CBMC model checker [26].

A two-step verification in [42] compares the proof failures of an Eiffel program with those of its variant where called functions are inlined and loops are unrolled. It reports code and contract revision suggestions from this comparison. Inlining and unrolling are respectively limited to a given number of nested calls and explicit iterations. If that number is too small the semantics is lost and a warning of unsoundness is reported. A bigger number of inlinings often overpasses the capacity of the solver, while DSE, focusing on one path at a time, can be expected to be more efficient. Another benefit of DSE is the possibility to use concrete values (e.g. discovered in a previous execution) even when the constraints become very complex and the solver cannot generate a counterexample.

DAFNY has also been recently extended with tools for diagnosing proof failures [12]. When the proof times out, an algorithm decomposes it and tries to diagnose on which part the user has to focus to prevent the timeout. Then, if the proof fails, following the approach we proposed in our previous work [37], a DSE tool is used to try to find counterexamples demonstrating non-compliance between program and specification. But, when no counterexample is found, the user must manually try to find the reason of the proof failure (with the Boogie Verification Debugger), whereas we extend the approach by further exploiting DSE to automatically identify subcontract weaknesses. The notions of global and single SW and their comparison are also new.

Proof Tree Analysis. More precision can be statically obtained by analyzing the unclosed branches of a proof tree. The work [24] is performed in the context of KEY and its verification calculus that applies deduction rules to a dynamic formula mixing a program and its specification. It proposes *falsifiability preservation checking* that helps to distinguish whether the branch failure comes from a programming error or from a contract weakness. However this technique can detect bugs only if contracts are strong enough. Moreover it is automatic only if a prover (typically, an SMT solver) can decide the non-satisfiability of the first-order formula expressing the falsifiability preservation condition. The test generation proposed in [22] exploits the proof trees built by the KEY prover during a proof attempt. The relevance of generated tests depends on the quality of the provided specification, and it does not allow to distinguish non-compliances from specification weaknesses.

Combination of Static and Dynamic Analysis. Static and dynamic analysis work better when used together, as in SYNERGY [27], its interprocedural and compositional extension in SMASH [25], the method SANTE [9] and the present method. Static analysis maintains an over-approximation that aims at verifying the correctness of the system, while dynamic analysis maintains an under-approximation trying to detect an error. Both abstractions help each other in a way similar to the counterexample guided abstraction refinement method (CEGAR) [16]. The work [10] combines symbolic execution, testing and automatic debugging, through the identification of counterexamples violating metamorphic relations for the program under test. The debugging builds a cause-effect chain to a failure, by analysis of some path conditions. Comparatively, our method focuses on deductive verification rather than on symbolic execution, and aims at verifying behavioral pre-post specifications rather than metamorphic relations.

Counterexamples for Non-inductive Invariants. Counterexamples can be generated to show that invariants proposed for transition systems are too strong or too weak [15]. Differences with our work are the focus on invariants, the formalism of transition systems, and the use of random testing (with QUICKCHECK).

Other Verification Feedbacks. Our goal was to find input data to illustrate proof failures. A complementary work [35] proposed to extend a runtime assertion checker to use it as a debugger to help the user understand complex counterexamples. For NC errors in the code, [11] proposed to analyze a trace formula to identify the fragments of code that can cause them. Our approach is complementary on two points. First, we detect either NC or SW errors. Second, we consider that the origin of an NC can be either in the code or in the specifications. Combining our method with such a localization of causes of NC errors, extended to specifications, would be another contribution.

Checking Prover Assumptions. Axioms are logic properties used as hypotheses by provers and thus usually not checked. Model-based testing applied to a computational model of an axiom can permit to detect errors in axioms and thus to maintain the soundness of the axiomatization [1]. This work is complementary to ours because it tackles the case of deductive verification trivially succeeding due to an invalid axiomatization, whereas we tackle the case of inconclusive deductive verification. [14] proposed to complete the results of static checkers with dynamic symbolic execution using PEX. The explicit assumptions used by the verifier (absence of overflows, non-aliasing, etc.) create new branches in the program's control flow graph which PEX tries to explore. This approach permits to detect errors out of the scope of the considered static checkers, but does not provide counterexamples in case of a specification weakness.

The present work continues previous efforts to facilitate deductive verification by generating counterexamples. We propose an original detection technique of three categories of proof failure that gives a more precise diagnosis than in the previous work using testing. That is due to dedicated detection methods for non-compliances and subcontract weaknesses, as well as the definition and detection of single and global subcontract weaknesses. To the best of our knowledge, such a complete testing-based methodology, automatically providing the verification engineer with a precise feedback on proof failures was not studied, implemented and evaluated before.

The different techniques of assisting deductive verification (in particular, by generating counterexamples using solvers' counter-models or by test generation) being relatively recent and intrinsically incomplete, further work is still required to better compare them and understand in which cases which technique is more practical.

7 Conclusion and Future Work

We proposed a new approach to improve the user feedback in case of a proof failure. Our method relies on test generation and helps to decide whether the proof has failed or timed out due to a non-compliance (NC) between the code and the specification, a subcontract weakness (SW), or a prover weakness. This approach is based on a spec-to-code program transformation that produces an input program for the test generation tool. Our experiments show that our implementation—in a FRAMA-C plugin, STADY—was able to diagnose over 97 % of unproven programs. In particular, the subcontract weakness detection ($\mathfrak{D}^{SW}$) proposed in this paper was able to diagnose 66.7 % of proof failures that remained unclassified after the non-compliance detection ($\mathfrak{D}^{NC}$).

One benefit of the proposed approach is the ability to provide the verification engineer with a precise reason and a counterexample that facilitate the processing of proof failures. Generated counterexamples illustrate the issue on concrete values and help to find out more easily why the proof fails. The method is completely automatic, relies on the existing specification and does not require any additional manual specification or instrumentation task. As a consequence, this method can be adopted by less experienced verification engineers and software developers.

While the complete method requires to have the source code of called functions, the global subcontract weakness detection ($\mathfrak{D}^{SW}_{global}$) remains applicable even without their source code. Another limitation is related to a potentially big number of program paths, which cannot be explored. However, our initial experiments show that in practice most proof failures can be automatically classified even after test generation with a partial test coverage, within a testing time comparable to the time of the proof attempt.

We are convinced that the proposed methodology facilitates the verification task and lowers the level of expertise required to conduct deductive verification, removing one of the major obstacles for its wider use in industry. Future work includes further evaluation of the proposed technique, a study of optimized combinations of $\mathfrak{D}^{NC}$ and $\mathfrak{D}^{SW}$ for subsets of annotations and subcontracts, experiments on a larger class of programs and a better support of E-ACSL constructs in our implementation. In the DEWI project, we apply STADY to verification of protocols of wireless sensor networks. An experimental comparison of STADY with the inlining-based technique of [42] is another work perspective that will require the implementation of that technique in FRAMA-C.

Acknowledgment. Part of the research work leading to these results has received funding for DEWI project (www.dewi-project.eu) from the ARTEMIS Joint Undertaking under grant agreement No. 621353. The authors thank the FRAMA-C and PATH-CRAWLER teams for providing the tools and support. Special thanks to François Bobot, Loïc Correnson, Julien Signoles and Nicky Williams for many fruitful discussions, suggestions and advice.

References

1. Ahn, K.Y., Denney, E.: Testing first-order logic axioms in program verification. In: Fraser, G., Gargantini, A. (eds.) TAP 2010. LNCS, vol. 6143, pp. 22–37. Springer, Heidelberg (2010)
2. Arlt, S., Arenis, S.F., Podelski, A., Wehrle, M.: System testing and program verification. In: Software Engineering & Management (2015)
3. Arndt, J.: Matters Computational-Ideas, Algorithms, Source Code [The fxtbook] (2010). http://www.jjj.de
4. Baudin, P., Cuoq, P., Filliâtre, J.C., Marché, C., Monate, B., Moy, Y., Prevosto, V.: ACSL: ANSI/ISO C Specification Language. http://frama-c.com/acsl.html
5. Berghofer, S., Nipkow, T.: Random testing in Isabelle/HOL. In: SEFM (2004)

6. Botella, B., Delahaye, M., Hong-Tuan-Ha, S., Kosmatov, N., Mouy, P., Roger, M., Williams, N.: Automating structural testing of C programs: experience with PathCrawler. In: AST (2009)
7. Burghardt, J., Gerlach, J., Lapawczyk, T.: ACSL by Example (2016). https:// gitlab.fokus.fraunhofer.de/verification/open-acslbyexample/blob/master/ ACSL-by-Example.pdf
8. Chamarthi, H.R., Dillinger, P.C., Kaufmann, M., Manolios, P.: Integrating testing and interactive theorem proving. In: ACL2 (2011)
9. Chebaro, O., Kosmatov, N., Giorgetti, A., Julliand, J.: Program slicing enhances a verification technique combining static and dynamic analysis. In: SAC (2012)
10. Chen, T.Y., Tse, T.H., Zhou, Z.Q.: Semi-proving: an integrated method for program proving, testing, and debugging. IEEE Trans. Softw. Eng. **37**, 109 (2011)
11. Christ, J., Ermis, E., Schäf, M., Wies, T.: Flow-sensitive fault localization. In: Giacobazzi, R., Berdine, J., Mastroeni, I. (eds.) VMCAI 2013. LNCS, vol. 7737, pp. 189–208. Springer, Heidelberg (2013)
12. Christakis, M., Leino, K.R.M., Müller, P., Wüstholz, V.: Integrated environment for diagnosing verification errors. In: Chechik, M., Raskin, J.-F. (eds.) TACAS 2016. LNCS, vol. 9636, pp. 424–441. Springer, Heidelberg (2016). doi:10.1007/ 978-3-662-49674-9_25
13. Christakis, M., Emmisberger, P., Müller, P.: Dynamic test generation with static fields and initializers. In: RV (2014)
14. Christakis, M., Müller, P., Wüstholz, V.: Collaborative verification and testing with explicit assumptions. In: FM (2012)
15. Claessen, K., Svensson, H.: Finding counter examples in induction proofs. In: Beckert, B., Hähnle, R. (eds.) TAP 2008. LNCS, vol. 4966, pp. 48–65. Springer, Heidelberg (2008)
16. Clarke, E., Grumberg, O., Jha, S., Lu, Y., Veith, H.: Counterexample-guided abstraction refinement for symbolic model checking. J. ACM **50**, 752 (2003)
17. Cousot, P., Cousot, R., Fähndrich, M., Logozzo, F.: Automatic inference of necessary preconditions. In: Giacobazzi, R., Berdine, J., Mastroeni, I. (eds.) VMCAI 2013. LNCS, vol. 7737, pp. 128–148. Springer, Heidelberg (2013)
18. Delahaye, M., Kosmatov, N., Signoles, J.: Common specification language for static and dynamic analysis of C programs. In: SAC (2013)
19. Dijkstra, E.W.: A Discipline of Programming. Series in Automatic Computation. Prentice Hall, Englewood Cliffs (1976)
20. Dimitrova, R., Finkbeiner, B.: Counterexample-guided synthesis of observation predicates. In: Jurdziński, M., Ničković, D. (eds.) FORMATS 2012. LNCS, vol. 7595, pp. 107–122. Springer, Heidelberg (2012)
21. Dybjer, P., Haiyan, Q., Takeyama, M.: Combining testing and proving in dependent type theory. In: Basin, D., Wolff, B. (eds.) TPHOLs 2003. LNCS, vol. 2758, pp. 188–203. Springer, Heidelberg (2003)
22. Engel, C., Hähnle, R.: Generating unit tests from formal proofs. In: Gurevich, Y., Meyer, B. (eds.) TAP 2007. LNCS, vol. 4454, pp. 169–188. Springer, Heidelberg (2007)
23. Genestier, R., Giorgetti, A., Petiot, G.: Sequential generation of structured arrays and its deductive verification. In: Blanchette, J.C., Kosmatov, N. (eds.) TAP 2015. LNCS, vol. 9154, pp. 109–128. Springer, Heidelberg (2015)
24. Gladisch, C.: Could we have chosen a better loop invariant or method contract? In: Dubois, C. (ed.) TAP 2009. LNCS, vol. 5668, pp. 74–89. Springer, Heidelberg (2009)
25. Godefroid, P., Nori, A.V., Rajamani, S.K., Tetali, S.D.: Compositional may-must program analysis: unleashing the power of alternation. In: POPL (2010)

26. Groce, A., Kroening, D., Lerda, F.: Understanding counterexamples with explain. In: CAV (2004)
27. Gulavani, B.S., Henzinger, T.A., Kannan, Y., Nori, A.V., Rajamani, S.K.: SYNERGY: a new algorithm for property checking. In: FSE (2006)
28. Guo, S., Kusano, M., Wang, C., Yang, Z., Gupta, A.: Assertion guided symbolic execution of multithreaded programs. In: ESEC/FSE (2015)
29. Hauzar, D., Marché, C., Moy, Y.: Counterexamples from proof failures in SPARK. In: SEFM (to appear, 2016)
30. Jakobsson, A., Kosmatov, N., Signoles, J.: Fast as a shadow, expressive as a tree: hybrid memory monitoring for C. In: SAC (2015)
31. Kirchner, F., Kosmatov, N., Prevosto, V., Signoles, J., Yakobowski, B.: Frama-C: a software analysis perspective. Formal Asp. Comput. **27**(3), 573–609 (2015). http://frama-c.com
32. Kosmatov, N.: Online version of PathCrawler (2010–2015). http://pathcrawler-online.com/
33. Kosmatov, N., Petiot, G., Signoles, J.: An optimized memory monitoring for runtime assertion checking of C programs. In: RV (2013)
34. Kovács, L., Voronkov, A.: Finding loop invariants for programs over arrays using a theorem prover. In: Chechik, M., Wirsing, M. (eds.) FASE 2009. LNCS, vol. 5503, pp. 470–485. Springer, Heidelberg (2009)
35. Müller, P., Ruskiewicz, J.N.: Using debuggers to understand failed verification attempts. In: FM (2011)
36. Owre, S.: Random testing in PVS. In: AFM (2006)
37. Petiot, G., Botella, B., Julliand, J., Kosmatov, N., Signoles, J.: Instrumentation of annotated C programs for test generation. In: SCAM (2014)
38. Petiot, G., Kosmatov, N., Giorgetti, A., Julliand, J.: How test generation helps software specification and deductive verification in Frama-C. In: Seidl, M., Tillmann, N. (eds.) TAP 2014. LNCS, vol. 8570, pp. 204–211. Springer, Heidelberg (2014)
39. Podelski, A., Wies, T.: Counterexample-guided focus. In: POPL (2010)
40. Signoles, J.: E-ACSL: Executable ANSI/ISO C Specification Language. http://frama-c.com/download/e-acsl/e-acsl.pdf
41. The Coq Development Team: The Coq proof assistant. http://coq.inria.fr
42. Tschannen, J., Furia, C.A., Nordio, M., Meyer, B.: Program checking with less hassle. In: Cohen, E., Rybalchenko, A. (eds.) VSTTE 2013. LNCS, vol. 8164, pp. 149–169. Springer, Heidelberg (2014)
43. Williams, N., Marre, B., Mouy, P., Roger, M.: PathCrawler: automatic generation of path tests by combining static and dynamic analysis. In: Dal Cin, M., Kaâniche, M., Pataricza, A. (eds.) EDCC 2005. LNCS, vol. 3463, pp. 281–292. Springer, Heidelberg (2005)

Classifying Bugs with Interpolants

Andreas Podelski[1], Martin Schäf[2]([✉]), and Thomas Wies[3]

[1] University of Freiburg, Freiburg im Breisgau, Germany
[2] SRI International, Menlo Park, USA
martinschaef@gmail.com
[3] New York University, New York, USA

Abstract. We present an approach to the classification of error messages in the context of static checking in the style of ESC/Java. The idea is to compute a semantics-based signature for each error message and then group together error messages with the same signature. The approach aims at exploiting modern verification techniques based on, e.g., Craig interpolation in order to generate small but significant signatures. We have implemented the approach and applied it to three benchmark sets (from Apache Ant, Apache Cassandra, and our own tool). Our experiments indicate an interesting practical potential. More than half of the considered error messages (for procedures with more than just one error message) can be grouped together with another error message.

1 Introduction

The classification of error messages, bug reports, exception warnings, etc. is an active research topic [1,3,5,13,16,25,30]. The underlying motivation is that grouping related error messages together will help with their analysis. The problem of classification is to infer what error messages are related (and, in what sense).

In this paper, we address the problem of classification in the context of static checking of sequential procedural programs in the style of ESC/Java, as in [4,15,21]. Although in this context error messages may refer to an error in the specification rather than the code, the same motivation applies. The error messages may come in batches of, say, thousands, and they have to be analyzed, if only to debug the specification.

In the context of static checking, it seems natural to explore whether concepts and techniques from semantics and verification can be put to use for the classification of error messages.

In this paper, we present an approach to *semantics-based* classification of error messages which come in the form of a sequence of statements along with a witness; a witness here is an initial state from which the execution of the sequence of statements leads to the violation of a specified assertion. As in verification, semantics here is used to abstract away from syntactical details. For example, we can abstract a statement (or a sequence of statements) by its *summary* in the form of a pre-and postcondition pair.

© Springer International Publishing Switzerland 2016
B.K. Aichernig and C.A. Furia (Eds.): TAP 2016, LNCS 9762, pp. 151–168, 2016.
DOI: 10.1007/978-3-319-41135-4_9

The idea behind the approach is to compute a semantics-based *signature* for each of the error messages and then group together error messages with the same signature. More concretely, we associate each error message with a new verification problem. We apply a verification engine to infer a proof in the form of Hoare triples. We remove the *invariant-type* Hoare triples (of the form $\{F\}$ *st* $\{F\}$, expressing that an assertion F is invariant under a statement *st*). We take the remaining *change-type* Hoare triples to construct the signature.

Intuitively, *the larger the number of invariant-type Hoare triples* (and the smaller the number of change-type Hoare triples), *the more error messages will be grouped together* under the resulting signature. The approach exploits the fact that modern verification engines can often be geared to produce proofs with a large number of invariant-type Hoare triples. (We here think of Craig interpolation, constraint solving, and static analysis [9,24,29].)

We have implemented the new approach to classification on top of our own extended static checker for Java. We have applied it to three benchmark sets (from Apache Ant, Apache Cassandra, and our own tool). Our experiments indicate an interesting practical potential of the approach. More than half of the considered error messages (for procedures with more than just one error message) can be grouped together with another error message.

The technical contribution of this paper is to introduce the approach and to present an experimental evaluation of its implementation. The conceptual contribution is the formal foundation of the approach which associates each error message with a verification problem and constructs a *small but significant* signature from a correctness proof.

Roadmap. The next section illustrates the approach on an example. Section 3 fixes the notation and terminology of standard concepts. Section 4 introduces the approach together with its formal foundation. Section 5 presents the experimental evaluation and Sect. 6 discusses the related work.

2   Overview

We motivate our approach to classifying bugs using interpolation with the illustrative example in Fig. 1. For simplicity of exposition, the example is constructed to be of reasonable size. However, real Java programs such as the ones used in our experiments show similar patterns in larger methods.

Figure 1 shows a method m that takes two objects a and b of type A, and one integer x as input. We analyze this method with a static checker such as ESC/Java [15] to obtain *error messages* that indicate uncaught exceptions[1]. In this paper, we consider an error message to consist of a specific initial state and an error trace whose execution from the initial state leads to a state that violates an assertion guarding an uncaught run-time exception.

---

[1] The fact that we use a static checker is not crucial for our discussion. The error messages could also be generated using a bounded model checker such as [14,20], or a testing tool such as Randoop [27].

```
1   void m(A a, A b, int x) {
2     if (x>0) {
3       A obj = null;
4       try {
5         obj = b.clone();
6       } catch (Exception e) {
7         e.printStackTrace();
8       }
9       obj.bar();
10      a.bar();
11    }
12    a.bar();
13  }
```

Fig. 1. Example procedure m.

For the method m, the error messages that are produced by the static checker can be classified according to the line in the method where the run-time error occurs as follows:

1. If $x \leq 0$, and a is null the execution of m leads to a NullPointerException on line 12.
2. If $x > 0$ and a==null, a NullPointerException is thrown on line 10.
3. If $x > 0$ and b==null, a NullPointerException is thrown on line 9

Figure 2 shows an example of an error message for each of these three types. Each error message starts from a given initial state, which is followed by the sequence of statements executed on the corresponding error traces, and ends in the (implicit) assertion that is violated when starting execution from the initial state. For convenience, the initial states of the error messages are described symbolically by an assume statement at the beginning of each trace. Note that if we used a random testing tool such as Randoop instead of a static checker, then several error messages of each type may be reported. For example, a testing tool might generate multiple test cases that invoke m with a==null and different values for x that satisfy $x > 0$.

Grouping error messages *syntactically* based on the line in the program where a run-time error occurs may seem appropriate at first. However, this strategy does not yield a meaningful classification of bugs on its own. Two error messages that fail at the same program location may do so for different reasons and should therefore not be grouped together. Conversely, two error messages that fail at different program locations may do so for the same reason and should therefore be grouped together. Specifically, in our example the error messages of type 1 and 2 capture cases in which an error occurs because m has been called with the value null passed to parameter a. That is, the parameter a will be dereferenced with a NullPointerException regardless of the value of x. It therefore seems more

```
assume(a == null          assume(a == null          assume(a == null
    && b == null              && b == A@15ce            && b == null
    && x == 0);               && x == 1);               && x == 1);
assume(x <= 0);           assume(x > 0);            assume(x > 0);
assert(a!=null);          A obj = null;            A obj = null;
                          obj = b.clone();         e.printStackTrace();
                          obj.bar();               assert(obj!=null);
         Type 1           assert(a!=null);
                                                            Type 3
                                  Type 2
```

Fig. 2. Different syntactic types of error messages for the method m in Fig. 1.

appropriate to take into account only the error-relevant condition a==null that
is common to the error messages of type 1 and 2 and group them together during
classification. On the other hand, type 3 error messages should still be grouped
separately. Our approach aims to infer such a semantics-based characterization
of what is essential for the reason why the assertion in an error message fails.

The approach groups error messages by computing an *error signature* for
each individual error message as follows. First, we replace the failing assert
statement at the end of the error message by an assume statement with the
same condition. The resulting trace will not have any feasible execution because
the final condition is always violated. That is, if τ is the trace resulting from
this transformation, then $\{\top\}\ \tau\ \{\bot\}$ is a valid Hoare triple, where $\top$ stands for
the assertion *true* and $\bot$ for *false*. We can thus use an interpolating theorem
prover to generate a Hoare proof for the validity of this triple. For instance, the
generated Hoare proof for the trace obtained from the error message of type 2
may look as follows:

```
{⊤}
    assume(a == null && b == A@15ce && x == 1);
{a == null}
    assume(x > 0);
{a == null}
    obj = null;
{a == null}
    obj = b.clone();
{a == null}
    obj.bar();
{a == null}
    assert(a != null);
{⊥}
```

Observe that the intermediate assertion a == null is maintained throughout
the trace after initialization. It captures the reason why the trace described by
the original error message fails.

The next step is to extract the sequence of intermediate assertions from the Hoare proof and replace all consecutive occurrences of the same assertion by just one copy of that assertion. We refer to the resulting condensed sequence of intermediate assertions as the error signature of the original error message. For our error messages of type 2, the error signature computed from the given Hoare proof only consists of the assertion `a == null`.

We group error messages that have identical error signatures together into equivalence classes. We refer to these equivalence classes as *buckets*. For example, the error signature for the error messages of type 1 is also `a == null`. Hence, all type 1 and type 2 error messages will be grouped together in the same bucket. On the other hand, the error signature of the type 3 error messages consists of the two assertions $\top$, `obj == null`. Type 3 error messages will therefore end up in a separate bucket.

In general, an error signature consists of a non-trivial sequence of assertions that captures how the error condition is propagated through the trace of the error message. Intuitively, an error signature abstracts away from the specific values of the initial state of an error message and the syntax of the statements in its error trace, including the specific location of the failing assertion. Error signatures only maintain the error-relevant semantic conditions that hold along the trace of the error message. For example, an error message has the error signature $\top$, `obj == null` if its initial state satisfies $\top$ (i.e., the initial state can be arbitrary). Moreover, its error trace contains one statement that establishes the postcondition `obj == null` from a state that satisfies $\top$, and if it ends with an assert statement whose execution fails if `obj == null` holds; it can contain an arbitrary number of additional statements as long as they leave the corresponding assertion (which is $\top$ or `obj == null` according to the position within the error trace) invariant. That is, an error message with the error signature $\top$, `obj ==null` consists of:

- an initial state that satisfies $\top$, which is the case for any initial state.
- a (possibly empty) sequence of statements st for which $\top$ is invariant, which is the case for every statement st (the Hoare triple $\{\top\}$ st $\{\top\}$ holds trivially),
- a statement st that establishes the postcondition `obj == null` (i.e., the Hoare triple $\{\top\}$ st $\{$`obj == null`$\}$ holds),
- a (possibly empty) sequence of statements st for which the assertion `obj == null` is invariant (i.e., the Hoare triple $\{$`obj == null`$\}$ st $\{$`obj == null`$\}$ holds), and finally
- an statement `assert(F)` that fails when executed in a state where the assertion `obj == null` is true (i.e., the Hoare triple $\{$`obj == null`$\}$ `assume`(F) $\{\bot\}$ holds).

Note that the first assertion of an error signature can generalize the initial state of an error message. This is needed in order to group together error messages with different initial states.

We have found that error signatures provide a useful classification mechanism in the context of static checking of Java programs if the classification is restricted to the error messages that belong to the same method, i.e., if it is combined with a coarse syntactic classification mechanism based on method affiliation.

3 Preliminaries

The purpose of this section is to fix the notation and terminology for existing, standard concepts.

We assume a simple imperative language whose basic statements st consist of assignments as well as assume and assert statements:

$$x \in \mathcal{X} \qquad\qquad\qquad \text{program variables}$$
$$e \in \mathcal{E} \qquad\qquad\qquad \text{expressions}$$
$$F \in \mathcal{F} \qquad\qquad\qquad \text{formulas}$$
$$st ::= \texttt{assume}(F) \mid \texttt{assert}(F) \mid x := e \qquad \text{(basic) statements}$$

We do not define the syntax of expressions $e \in \mathcal{E}$ and formulas $F \in \mathcal{F}$. We only require that they fall into quantifier-free first-order logic for a signature that is defined by a suitable theory $\mathcal{T}$ (e.g., linear integer arithmetic). Moreover, we require that the variables appearing in e and F are drawn from the set $\mathcal{X}$. We assume standard syntax and semantics of first-order logic and use $\top$ and $\bot$ to denote the Boolean constants for *true* and *false*, respectively.

A *state* $s = (M, \beta)$ consists of a model M of the theory $\mathcal{T}$ and an assignment β of the variables in $\mathcal{X}$ to values drawn from the universe of M. The model M may be fixed for all states if M is the *canonical model* of the theory $\mathcal{T}$ (e.g., the integer numbers in the case of linear integer arithmetic). For an expression e, we denote by $s(e)$ the value obtained by interpreting e in s and we use similar notation for formulas. We write $s \models F$ to say that s satisfies F, i.e., $s(F) = \top$. A formula is valid if $s \models F$ for all states s and it is called unsatisfiable if $\neg F$ is valid.

Following the presentation in [11,26], we define the semantics of statements using the weakest precondition transformer wp, which maps a pair of a statement st and a formula F to another formula:

$$\mathsf{wp}(\texttt{assume}(G), F) = G \Rightarrow F$$
$$\mathsf{wp}(\texttt{assert}(G), F) = G \wedge F$$
$$\mathsf{wp}(x := e, F) = F[e/x]$$

The Hoare triple $\{F\}\, st\, \{F'\}$ stands for the formula $F \Rightarrow \mathsf{wp}(st, F')$.

For example, the Hoare triple $\{x = 0\}\, \texttt{assume}(x \neq 0)\, \{\bot\}$ is valid, whereas the Hoare triple $\{x = 0\}\, \texttt{assert}(x \neq 0)\, \{\bot\}$ is not valid.

A *trace* τ is a finite sequence of basic statements $\tau = st_1; \ldots; st_n$. We extend both wp and Hoare triples from statements st to traces τ in the expected way.

A sequence of formulas and statements $F_1, st_1, F_2, \ldots, st_n, F_{n+1}$ is called a *Hoare sequence* if for all $i \in [1, n]$, $\{F_i\}\, st_i\, \{F_{i+1}\}$ is valid. Intuitively, the Hoare sequence corresponds to an annotation or proof outline to prove the Hoare triple $\{F_1\}\, \tau\, \{F_{n+1}\}$ for the trace $\tau = st_1, \ldots, st_n$.

A trace τ is called *infeasible* if $\{\top\}\, \tau\, \{\bot\}$ is valid. Intuitively, the execution of the sequence of statements of an infeasible trace always (i.e., for every starting state) blocks on some assume statement in the sequence.

4 Classifying Error Traces Through Error Signatures

The purpose of this section is to introduce the formal foundation for an approach to the classification of error traces based on concepts and techniques from verification.

Definition 1. *A trace τ is called* error trace *if $\neg(\{\top\} \tau \{\top\})$ is satisfiable. An* error message *is a pair $\epsilon = (\tau, s_0)$ of an error trace τ and a state s_0 such that $s_0 \models \neg(\{\top\} \tau \{\top\})$.*

Intuitively, an error trace has at least one execution that violates an assert statement in the trace. Every state s_0 such that $s_0 \models \neg(\{\top\} \tau \{\top\})$ is the initial state s_0 of such a faulty execution of τ. The initial state s_0 may be obtained from the satisfiable formula $\neg(\{\top\} \tau \{\top\})$ by using a model-generating theorem prover. It could also be obtained directly (together with τ) from a failed test or a bug report.

An error trace has at least one execution that does not block on any assume statement (namely, the faulty execution). This fact may help to avoid the confusion with the terminology of error trace in software model checking as in [17].

The definition implies that an error trace must contain at least one assert statement. To simplify the discussion, we will restrict ourselves to error traces that contain exactly one assert statement and assume that this statement is the last statement in the trace.

4.1 From Error Messages to Proofs

The notion of error trace is not directly amenable to the use of verification technology and to the concept of proof. Recall that an error trace has some execution that violates an assert statement, which also means that it may still have normally terminating executions. The notion of an error trace is thus incompatible with the notion of an infeasible trace. We know that the infeasiblity of a trace can be tied to a proof. In order to make the connection from error traces to proofs, we transform error traces to infeasible traces. Intuitively, the transformation of an error trace eliminates all normally terminating executions from them. Given an error message (τ, s_0), the first step of the transformation is to encode the given initial state s_0 of a faulty execution of τ into an assume statement that is prepended to τ. The resulting trace is still feasible.[2] In fact, the trace has exactly one execution. The execution must start in the state s_0 (otherwise the newly added assume statement would immediately block the execution). The execution fails the assert statement in the trace. The second step of the transformation is to replace the assert statement in the trace is by an assume statement. The resulting trace is infeasible.

Notation $\bar{\tau}$: For a trace τ, we denote by $\bar{\tau}$ the trace obtained from τ by replacing every assert statement of the form $\texttt{assert}(F)$ in τ by $\texttt{assume}(F)$.

---

[2] Note that we use weakest preconditions, as opposed to weakest liberal preconditions; see Sect. 4. For example, the trace $\texttt{assume}(x = 0); \texttt{assert}(x \neq 0)$ is not infeasible since $\textsf{wp}(\texttt{assume}(x = 0); \texttt{assert}(x \neq 0), \bot) = (x = 0 \Rightarrow (x \neq 0 \wedge \bot)) = (x \neq 0)$.

Definition 2 (Infeasible Extension of Error Messages). *Let $\epsilon = (\tau, s_0)$ be an error message and let $\{x_1, \ldots, x_k\}$ be the (finite) set of variables occurring in the statements of τ. Let further $e_1, \ldots, e_k$ be expressions that define the values of $x_1, \ldots, x_k$ in the state s_0.[3] Then the trace τ' of the form*

$$\tau' = \texttt{assume}(x_1 = e_1 \wedge \cdots \wedge x_k = e_k); \bar{\tau}$$

is the infeasible extension *of the error message ϵ.*

Remark 3 (Infeasibility of infeasible extension of error message). If ϵ is an error message and τ' its infeasible extension, then τ' is infeasible.

Note that, in the formal setting as introduced in Sect. 3, all three kinds of statements are deterministic. In the presence of a non-deterministic statement such as `havoc(x)`, we would need to add an assume statement to encode the non-deterministically chosen value for x in the faulty execution of an error trace τ. Definition 2 would accommodate this in the setting where each non-deterministic assignment statement in a trace is of the form $x := x^{(i)}$ with each $x^{(i)}$ a fresh renaming of x.

4.2 Error Signatures

Let ϵ be an error message and τ its infeasible extension. An error signature σ for ϵ is a sequence of formulas that can be extended to form a Hoare sequence with τ by allowing each formula in σ to be repeated for some (possibly empty) subtrace of τ. That is, each formula in σ is invariant for some subtrace of τ and each consecutive pair of formulas in σ is inductive for some statement in τ that connects the respective invariant subtraces. The intuition behind this definition is that the error signature abstracts the irrelevant statements in the trace (those contained in the invariant subtraces) while keeping the statements that are relevant for understanding the error (those connecting the invariant subtraces). The following definition makes this notion formally precise.

Definition 4 (Error Signatures). *Let $\tau = st_1; \ldots; st_n$ be an infeasible extension of an error message ϵ. A sequence of formulas $\sigma = F_1, \ldots, F_{m-1}$ with $m \leq n$ is an error signature of ϵ if there exists a strictly monotone function $h : [1, m] \to [1, n]$ such that:*

– *the sequence*

$$\top, st_{h(1)}, F_1, st_{h(2)}, F_2, \ldots, st_{h(m-1)}, F_{m-1} st_{h(m)}, \bot$$

is a Hoare sequence,

---

[3] In the general case, we may not be able to describe s_0 using simple equalities and instead must consider its *diagram* [6]. For the sake of the clarity of presentation, we skim over these technicalities.

– every F_i is invariant on the subtrace from $st_{h(i)}$ to the last statement before $st_{h(i+1)}$, i.e., for every $i \in [1, m-1]$, the sequence

$$F_i, st_{h(i)}, F_i, st_{h(i)+1}, F_i, \dots, st_{h(i+1)-1}, F_i$$

is a Hoare sequence.

We call the trace $st_{h(1)}, \dots, st_{h(m)}$ the abstract slice of ϵ induced by σ and h.

Remark 5. Let $\epsilon = (\tau, s_0)$ be an error message and σ an error signature of ϵ. Then the formulas in σ are all different from $\bot$. This means that σ corresponds to a proof that the execution of τ that starts in s_0 is non-blocking and fails the final assert statement in τ.

Note that error signatures always exist. In particular, for the infeasible extension $\tau = st_1; \dots; st_n$ of an error message ϵ, the sequence of formulas

$$\sigma = \mathsf{wp}(st_2; \dots; st_n, \bot), \dots, \mathsf{wp}(st_n, \bot)$$

is an error signature of ϵ. Evidently this error signature is not very informative, as the abstract slice of ϵ induced by σ is identical to τ. We will discuss below how to compute error signatures that yield proper abstract slices.

4.3   Classifying Error Messages

In the following, let sig be a function that maps error messages to error signatures. Then sig defines an equivalence relation $=_{\mathsf{sig}}$ on error messages. Two error messages ϵ_1 and ϵ_2 are equivalent with respect to sig if sig maps them to the same error signature:

$$\epsilon_1 =_{\mathsf{sig}} \epsilon_2 \iff \mathsf{sig}(\epsilon_1) = \mathsf{sig}(\epsilon_2).$$

Definition 6 (Buckets). *Given a set of error message E and a function* sig *mapping the elements of E to error signatures, we refer to the equivalence classes in the quotient $E/ =_{\mathsf{sig}}$ as* buckets.

We now have everything in place to give the classification algorithm, which is shown in Algorithm 1. The algorithm takes as input a set E of error messages. The output of the algorithm is the map *Buckets* whose domain is a set of error signatures (such that every error message in E is covered by some error signature in the domain). Each error signature σ in the domain is mapped to the corresponding *bucket*, i.e., a set of error messages which all have the error signature σ.

The algorithm computes a function sig mapping error messages to error signatures, as follows. For every error message $\epsilon = (\tau, s_0)$ in E, we first compute its infeasible extension τ' using the helper function `InfeasibleExtension`. Suppose τ' is of length n. Then we compute the formulas $F_0, \dots, F_{n+1}$ for a Hoare sequence of τ' by applying an interpolating theorem prover to the path formula

---

Algorithm 1. Classification of error messages.

   Input: E: set of error messages
   Output: *Buckets*: map from error signatures to buckets of error messages from E

```
 1 begin
 2     for ε ∈ E do
 3         (τ, s₀) ← ε ;
 4         τ' ← InfeasibleExtension(τ, s₀) ;
 5         F₀, ..., Fₙ₊₁ ← Interpolate(τ') ;
 6         // remove successive duplicates in F₁, ..., Fₙ ;
 7         curr ← 1 ;
 8         σ ← F₁ ;
 9         for i from 1 to n do
10             if Fᵢ ≠ F_curr then
11                 σ ← σ, Fᵢ ;
12                 curr ← i ;
13             end if
14         end for
15         if σ ∉ dom(Buckets) then
16             Buckets[σ] ← ∅;
17         end if
18         Buckets[σ] ← Buckets[σ] ∪ {ε};
19     end for
20 end
```

---

constructed from τ'. This step is implemented by the function `Interpolate`. Note that the resulting interpolant sequence always satisfies $F_0 = \top$ and $F_{n+1} = \bot$. Moreover, the subsequence $F_1, \ldots, F_n$ is guaranteed to be an error signature for ϵ. However, it is not yet abstracting any statements in τ'. To obtain a proper error signature, we exploit the observation that interpolating theorem provers often produce interpolant sequences that consecutively repeat the same interpolant. Thus, we simply iterate over the formulas $F_1, \ldots, F_n$ and remove consecutive duplicates of formulas F_i to obtain the actual error signature σ for ϵ. The obtained error signature is then used to insert the current error message into its bucket.

5   Evaluation

Our approach to categorize error messages is embodied in a tool called Bucketeer. More precisely, the tool implements Algorithm 1 where the helper procedure `Interpolate` is implemented using the interpolation procedure of Princess [28]. The tool is available online, together with the benchmarks discussed in this paper.[4]

We have implemented the tool on top of a (prototype of a) static checker for Java [2]. The static checker is similar to OpenJML [8]. It uses Princess [28] to test

---

[4] http://www.csl.sri.com/~schaef/experiments.zip.

an SMT formula for satisfiability and to compute a model if possible. It checks for null pointer dereferences, out-of-bound access to arrays, and division by zero errors. The checks are realized by inserting assertions into the code. Assertion violations are detected by translating the transition relation of each method into an SMT formula; a model of the SMT formula corresponds to an execution that violates an assertion (during the construction of the SMT formula, the checker unwinds loops (twice), and it replaces method calls by the specified (possibly trivial) contracts). The corresponding error message, i.e., the error trace for the failing execution together with the computed model, is fed to Bucketeer. For performance reasons, the static checker ensures that no two error messages share the same sequence of statements in the error trace (otherwise, we might find an infinite number of error messages). Bucketeer, however, does not require that error messages exercise different paths. Bucketeer categories error messages which belong to the same method (which makes sense only if more than one error message belongs to the method).

For the test of equality between formulas used in Line 10 of Algorithm 1 ("$F_i \neq F_{curr}$"), we use syntactic equality. In our experiments, using the more costly test of logical equivalence instead of syntactic equality does not change the outcome of the tests. The reason lies in the fact that the generation of the formulas by the interpolation procedure is optimized towards using the same formula whenever possible. This means in particular that the generation of a syntactically new but logically equivalent formula is unlikely.

Experimental Setup. To evaluate our approach we conducted two experimental analyses: a quantitative analysis to evaluate if the number of buckets that have to be investigated by the user is significantly lower than the number of original error traces, and a qualitative analysis where we analyze the buckets for one application in-depth to assess if the error traces that are grouped in one bucket actually share properties that make it easier to fix them together.

For the quantitative analysis, we evaluate Bucketeer approach on three open-source Java applications: the build system Apache Ant, the database Cassandra, and on our own tool, Bucketeer. Table 1 shows an overview of the benchmarks and a summary of some of the raw data of our evaluation.

Applied to Ant, the static checker finds 2470 methods with error traces, out of which 820 methods have more than one error trace. Bucketeer is applied to the in total 2715 error traces of those 820 methods. Applied to Cassandra, the static checker finds 2190 methods with error traces, out of which 937 methods have more than one error trace. Bucketeer is applied to the in total 3243 error traces of those 937 methods. Applied to Bucketeer itself, the static checker finds 203 methods with error traces, out of which 102 methods have more than one error trace. Bucketeer is applied to the in total 376 error traces of those 102 methods. Summarizing over all three benchmark sets, Bucketeer is applied to 6333 error traces of 1859 methods.

We discuss the results of the quantitative analysis in Sect. 5.1. For the qualitative analysis, which we discuss in Sect. 5.2, we manually inspected all buckets produced by running Bucketeer on its own source code.

Table 1. Raw data of the experimental evaluation

Benchmarks	Ant	Cassandra	Bucketeer
Lines of code	271k	299k	15k
# of methods	7847	9373	331
Time for static checking (min)	87.35	55.65	6.00
# of methods with error traces	2470	2190	203
# of methods with multiple error traces	820	937	102
Sum of error traces in methods with multiple traces	2715	3243	376
Time for categorization (min)	25.23	54.78	6.06
Number of Buckets	1595	2041	258

The experiments were run on a 2.7 GHz i7 machine with 16 GB memory and an initial size of 4 GB for the Java virtual machine. We used an analysis timeout of 30 s per method. We experimented with larger timeouts up to five minutes per method but it had no significant effect on the number of methods that could be analyzed.

The time for the static checking and the time for categorization given in Table 1 does not account for the time spent on methods that time out or where the interpolant generation crashes.

Due to the timeout we were not able to analyze 1053 methods in Ant, 346 methods in Cassandra, and 132 methods in Bucketeer. These methods are not included in the numbers reported above.

The interpolating prover crashed for all methods where interpolation involved reasoning about the sub-typing relation used in our encoding of Java programs. We excluded these methods from our evaluation (1012 methods for Ant, 896 methods for Cassandra, and 80 methods for Bucketeer). These methods are not included in the numbers reported above.

5.1 Quantitative Analysis

The distribution of the numbers n of error traces across the methods of a benchmark program is needed in order to interpret the performance of a classification tool on the benchmark program (in principle, the lower the number of error traces, the lower are the chances that some of them can be grouped together). Figure 3 shows, for $n = 2, 3, \ldots$, how many methods contain n error traces (the number of methods with $n = 1$ error traces (which is available in Table 1) is not present here because the classification tool is not applied to such methods). As expected, the number of methods decreases with increasing n.

We observe that the number of methods containing four or more error traces almost adds up to the number of methods containing only two error traces. This indicates that a user of a static checker will encounter methods with more than four error traces relatively frequently.

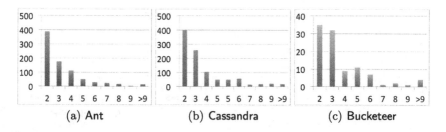

Fig. 3. Number of methods (on y-axis) with n error traces (x-axis).

We can see that the distribution of error traces across methods is similar for Ant and Cassandra, while for Bucketeer there are more methods with three or more error traces. The difference may stem from the fact that the code of Bucketeer implements more involved algorithms.

As shown in Table 1, the overall time cost may almost double when one adds classification to static checking. The cost for classification lies in the interpolant generation, which is a relatively new technique in SMT solving, with a high potential for optimization. In any case, the cost for classification seems acceptable.

We next evaluate how many error traces can be categorized in buckets of a given size. For Ant, 1595 buckets are generated, which means that, on average, each bucket contains 1.7 error traces. For Cassandra, 2041 buckets are generated, which means an average of 1.6 error traces per bucket. For Bucketeer, 258 buckets are generated, which means an average of 1.45 error traces per bucket.

One way to evaluate the effectiveness of our tool for classification is to measure its behavior in view of the two extreme cases of unsatisfactory behavior. The two extreme cases are the scenario (a) where each trace ends up in a separate bucket (no trace is grouped together with another one), and the scenario (b) where all traces of a method are grouped together into one single bucket. To compare against scenario (a), we count how many traces are grouped in buckets of a given size n, for $n = 1, 2, \ldots$. Figure 4 shows the percentage of error traces that are grouped in buckets of size n. More than half of the error traces (from 50 % to 65 %) are categorized in a bucket of size $n \geq 2$, i.e., more than half of

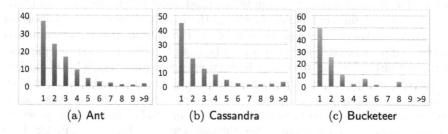

Fig. 4. Percentage of trace (y-axis) grouped in a bucket of size n (x-axis).

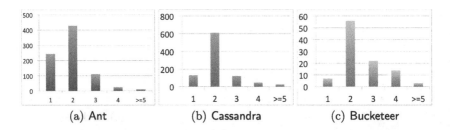

Fig. 5. Number of methods that (y-axis) contain n buckets (x-axis).

the error traces are grouped together with at least one other error trace. This means that we are rather far away from the scenario (a).

To compare against the scenario (b), we count the number of methods containing n buckets, for $n = 1, 2, \ldots$. Figure 5 shows that a very large portion of the methods have two or more buckets. In other words, we are rather far away from the scenario (b).

5.2   Qualitative Analysis

The goal of our qualitative analysis was to evaluate if the error messages grouped in one bucket have a common root cause and, thus, the grouping helps to reduce redundant work for the user. To this end, we manually investigated the buckets that Bucketeer produced when we applied it to its own source code. Evaluating the tool on the code written by us introduces some confirmation bias. On the other hand, since we are familiar with the code it also increases our confidence in judging if error messages in a bucket have a common root cause.

We inspected all 65 buckets generated for Bucketeer that contained at least two error messages. These buckets can be grouped into two categories. The first category consists of buckets that contain error messages that fail because the initial state of the method sets one of the method parameters to null which is dereferenced later in the method body. 73 % of the buckets in Bucketeer are of that form. These buckets contain between two and seven error messages (the average is 3 error messages per bucket). All these error messages have in common that the initial state sets a particular method parameter to null, which triggers a run-time exception somewhere in the method body. Often the actual run-time error occurs at different points in the method body. However, the important observation is that these error messages share the initialization statement of the specific input parameter and they all can be fixed by enforcing that this parameter is not null. That is, instead of inspecting each error message in the bucket, a user of Bucketeer can pick any error message in one of these buckets, fix it by adding an adequate precondition, and thus eliminate all other error messages in the bucket without further inspection. The grouping of error messages provided by our approach can therefore reduce the user's workload substantially for these types of buckets.

The remaining 27 % of the buckets that we inspected contained error messages where the initial state assumes a field to be `null` which is dereferenced later on the trace. Again, each bucket contains between two and seven error messages with an average of 3 error messages per bucket. The error messages in each bucket share that the initial state sets a field of an object to `null` which is dereferenced later in the method body. All error messages in one bucket share the initial state that sets the field to `null`. Some error messages also share the statement that raises the run-time exception (but take different paths to get there). Others raise run-time exceptions at different statements but because of the same field. That is, all error messages in one bucket can be fixed by adding a precondition that ensures that the given field is not `null` (or, alternatively, by guarding all dereferencing expressions with an appropriate check if such a precondition cannot be established). Again, the grouping of the error messages helps the user of Bucketeer by reducing the number of error messages that she has to inspect.

Thus, for all the buckets that we inspected, the contained error messages had a common root cause that could be fixed after inspecting only one error message in the bucket. In summary, the qualitative analysis shows that the grouping of error error messages done by Bucketeer is useful.

6   Related Work

The classification and bucketing of error messages is an active research topic. We will discuss what seems the most relevant work in our context. In summary, no existing approach to classification and bucketing addresses the question whether the comparison between error messages can be based on criteria other than syntactic or statistical criteria (as opposed to criteria based on the semantics of statements as in our work).

The original motivation for our work stems from the work in [3] which addresses the error traces generated by a software model checker (somewhat confusingly, the existing notions of error trace are subtly but substantially different from each other). The classification of error traces in [3] is based on common statements that have been identified as a possible *root cause*. The software model checker then only reports one error trace per root cause. The identification of the root cause works by comparing error traces to non-error traces which are obtained from correct executions of the program (in this it is similar to dynamic fault localization techniques such as delta debugging [31]). Our approach does not require any successful executions of a program to compare against.

A static approach to cluster static analysis errors is presented in [23]. They introduce the notion of sound dependency of alarms which is based on the trace partitioning abstract domain. An alarm depends on another alarm if it spuriousness implies the spuriousness of the other alarm. This is different from our error signatures which can, in general, group arbitrary traces, even if they do not share control locations.

Other approaches, such as [19] or [22] cluster static analysis alarms (not necessarily only error traces) using unsound techniques. That is, their approaches may suppress alarms related to genuine errors, or highlight alarms that are actually false positives. Our approach just groups error traces. It does not suppress or highlight particular error traces, and genuine errors and false alarms may be grouped in the same bucket if they share the same error signature.

Most industrial static analyzers such as Coverity, HP Fortify, Facebook Infer, or Red Lizards Goanna have complex systems to categorize error messages, group them into buckets, and eliminate potential false alarms. These approaches usually combine statistical analysis, feasibility checks, and data-flow analysis and are heavily customized. While our approach is similar in spirit, we try to obtain a more semantic categorization of error traces with our error signatures. Existing approaches tend to group traces that violate the same property, while the error signatures capture that traces perform similar computations. That is, using error signatures is conceptually different from existing approaches.

A related problem to classification of error messages is duplicate analysis of bug reports in bug tracking systems [1, 30]. Existing techniques for automating the analysis of bug reports focus on the verbal description of the bug that is provided by the bug reporter. The information in the bug report that describes the actual error trace is typically incomplete and not amenable to automated analysis. For example, in a bug report for a program crash, one will at most find a stack trace of the program state when the crash occurred but no further information about the actual execution leading to that state. Recently, techniques have been explored to automatically reconstruct the actual error trace from a field failure by using symbolic execution [18].

The focus of our classification approach is on error traces of sequential programs. This is different in the work on the classification of concurrency bugs to identify the type of concurrency violation (out of order violation, atomicity violation, deadlocks, etc.); see, e.g., [5, 16]. The approach in [16] is related to our tool in that it also uses an SMT solver to perform this type of classification.

The notion of error signature that we introduce in this paper is somewhat related to the notion of error invariants and abstract slices explored in [7, 13, 25]. There, the goal is to obtain an explanation of a bug in an individual error trace. In contrast, the work of this paper is about the classification of a set of error traces.

The work on tools to infer preconditions such as [10] and [12] is related to our work in the sense that it may be conceivable to classify error messages according to the same precondition. In comparison, error signatures are strictly more fine grained (i.e., error messages with different error signatures may still share the same precondition; e.g., the precondition can always be ⊤ if the initial state is irrelevant for reaching the error).

7   Conclusion

We have presented an approach that uses concepts and techniques from semantics and verification in order to classify error messages in the context of static checking. We have presented the formal foundation that allows us to associate each error message with a verification problem whose solution (i.e., the proof of validity of a certain correctness property for a program derived from the error message) can be used to construct a small but significant *error signature* (on which the classification is based). We have implemented the approach and applied it to three benchmark sets. Our experiments indicate an interesting practical potential.

While our motivation stems from the context of extended static checking, it may be interesting to explore how the approach can be used to complement existing approaches to classification in other contexts (abstract interpretation, bounded model checking, testing, ...).

A more fundamental question for future research concerns the existence of a metric for error signatures in order to define a *distance between error messages*.

Acknowledgement. This work is funded in parts by AFRL contract No. FA8750-15-C-0010 and the National Science Foundation under grant CCF-1350574.

References

1. Anvik, J., Hiew, L., Murphy, G.C.: Who should fix this bug? In: ICSE, pp. 361–370. ACM (2006)
2. Arlt, S., Rubio-González, C., Rümmer, P., Schäf, M., Shankar, N.: The gradual verifier. In: Badger, J.M., Rozier, K.Y. (eds.) NFM 2014. LNCS, vol. 8430, pp. 313–327. Springer, Heidelberg (2014)
3. Ball, T., Naik, M., Rajamani, S.K.: From symptom to cause: localizing errors in counterexample traces. SIGPLAN Not. **38**, 97–105 (2003)
4. Barnett, M., Fähndrich, M., Leino, K.R.M., Müller, P., Schulte, W., Venter, H.: Specification and verification: the Spec# experience. Commun. ACM **54**(6), 81–91 (2011)
5. Tabaei Befrouei, M., Wang, C., Weissenbacher, G.: Abstraction and mining of traces to explain concurrency bugs. In: Bonakdarpour, B., Smolka, S.A. (eds.) RV 2014. LNCS, vol. 8734, pp. 162–177. Springer, Heidelberg (2014)
6. Chang, C., Keisler, H.J.: Model Theory. Studies in Logic and the Foundations of Mathematics. Elsevier Science, North-Holland (1990)
7. Christ, J., Ermis, E., Schäf, M., Wies, T.: Flow-sensitive fault localization. In: Giacobazzi, R., Berdine, J., Mastroeni, I. (eds.) VMCAI 2013. LNCS, vol. 7737, pp. 189–208. Springer, Heidelberg (2013)
8. Cok, D.R.: OpenJML: JML for Java 7 by extending OpenJDK. In: Bobaru, M., Havelund, K., Holzmann, G.J., Joshi, R. (eds.) NFM 2011. LNCS, vol. 6617, pp. 472–479. Springer, Heidelberg (2011)
9. Cousot, P., Cousot, R.: Systematic design of program analysis frameworks. In: POPL, pp. 269–282. ACM (1979)
10. Cousot, P., Cousot, R., Fähndrich, M., Logozzo, F.: Automatic inference of necessary preconditions. In: Giacobazzi, R., Berdine, J., Mastroeni, I. (eds.) VMCAI 2013. LNCS, vol. 7737, pp. 128–148. Springer, Heidelberg (2013)
11. Dijkstra, E.W.: A Discipline of Programming. Prentice-Hall, Englewood Cliffs (1976)
12. Dillig, I., Dillig, T., Aiken, A.: Automated error diagnosis using abductive inference. In: PLDI, pp. 181–192 (2012)

13. Ermis, E., Schäf, M., Wies, T.: Error invariants. In: Giannakopoulou, D., Méry, D. (eds.) FM 2012. LNCS, vol. 7436, pp. 187–201. Springer, Heidelberg (2012)

14. Falke, S., Merz, F., Sinz, C.: LLBMC: improved bounded model checking of C programs using LLVM. In: Piterman, N., Smolka, S.A. (eds.) TACAS 2013 (ETAPS 2013). LNCS, vol. 7795, pp. 623–626. Springer, Heidelberg (2013)

15. Flanagan, C., Leino, K.R.M., Lillibridge, M., Nelson, G., Saxe, J.B., Stata, R.: Extended static checking for Java. SIGPLAN Not. **37**, 234–245 (2002)

16. Gupta, A., Henzinger, T.A., Radhakrishna, A., Samanta, R., Tarrach, T.: Succinct representation of concurrent trace sets. In: POPL, pp. 433–444. ACM (2015)

17. Heizmann, M., Hoenicke, J., Podelski, A.: Software model checking for people who love automata. In: Sharygina, N., Veith, H. (eds.) CAV 2013. LNCS, vol. 8044, pp. 36–52. Springer, Heidelberg (2013)

18. Jin, W., Orso, A.: Bugredux: reproducing field failures for in-house debugging. In: ICSE, pp. 474–484. IEEE (2012)

19. Kremenek, T., Engler, D.: Z-ranking: using statistical analysis to counter the impact of static analysis approximations. In: SAS, pp. 295–315 (2003)

20. Kroening, D., Tautschnig, M.: CBMC – C bounded model checker. In: Ábrahám, E., Havelund, K. (eds.) TACAS 2014 (ETAPS). LNCS, vol. 8413, pp. 389–391. Springer, Heidelberg (2014)

21. Lal, A., Qadeer, S.: Powering the static driver verifier using corral. In: FSE, pp. 202–212. ACM (2014)

22. Le, W., Soffa, M.L.: Path-based fault correlations. In: FSE, pp. 307–316 (2010)

23. Lee, W., Lee, W., Yi, K.: Sound non-statistical clustering of static analysis alarms. In: Kuncak, V., Rybalchenko, A. (eds.) VMCAI 2012. LNCS, vol. 7148, pp. 299–314. Springer, Heidelberg (2012)

24. McMillan, K.L.: An interpolating theorem prover. Theor. Comput. Sci. **345**, 101–121 (2005)

25. Murali, V., Sinha, N., Torlak, E., Chandra, S.: What gives? a hybrid algorithm for error trace explanation. In: Giannakopoulou, D., Kroening, D. (eds.) VSTTE 2014. LNCS, vol. 8471, pp. 270–286. Springer, Heidelberg (2014)

26. Nelson, G.: A generalization of Dijkstra's calculus. ACM Trans. Program. Lang. Syst. **11**(4), 517–561 (1989)

27. Pacheco, C., Ernst, M.D.: Randoop: feedback-directed random testing for java. In: Companion to the 22nd ACM SIGPLAN Conference on Object-oriented Programming Systems and Applications Companion, OOPSLA 2007, New York, NY, USA, pp. 815–816. ACM (2007)

28. Rümmer, P.: A constraint sequent calculus for first-order logic with linear integer arithmetic. In: Cervesato, I., Veith, H., Voronkov, A. (eds.) LPAR 2008. LNCS (LNAI), vol. 5330, pp. 274–289. Springer, Heidelberg (2008)

29. Sankaranarayanan, S., Sipma, H., Manna, Z.: Non-linear loop invariant generation using Gröbner bases. In: POPL, pp. 318–329. ACM (2004)

30. Wang, X., Zhang, L., Xie, T., Anvik, J., Sun, J.: An approach to detecting duplicate bug reports using natural language and execution information. In: ICSE, pp. 461–470. ACM (2008)

31. Zeller, A.: Isolating cause-effect chains from computer programs. In: SIGSOFT FSE, pp. 1–10 (2002)

Tool Demonstration

Debugging Meets Testing in Erlang

Salvador Tamarit[1], Adrián Riesco[2], Enrique Martin-Martin[2],
and Rafael Caballero[2(✉)]

[1] Babel Research Group, Universidad Politécnica de Madrid, Madrid, Spain
stamarit@fi.upm.es
[2] Universidad Complutense de Madrid, Madrid, Spain
ariesco@fdi.ucm.es, emartinm@ucm.es, rafa@sip.ucm.es

Abstract. We propose a bidirectional collaboration between declarative debugging and testing for detecting errors in the sequential subset of the programming language Erlang. In our proposal, the information obtained from the user during a debugging session is stored in form of unit tests. These test cases can be employed afterwards to check, through testing, if the bug has been actually corrected. Moreover, the debugger employs already existing tests to determine the correctness of some subcomputations, helping the user to locate the error readily. The process, contrarily to usual debugger frameworks is cumulative: if later we find a new bug we have more information from the previous debugging and testing iterations that can contribute to find the error readily.

1 Introduction

One of the most important underlying ideas of the software development life cycle [1] is that the assets from one phase can be employed both in the next phases and in successive iterations of the cycle. For instance, the testing phase produces test cases that allow checking whether the system satisfies the initial requirements. If later the system is modified, for instance to improve its efficiency, the initial tests (or at least part of them) can be employed again to check whether the initial requirements are still verified.

However, there is a task in the software development cycle that often constitutes the exception to this rule: debugging. In spite of the introduction of tools that try to automatize the location of errors, debugging is still a manual and very time-consuming non-trivial task that requires a careful comparison between the actual and the expected results of some subcomputations. Unfortunately, the very useful information gathered during a debugging session is usually thrown away once the debugging session is finished.

Research supported by the Comunidad de Madrid project N-Greens Software-CM (S2013/ICE-2731), by the MINECO Spanish projects *StrongSoft* (TIN2012-39391-C04-04), *VIVAC* (TIN2012-38137), *CAVI-(ROSE/ART)* (TIN2013-44742-C4-(1/3)-R), *LOBASS* (TIN2015-69175-C4-2-R), and *TRACES* (TIN2015-67522-C3-3-R), and by the European Union project POLCA (STREP FP7-ICT-2013.3.4 610686).

B.K. Aichernig and C.A. Furia (Eds.): TAP 2016, LNCS 9762, pp. 171–180, 2016.
DOI: 10.1007/978-3-319-41135-4_10

We propose a modification of the general framework followed in *declarative debugging*, also known as *algorithmic debugging* [9], a debugging technique that asks questions to the user until a bug is found. In our proposal the answers given by the user are stored in the form of test cases that make persistent the valuable information obtained during a debugging session. In order to prove the applicability of the new debugging schema, we have implemented the new schema in the Erlang Declarative Debugger EDD [3]. The same ideas can enhance any declarative debugger implemented for a system allowing unit tests.

Furthermore, the relation between debugging and testing can be seen as a bidirectional collaboration. One of the major complaints about declarative debugging is the large number of questions asked to the user in order to find the bug. In our proposals, each question is compared in advance with the existing test cases, in order to determine if the answer can be entailed without further assistance from the user. We have observed that this feature is very helpful in practice, especially if there are more than one bug in the system, since the user can focus directly on the code affected by the error, disregarding the fragments of code that have been checked and found correct in previous debugging sessions.

The rest of the paper is structured as follows: Sect. 2 presents our proposal as a new general debugging framework. Section 3 describes how our tool takes advantage of test cases to improve declarative debugging, while Sect. 4 shows how test cases are generated by our declarative debugger. Finally, Sect. 5 concludes and discusses some lines of future work. The tool EDD, modified to take into account the generation and use of test cases, is publicly available at https://github.com/tamarit/edd.

2   A New General Debugging Schema

Declarative debugging is a semi-automatic debugging technique that abstracts the execution details to focus on results. It can be presented as a general schema with the following structure:

```
declarative_debugger(initialSymptom) −>
    T = execution_tree(initialSymptom)
    while (|T| ≠ 1)
        pick up a node N in T with N ≠ root(T)
        ask the oracle whether N is valid/invalid
        if N is valid:
            remove N and its subtree from T
        else
            T = subtree rooted by N
    return root(T)
```

The debugger starts when the user detects a computation returning an unexpected result, the initialSymptom. Then, it builds an *execution tree* representing the initial symptom. The nodes of the tree can be depicted with the form $C = V$, with C a computation (function evaluation) and V its computed result. A node is considered *valid* if its result is the expected for the associated computation, and *invalid* otherwise. In particular, the root of the tree represents the computation of the initial symptom and thus it is invalid. The children of each node correspond to the subcomputations needed to obtain the result at the parent. The final goal is to locate a *buggy node*, an invalid node with valid children. The fragment of code represented by this node is then considered as the source of the error, because it has produced an erroneous output from valid inputs (the children results). Each iteration of the main loop chooses an *unknown* node N, possibly following some strategy [10], and asks to the user about its validity. If N is valid, the subtree rooted by N is removed from the tree. If it is invalid then the subtree rooted by N becomes the new debugging tree. Observe that after each iteration the size of the tree decreases, and that in every iteration its root is invalid. Then, it is possible to ensure that in a finite number of iterations we will get a tree with only one node ($|T| = 1$), and that this node is a buggy node. Both operations, removing subtrees rooted by valid nodes, and replacing the tree by a subtree rooted by an invalid node, are safe, in the sense that the tree obtained after the operation contains at least one buggy node, and every buggy node in the new tree is also buggy in the original tree.

In this paper, we consider EDD [3], a declarative debugger for the sequential subset of the programming language Erlang [6] that follows this schema. The nodes of the execution trees in EDD have the form $m : f(t_1, \ldots, t_n) = r$, with m the name of an Erlang module, f a function defined in $m, t_1, \ldots, t_n$ the arguments of a call to f occurred during the computation, and r the computed result. EDD also debugs anonymous functions, and allows the user inspecting the body of functions looking for more particular errors [4] but these features are not used in this paper.

Our proposal extends the initial framework by taking into account existing test cases and also by generating new test cases following the information gathered from the user. We distinguish two kinds of test cases:[1]

- *Positive* test cases, depicted as **?assertEqual**(C,V), indicating that V is the expected result for computation C.
- *Negative* test cases **?assertNotEqual**(C,V'), indicate that V' is *not* the expected result for C.

The extended framework that we propose is presented in Fig. 1. It takes as additional input parameter a set of test cases inputTCs, used to decide initially that some of the nodes of the execution tree are valid or invalid. In particular, the lines 5 and 6 look for positive test cases that occur in the tree. These nodes are valid, and their subtrees can be safely removed. Lines 7–10 initialize outputTCs, the list that stores the new test cases obtained after each question answered by the user. It takes the initial symptom with its value as first negative test case if there is not a positive test case for the same call in the initial set of

---

[1] Erlang also supports test cases ?assert(...) with predicates. Our system can handle these test cases when their predicates involve equality or inequality operators, but we will focus only on **?assertEqual** and **?assertNotEqual** for simplicity in the presentation.

```
 1  declarative_debugger(initialSymptom, inputTCs) −>
 2
 3      T = execution_tree(initialSymptom)
 4
 5      for  ?assertEqual(C,V) ∈ inputTCs
 6          remove from T every subtree rooted by C=V
 7      if ∄ ?assertEqual(initialSymptom, V) ∈ inputTCs
 8          outputTCs = [?assertNotEqual(initialSymptom, value(initialSymptom))]
 9      else
10          outputTCs = []
11
12      let T' be the smallest subtree of T verifying
13          invalidTC(root(T'),inputTCs ∪ outputTCs)
14      T=T'
15
16      while (|T| ≠ 1)
17          pick up a node N ≡ (C=V) from T with N ≠ root(T)
18          ask the oracle whether N is valid/invalid
19
20          if N is valid
21              outputTCs = [?assertEqual(C,V) | outputTCs]
22              remove from T the subtree rooted by N
23          else
24              outputTCs = [?assertNotEqual(C,V) | outputTCs]
25              T = subtree rooted by N
26
27      return (root(T), outputTCs \ inputTCs)
28
29  invalidTC(C=V,inputTCs ) −>
30    return (?assertEqual(C,V') ∈ inputTCs and V'≠V) or
31            (?assertNotEqual(C,V) ∈ inputTCs)
```

Fig. 1. Declarative debugging with test cases

test cases.[2] Line 13 looks for nodes that can be detected as invalid from the information contained in the test cases. This is the task of the Boolean function invalidTC defined in lines 29–31, which receives a node and a set of input test cases and return **true** if it is possible to determine that the node is invalid from the information contained in the test cases. As the function indicates, a node in the tree can be pointed out as invalid in two situations:

1. If there is a positive test case for the same computation but with a different associated value (then the value contained in the node is not the correct result).
2. If there is a negative test case for the same computation and for the same value, that is, the test case indicates directly that the result is unexpected.

---

[2] The positive test case, if exists, indicates that the initial symptom is wrong indicating also the expected value. This makes the addition of the negative test case redundant.

It is safe to replace the tree T by the subtree T' rooted by a node verifying any of these two conditions. Line 12 of Fig. 1 takes the smallest tree T' with these characteristics; although this tree might not be unique, the completeness property for debugging trees with an invalid root [4] ensures that any of these trees will reveal an error. This is important, because a smaller tree means, generally, less questions to the user. The rest of the code is similar to the original schema. Finally, both the buggy node and the new test cases are returned.

This general idea has been put into practice extending EDD using EUnit tests [5]. EUnit belongs to the general testing framework family known as *unit testing*, a well-established testing methodology that allows users to indicate the expected values obtained when executing a function with some specific arguments. Thus, the tests generated by EDD can be executed using EUnit, which allows the user to check that the problem has been actually solved after the error has been corrected, simply running the generated tests. Notice that the tests will check not only the main result, that could be checked readily by the user, but also all the intermediate results obtained during the debugging process. This is important because correcting an error sometimes introduces inadvertently a new one. The exhaustive checking of the computation helps to check that this is not the case. Note also that the tests generated are not affected by code changes since they are only expressing the intended interpretation of one particular function.

```
1  -module(quicksort).
2
3  qs(_, []) -> [];
4  qs(F, [E|R]) ->
5    {A, B} = partition(F, E, R),
6    qs(F, B) ++ [E] ++ qs(F, A).
7
8  leq(A, B) -> A =< B.
9
10 partition(_, _, []) -> {[], []};
11 partition(F, E, [H|T]) ->
12   {A, B} = partition(F, E, T),
13   case F(H, E) of
14     true  -> {[H|A], B};
15     false -> {A, B}
16   end.
17
18 quicksort_test() ->
19   ?assertEqual(qs(fun leq/2, []), []),
20   ?assertEqual(qs(fun leq/2, [1]), [1]),
21   ?assertEqual(qs(fun leq/2, [7,1]), [1,7]),
22   ?assertEqual(qs(fun leq/2, [7,8,1]),
                  [1,7,8]).
```

Fig. 2. Code for the quicksort function and its corresponding tests

3   When Declarative Debugging Met Testing

We illustrate these ideas with the quicksort module presented in Fig. 2, which is an adaptation of the code in [7]. The module contains 3 functions: qs, leq and partition. The function qs takes as arguments a binary predicate F representing the notion of *order* and a list, and returns the list ordered using the QuickSort algorithm. Lists in Erlang are represented as sequences of elements $[E_1, \ldots, E_n]$ or $[H|T]$ where H is the first element of the list (called *head*) and T is the rest of the list (called *tail*). Erlang also allows the use of *tuples*, represented as sequences of elements enclosed in curly braces: $\{E_1, \ldots, E_n\}$. As usual in functional languages, the function qs is defined by two clauses that are tried in top-down order by applying *pattern matching*. The first clause (line 3) returns the empty list if the argument is an empty list. The second clause (lines 4–6) accepts a non-empty list [E|R], splits the tail R using E as pivot and recursively sort the partitions A and B. The function leq is simply a wrapper of the predefined operator =<. Finally, the function partition takes as input parameters an order function F, a pivot element E and a list and divides the latter into two according to the pivot and the order function. Notice the usage of a **case** expression to decide in which partition the head H must be inserted. The module quicksort includes also a testing function (quicksort_test) defining four simple positive unit tests obtained from a previous debugging session. The third test in this function (line 21) fails, hence revealing that there is at least one error. We start the debugging process by introducing the failing test case in EDD:

> edd:dd("quicksort:qs(fun quicksort:leq/2, [7,1])").

Following the schema of Fig. 1, EDD builds the execution tree corresponding to this computation, which can be examined in Fig. 3(A),[3] and uses the same test cases to prune the tree, obtaining that nodes 3, 5, 6, and 7 are entailed as valid (marked with diagonals in the corners) and can be safely removed together with their subtrees. The pruning of the associated subtrees removes 5 of the 8 initial possible questions, and leaves only the shaded nodes in the debugging tree. Then, the following question about node 2 is asked to the user:

quicksort:partition(fun quicksort:leq/2, 7, [1]) = {[1], []}? y

The intended meaning of partition is to split the input list ([1]) into two lists, one containing the elements less than or equal to 7, and another one with the elements greater than 7. The result of the call is valid so the user answers y (*yes*). At this point, after just one user answer, the debugger identifies node 8 as buggy:

Call to a function that contains an **error**:
quicksort:qs(fun quicksort:leq/2, [7, 1]) = [7, 1]
Please, revise the second clause:
qs(F, [E | R]) −> {A, B} = partition(F, E, R),
                  qs(F, B) ++ [E] ++ qs(F, A).

The error is in line 6, which should be qs(F, A) ++ [E] ++ qs(F, B). Before starting the next section we assume that the error has been corrected.

It is important to note that, since EDD is based in a formal semantics, it is possible to prove the soundness and completeness of the technique. The key point for proving these properties is the existence of an *intended interpretation*, that corresponds with the semantics that the programmer had in mind when implementing the system; by comparing this intended interpretation with the actual execution we are able to discover the buggy node. In our work, the soundness and completeness results are easily extended by ensuring that the test cases are

---

[3] Nodes' modules are not shown for the sake of clarity.

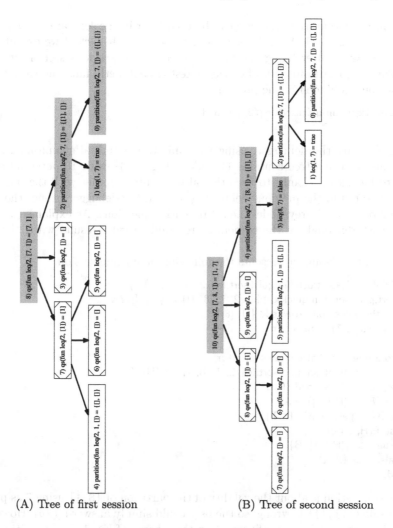

(A) Tree of first session   (B) Tree of second session

Fig. 3. Debugging trees of the EDD sessions

a subset of the intended interpretation, that can be used to appropriately prune the tree before asking the user to answer the rest of the questions. More details on the proofs are available in [4].

4 When Testing Met Declarative Debugging

The previous debugging session not only finds a bug but it also generates one new positive test case[4] **?assertEqual**(partition(fun leq/2, 7, [1]), {[1], [ ]}). As outlined

---

[4] Notice that, as explained in Sect. 2, a negative test case **?assertNotEqual** for the root qs(fun leq/2, [7,1]) is not generated as the test suite already contains a positive test for it (see line 21 in Fig. 2).

in the introduction, this test case can be used later in the software development cycle, as well as by EDD in later debugging sessions. In fact, if we execute the test cases again after fixing the bug detected in the previous section, we find out that the fourth unit test of quicksort_test (line 22) still fails, indicating that another bug is hidden in the program:

```
> quicksort:qs( fun quicksort:leq/2, [ 7, 8, 1 ] ).
[1,7]
```

Again we start the debugger, using this unit test as initial symptom. In this case, the execution tree contains 11 nodes—Fig. 3(B)—with 10 potential questions to be asked. Thanks to the original test suite together with the unit test case generated in the previous debugging session, the debugger prunes the tree, keeping only the 3 grey nodes, i.e., 2 potential questions. As explained before, nodes with diagonals in the corners correspond to valid results w.r.t. the test cases.

Hence, the debugger presents the following debugging session:

```
> edd:dd( "quicksort:qs( fun quicksort:leq/2 , [7,8,1 ] )" ).
quicksort:partition(fun quicksort:leq/2, 7, [8, 1]) = {[1], []}? v
What is the value you expected? {[1],[8]}
quicksort:leq(8, 7) = false?  t

Call to a function that contains an error:
quicksort:partition(fun quicksort:leq/2, 7, [8, 1]) = {[1], []}
Please, revise the second clause
partition(F, E, [H | T]) ->
    {A, B} = partition(F, E, T),
    case F(H, E) of
      true -> {[H | A], B};
      false -> {A, B}
    end.
```

The first question is about the validity of the partition of [8,1] using 7 as pivot. The result {[1], []} is wrong, so the user could simply answer n (no). However, our debugger introduces a refinement on the schema of Fig. 1. Since positive test cases are more informative than negative ones and they allow EDD to prune more nodes, we have introduced in EDD an option (letter v from *value*) that allows the user to type the correct value in addition to answering no. This command produces an **?assertEqual** test case instead of the negative one. In this session the user decides to use this option and indicates that the correct value should be {[1],[8]}. The second question is answered by the user with t, meaning *trusted*. In EDD this answer indicates that the user considers that function leq is correct so all the nodes containing a call to leq must be marked as valid, therefore generating as many positive **?assertEqual** unit tests as distinct calls to leq are found in the tree—in this case there are two calls. Finally, EDD points out to the second error (line 15 in Fig. 2). We realize that the **false** branch inside partition is incorrect: the first element H of the list, which is greater than the pivot E, must be appended to B. Fixing this second bug will result in replacing line 15 by **false** $->\{$A, [H|B]$\}$.

As well as detecting the buggy function, EDD has extended the test suite with four unit tests:

```
?assertEqual(partition(fun leq/2, 7, [1]), {[1], []}),
?assertEqual(partition(fun leq/2, 7, [8, 1]), {[1],[8]}),
?assertEqual(leq(8, 7), false),
?assertEqual(leq(1, 7), true).
```

Of course, although very useful, employing/generating test can be disabled in EDD using options:

- *not_load_tests*: do not use existing EUnit tests to prune the execution tree.
- *not_save_tests*: do not generate EUnit tests from the user answers.

5   Conclusions and Ongoing Work

Debugging is usually a manual task that involves the comparison of the actual and the expected behavior of the debugged system. Unfortunately, this very valuable information, which requires a great amount of time and effort, is discarded once the error is found. In fact, debuggers are often considered auxiliary tools and are not properly integrated in the software development cycle. In this paper we have shown how to improve this situation by employing an algorithmic debugger that stores the information extracted from the user during the debugging sessions in the form of unit tests. These tests are especially useful to check whether the error has been effectively corrected, and can become part of the tests produced during the testing phase.

Moreover, the result of this fruitful collaboration between testing and algorithmic debugging is also beneficial for the debugger, since the unit tests can be employed for automatically detecting if some subcomputations are valid or not, thus reducing the number of questions that the user must consider. The unit tests employed for this purpose can be both those generated in a previous debugging session and those produced during the testing phase. We have applied the new general framework to the EDD, an already existing declarative debugger for the sequential subset of the programming language Erlang. The result is a debugger that generates for free and uses unit tests in the format required by the EUnit tool.

It is worth mentioning that although generated automatically, our test cases are different from those generated by usual automated test case generators, where the user needs to examine the generated test suites looking for unit tests producing erroneous results. This is known as the *oracle problem* [2]. In our case, the test case output is obtained directly from the user during the debugging, and thus this problem does not occur.

As future work, it would be interesting to use and generate not just specific tests but properties, as those defined by PropEr [8], a QuickCheck-inspired property-based testing tool for Erlang. In this way we could further prune the debugging tree and store **trust** answers more accurately. Finally, it would also be interesting to apply the same framework to different languages, and performing an extensive experimental work to check the impact of the proposal.

Acknowledgments. We thank the anonymous reviewer of a previous work published in the journal *Science of Computer Programming for suggesting us this line of work.*

References

1. Alexander, I.F., Maiden, N.: Scenarios, Stories, Use Cases: Through the Systems Development Life-cycle. Wiley, New York (2005)
2. Barr, E., Harman, M., McMinn, P., Shahbaz, M., Yoo, S.: The oracle problem in software testing: a survey. IEEE Trans. Softw. Eng. **41**(5), 507–525 (2015)
3. Caballero, R., Martin-Martin, E., Riesco, A., Tamarit, S.: EDD: a declarative debugger for sequential erlang programs. In: Ábrahám, E., Havelund, K. (eds.) TACAS 2014 (ETAPS). LNCS, vol. 8413, pp. 581–586. Springer, Heidelberg (2014)
4. Caballero, R., Martin-Martin, E., Riesco, A., Tamarit, S.: A zoom-declarative debugger for sequential Erlang programs. Sci. Comput. Program. **110**, 104–118 (2015)
5. Carlsson, R., Rémond, M.: EUnit: a lightweight unit testing framework for Erlang. In: Proceedings of the 2006 ACM SIGPLAN Workshop on Erlang, ERLANG 2006, p. 1. ACM, New York (2006)
6. Cesarini, F., Thompson, S.: Programming Erlang: A Concurrent Approach to Software Development. O'Reilly Media Inc., Beijing (2009)
7. Hebert, F.: Learn You Some Erlang for Great Good!: A Beginner's Guide. No Starch Press (2013). http://learnyousomeerlang.com
8. Papadakis, M., Sagonas, K.: A PropEr integration of types and function specifications with property-based testing. In: Proceedings of the 2011 ACM SIGPLAN Erlang Workshop, pp. 39–50. ACM Press (2011)
9. Shapiro, E.Y.: Algorithmic Program Debugging. ACM Distinguished Dissertation. MIT Press, Cambridge (1983)
10. Silva, J.: A survey on algorithmic debugging strategies. Adv. Eng. Softw. **42**(11), 976–991 (2011)

Short Contributions

Combining Dynamic and Static Analysis to Help Develop Correct Graph Transformations

Amani Makhlouf[✉], Hanh Nhi Tran, Christian Percebois,
and Martin Strecker

Institut de Recherche en Informatique de Toulouse (IRIT),
University of Toulouse, Toulouse, France
{amani.makhlouf, tran, percebois, strecker}@irit.fr

Abstract. Developing provably correct graph transformations is not a trivial task. Besides writing the code, a developer must as well specify the pre- and post-conditions. The objective of our work is to assist developers in producing such a Hoare triple in order to submit it to a formal verification tool. By combining static and dynamic analysis, we aim at providing more useful feedback to developers. Dynamic analysis helps identify inconsistencies between the code and its specifications. Static analysis facilitates extracting the pre- and post-conditions from the code. Based on this proposal, we implemented a prototype that allows running, testing and proving graph transformations written in small-$t_{\mathcal{ALC}}$, our own transformation language.

Keywords: Symbolic execution · Test case generation · Graph transformation development

1 Introduction

For most of untrained developers, writing Hoare-style provably correct graph transformations is particularly demanding because besides the transformation code, they have to specify formally the pre- and post-conditions in a suitable logic.

Our ultimate goal is an integrated development environment that allows developing and reasoning about graph transformations written in small-$t_{\mathcal{ALC}}$, a logic-based graph transformation language. In the previous work [1], we focused on using a prover to verify a given Hoare triple presenting the transformation. However, in practice, a proof based on Hoare logic is difficult to perform and often many programing efforts are needed before submitting a transformation to the prover. Thus, in this work, we turn our attention to assisting developers in writing provably correct transformations.

Section 2 presents briefly our graph transformation language small-$t_{\mathcal{ALC}}$. Section 3 presents our approach to help developers analyzing better their transformations. On the one hand, we use dynamic analysis to detect inconsistencies between the code and its specifications (Sect. 3.1). On the other hand, we use static analysis to construct the pre- and post-conditions from a code (Sect. 3.2). This paper reports on how these techniques can complement each other in a testing environment to offer useful feedback to developers.

© Springer International Publishing Switzerland 2016
B.K. Aichernig and C.A. Furia (Eds.): TAP 2016, LNCS 9762, pp. 183–190, 2016.
DOI: 10.1007/978-3-319-41135-4_11

2 Small-t$_{\mathcal{ALC}}$ Environment for Graph Transformations

Our graph transformation language is based on $\mathcal{ALC}$ *(Attributive Language with Complements)* [2], a member of the *Description Logic* family. This logic uses a three-tier framework: *concepts, facts* and *formulae*. A concept represents a set of individuals and a role represents a binary relation between the individuals.

At the concept level, a concept C can be empty, atomic or built from other concepts. $\mathcal{ALC}$ provides the following concept constructors: intersection *(C1 ⊓ C2)*, union *(C1 ⊔ C2)*, complement *(¬C)* and existential or universal restrictions on roles *(∃r C* and *∀r C)*. The fact level allows making assertions about an individual owned by a concept, or involved in a role. The grammar of facts is summarized in the following: *(i:C)* asserts that an individual i is an instance of a concept C; *(i r j)* and *(i (¬r) j)* assert respectively that an instance of a role r exists or not between two individuals i and j. The final level is about formulae defined by a Boolean combination of $\mathcal{ALC}$ facts. This formula level includes negation *(¬f)*, conjunction *(f1 ∧ f2)* and disjunction *(f1 ∨ f2)* of formulae.

Concepts, facts and formulae are the core of small-t$_{\mathcal{ALC}}$, a rule-based imperative programming language that we've developed for specifying and reasoning about graph transformations [1]. Note that individuals of a concept can be represented as the nodes of a graph; in the same way, a role between two individuals corresponds to an edge. Thus, a graph can be described by a formula in which each node is represented by a fact *(i:C)* and each edge between two nodes i and j is represented by a fact *(i r j)*. Manipulating a graph results in modifying the formula representing it.

small-t$_{\mathcal{ALC}}$ provides statements to manipulate the structure of a graph: *add (i:C)* and *delete (i:C)* for adding and respectively deleting a node (an individual) from a concept[1]; *add (i r j)* and *delete (i r j)* for adding and respectively deleting an edge (a role) between two nodes. small-t$_{\mathcal{ALC}}$ also proposes *(select i with f)*, a non-deterministic assignment statement allowing to select a set of individuals satisfying a formula. In this work, we focus only on transformation of graph structure and do not deal with the values of attributes that maybe associated to graph's elements.

small-t$_{\mathcal{ALC}}$ enables sequential composition, branching, iteration and modularity. A small-t$_{\mathcal{ALC}}$ program comprises transformation rules and a *main* function, as the program's entry, that orders the rules to be executed. To allow reasoning about graph transformation programs, a rule is annotated with assertions specifying its pre- and post-conditions. The distinctive feature of small-t$_{\mathcal{ALC}}$ is that formulae occur not only in assertions (such as pre- and post-conditions or loop invariants), but also in statements (branching and iteration conditions, *select* conditions). In this way, assertions are akin to graph manipulation statements and based on the same logic dialect. Assertions lead to a Hoare-like calculus for small-t$_{\mathcal{ALC}}$ with potential tests and proofs.

Figure 1 gives an example of a small-t$_{\mathcal{ALC}}$ rule which redirects the edges between nodes of concept A and nodes of concept B to the edges between nodes of concept A and new nodes of concept C. The rule is structured into three parts: a pre-condition, the code (a set of statements) and a post-condition. small-t$_{\mathcal{ALC}}$ is designed as a domain

---

[1] The individual is not deleted from the graph because it can be still owned by other concepts.

```
rule EdgeRedirection {
    pre : a : A and b : B and a r b
    post : a : A and b : B and c : C and a r c
    while (a : A and b : B and a r b) do {
        select a, b with a : A and b : B and a r b;
        add(c : C);
        delete(a r b);
        add(a r c);
    }
}
```

Fig. 1. Rule redirecting *(a r b)* to *(a r c)*

specific language, not a general purpose one. Thus, to simplify its syntax, all rules work on the same input and output graphs and the pre- and post-conditions are specified on these global graphs. In this example, the pre-condition expresses that *a* is a node of concept *A*, *b* a node of concept *B* and that *a* is linked to *b* via role (or edge) *r*. While there are nodes *a* and *b* satisfying the while condition, the rule selects these nodes, deletes the link between them, add a new node *c* of concept *C*, then connects the selected node *a* with the new node *c* via the role *r*. The post-condition expresses that there are three nodes *a*, *b* and *c* of concepts *A, B* and *C* respectively and that *a* is connected to *c* via role r^2.

For executing and reasoning on small-t$_{ALC}$ programs, we developed an environment composed of a Java code generator to enable executing small-t$_{ALC}$ rules, a JUnit test case generator for rule testing and an Isabelle/HOL verification condition generator coupled to a tableau prover for Hoare triples.

3   Assistance for Writing Small-t$_{ALC}$ Programs

Our objective is to provide assistance on writing both small-t$_{ALC}$ code and specifications by combining static and dynamic analysis [3]. In Sect. 3.1 we report how testing can help developers correct their code with respect to given specifications. In Sect. 3.2 we investigate the symbolic execution technique to help a developer construct pre- and post-conditions from a given code.

3.1   Dynamic Analysis for Detecting Defects in Transformation Code

We consider a situation where the correct specifications of a code are given, especially the pre-condition. As presented in Sect. 2, the pre- and post-conditions are formulae specifying graphs before and after a transformation. Each fact of the pre-condition represents the existence of a node or an edge in the source graph. Each fact of the

---

[2] We can strengthen the post-condition by adding the fact *(a ¬r b)* to insist that there is no edge between *a* and *b*. However, we intentionally keep it weak to illustrate that developers can write any post-condition, not exactly the strongest post condition *wrt.* the given pre-condition.

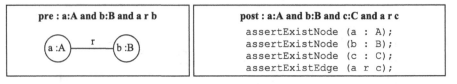

pre : a:A and b:B and a r b	**post : a:A and b:B and c:C and a r c**

	`assertExistNode (a : A);`
	`assertExistNode (b : B);`
	`assertExistNode (c : C);`
	`assertExistEdge (a r c);`

Fig. 2. Source graph and test cases generated from the running example

post-condition represents the existence of a node or an edge in the target graph. Thus, from the given pre-condition we can generate a source graph and, from the given post-condition, generate a set of test cases for the required properties. In our framework, dynamic analysis consists in testing the target graph obtained by the transformation with the generated test cases which are expressed in JUnit. In this context, we defined and implemented a unit testing library for small-t_{ACC} having about twenty assertion methods allowing testing the existence and multiplicity of nodes and edges.

Figure 2 shows the result of the generation of a source graph and the test cases corresponding to the pre- and post-conditions of the example in Fig. 1. The generated source graph represents the minimal graph configuration satisfying the pre-condition.

Suppose that the developer did not write the statement *add(a r c)* in the code. Because of this missing statement, the corresponding test *assertExistEdge(a r c)* fails. This test result reveals then an inconsistency between the code and its specifications. Moreover, it informs the developer about the non-existence of the edge *r* between *a* and *c*[3].

When the proof fails on verifying a program, the prover can give a counter example without further suggestions about the code's inconsistencies. This counterexample can be used as the program's graph input instead of a graph generated from the precondition to provide more feedback about the behavior of the code in such situation.

3.2   Static Analysis for Constructing Specifications from Code

Assume now that a code is correct, but developers need help to define the formal specification. We aim at computing, from the given code, conditions that must be satisfied before and after applying the transformation. For small-t_{ACC} programs whose symbolic values are explicitly defined in the code's formulae, such computation can be easily done by using a technique based on symbolic execution. We analyze the code's control flows to generate all possible execution paths and then execute each path symbolically to construct incrementally the pre- and post-conditions by considering the required conditions of each path.

We recall that the axiomatic semantics of each small-t_{ACC} statement is defined by the formulae representing its pre- and post-conditions, which specify a graph before and after executing the statement. Thus, on tracing the path's statements, we can compute progressively the formulae representing the pre- and post-conditions of the path by updating them according to the pre- or post-conditions of each encountered

---

[3] If the post-condition was strengthened by the fact *(a ¬r b)*, the corresponding test *assertNotExistEdge(a r b)* will have been also generated.

Forward computation
`FC (add(f), Q)   = delFM (addFM(Q, post(add(f))), pre(add(f)))`
`FC (delete(f), Q) = delFM (Q, pre(delete(f)))`
`FC (select(f), Q) = addFM (Q, post(select(f)))`
Backward computation
`BC (add(f), P)   = addFM (delFM (P, post(add(f))), pre(add(f)))`
`BC (delete(f), P) = addFM (P, pre(delete(f)))`
`BC (select(f), P) = addFM (P, pre(select(f)))`

Fig. 3. Forward and Backward computations for analyzing small-t$_{ACC}$ statements

statement. An execution path is analyzed in two directions. A forward computation extracts a formula representing the post-condition and a backward computation extracts a formula representing the pre-condition. Path statements are processed differently in each computation mode. Figure 3 presents, in a simplified functional style, the algorithms to update the extracted specification according to the semantics of the encountered statement.

In this figure, *FC* represents the Forward Condition formula and *BC* the Backward Condition formula. *st(f)* denotes a small-t$_{ACC}$ statement, where *st* can be *add*, *delete* or *select* and *f* is the formula specifying the manipulated graph element. If *st* is *add* or *delete*, *f* can be *(i:C)* to represent a node, or *(i r j)* to represent an edge. The auxiliary functions *pre(st(f))* and *post(st(f))* extract respectively the pre- and post-conditions of *st* (*f*). For example, *pre(add(i r j)) = (i (¬r) j)* and *post(add(i r j)) = (i r j)* as we allow only one edge of a given relation between two nodes. For the *select* statement, *pre (select(f)) = post(select(f)) = f*. The auxiliary functions *addFM(C, f)* and *delFM(C, f)* are used respectively to add the formula *f* into the path's conjunction *C* (if *C* does not already contain *f*) or delete the formula *f* in the conjunction (if *C* contains *f*). *C* denotes a post-condition *Q* in a forward computation, or a pre-condition *P* in a backward computation.

For a given path, *FC* and *BC* of the classic control statements are computed in the same way as strongest post-condition and weakest pre-condition computations respectively [4]. Figure 4 illustrates the FC computation for the post-condition *Q* of the example in Fig. 1. We consider only the execution path in which the *while* condition is true.

The computed formula is then presented to developers in the testing framework (c.f. Sect. 3.3) to allow them to verify if the conditions of the analyzed path are respected in the current rule's pre- and post-conditions issued from analyzing previous execution paths or written by developers themselves.

while condition
Q = true $\xrightarrow{}$ Q = a : A and b : B and a r b $\xrightarrow{FC(select,Q)}$ Q = a : A and b : B and a r b

$\xrightarrow{FC(add,Q)}$ Q = a : A and b : B and a r b and c : C $\xrightarrow{FC(delete,Q)}$ Q = a : A and b : B and c : C

$\xrightarrow{FC(add,Q)}$ Q = a : A and b : B and c : C and a r c

Fig. 4. FC computation for the example

The consequence rule of Hoare logic rule allows to strengthen the precondition and/or to weaken the post-condition of a Hoare triple: given $P1 \rightarrow P2$ and $Q2 \rightarrow Q1$, if $\{P2\}\ S\ \{Q2\}$ then $\{P1\}\ S\ \{Q1\}$. Ideally $P1$ should be the weakest precondition $wp(S, Q1)$ of S with respect to $Q1$ and vice versa (i.e. $Q1$ should be the strongest post-condition $sp(S, P)$ of S with respect to $P1$). However, developers can write a rule with the independent specifications $P2$ and $Q2$ where some facts of the precondition $P2$ are not necessarily considered for the post-condition $Q2$. Considering the rule in Fig. 1, $(a\ r\ b)$ in the pre-condition has been translated into $(a\ r\ c)$ without considering $(a \neg r\ b)$ in the post-condition.

3.3 Combining Dynamic and Static Analysis

The two scenarios represented in Sects. 3.1 and 3.2 are the borderline cases of small-t_{ACC} transformations development. In practice, both of specifications and code are partially and imprecisely defined. Complementary to the diagnostics provided by a prover, we propose an approach that allows treating an incomplete Hoare triple by verifying its consistency in an incremental manner. In general developers prefer testing to proving, so our assistance provides them feedback via a testing framework combining white-box testing and black-box testing [5].

A developer may write a code and weak specifications, apply the white-box testing to detect inconsistencies between them and use the static analysis technique to complete them. On the basis of the static analysis technique, extracted specifications from the code are compared to pre- and post-conditions given by the developer to help him correct or complete his specifications. This comparison yields black-box test cases generated from the extracted pre- and post-conditions then executed on a graph generated from the given pre- and post-conditions respectively. Each test which fails corresponds to a missing or an incorrect fact in the formula representing the given specification. Therefore, during the development of a transformation program, in each iteration, a developer can alternate between the two approaches depending on his needs.

4 Discussion

Our small-t_{ACC} environment combines two techniques for verifying a Hoare triple. The prover we developed [1] can prove the correctness of a transformation for all arbitrary graphs satisfying the pre-condition without executing the transformation. This formal verification technique, although has been well developed [6, 7], is not really applicable during the transformation development where the Hoare triple is often still incomplete. The testing environment presented in this paper proposes a more pragmatic solution, from the developer's point of view, to detect inconsistencies in an under-developed transformation. By using both of the above techniques, we try to take advantage of multiple complementary approaches [3, 8, 9] for assisting transformation developers.

To assist developers, testing has been used for generic imperative languages. Our approach shares with [5] the idea to use a deductive program verification mechanism for extracting specification by symbolically executing small-t_{ACC} rules. Our forward and backward test cases generations are based on code-driven paths exploration as in [5, 10]. The transitions from code to specification and vice versa are straightforward with small-t_{ALC} because it uses the same logic to specify programs and properties to be verified. This is often less direct for conventional imperative languages where there is a possible gap between the logic defining the semantics of the language and the logic used for formalizing the correctness of programs. In such cases, sometimes it is difficult to identify symbolic values [11] and symbolic execution is often achieved for only a limited subset of the target language features [10].

The design of language GP2 [12] is close to small-t_{ALC}. Building blocks in GP programs are conditional rule schemata whose nodes and edges are labeled by sequences of expressions over parameters of type integer, string and list. Condition of a rule schema can be expressed then on the existence of a specific labeled edge or the in/out degree of a node. small-t_{ALC} does not propose such computations on nodes and edges: individuals (nodes) and roles (edges) within a rule define only local structural properties of a graph. We do not define variables and values in order to simplify the small-t_{ALC}'s computation model. The conditions of our calculus are $ALCQ$ formulae while GP uses E-conditions [6], i.e. nested graph conditions extended with expressions as labels and assignment constraints for specifying properties of labels [7]. Tools to help the designer when a fail occurs are not addressed in GP.

Few works have been proposed for testing graph transformation implementations. Close to our work, [13] generates test cases for the graph pattern matching phase; [14] generates JUnit test cases from a Fujaba graphical story diagram. Both approaches are based on the graph pattern matching phase of the transformation rule to generate test cases, not on logical rule specifications as we propose.

5 Conclusion

Thanks to the formal semantic basis of small-t_{ALC}, we can apply both dynamic and static analysis techniques in an effortless way to reason about small-t_{ALC} programs and give useful feedback to developers during the transformation development.

Our current test data generation is rather simplistic and just covers a minimal configuration of possible source graphs. We are improving our algorithm for generating more graphs from the typical graph on the basis of Molloy-Reed algorithm [15, 16] and allowing also graph inputs provided by developers as the prover's counterexample.

In this paper we did not deal with loop invariants as conditions of a transformation, we plan to automatically infer and test invariant candidates gathered from their corresponding post-condition as proposed in [17]. This attempt is based on the fact that a small-t_{ALC} loop iterates on all individuals selected from a logic formula in order to achieve the same logic property for all transformed elements. We also aim at enhancing interface functionalities between test and proof processes. For instance, suppose that our testing environment validates a rule's post-condition on a given path. One can imagine, with the help of a prover, computing the strongest post-condition of this path by symbolic execution. The correctness of the path can be proven if the strongest post-condition implies the given post-condition. If this implication holds for all paths in the code, then the original Hoare triple is valid [4].

Acknowledgment. Part of this research has been supported by the *Climt* (Categorical and Logical Methods in Model Transformation) project (ANR-11-BS02-016).

References

1. Baklanova, N., Brenas, J.H., Echahed, R., Percebois, C., Strecker, M., Tran, H.N.: Provably correct graph transformations with small-tALC. In: ICTERI 2015, pp. 78–93 (2015)
2. Schmidt-Schauß, M., Smolka, G.: Attributive concept descriptions with complements. Artif. Intell. **48**(1), 1–26 (1991)
3. Smaragdakis, Y., Csallner, C.: Combining static and dynamic reasoning for bug detection. In: Gurevich, Y., Meyer, B. (eds.) TAP 2007. LNCS, vol. 4454, pp. 1–16. Springer, Heidelberg (2007)
4. Gordon, M., Collavizza, H.: Forward with Hoare. In: Roscoe, A.W., Jones, C.B., Wood, K.R. (eds.) Reflections on the Work of C.A.R. Hoare. History of Computing Series, pp. 101–121. Springer, London (2010)
5. Beckert, B., Gladisch, C.: White-box testing by combining deduction-based specification extraction and black-box testing. In: Gurevich, Y., Meyer, B. (eds.) TAP 2007. LNCS, vol. 4454, pp. 207–216. Springer, Heidelberg (2007)
6. Habel, A., Pennemann, K.H.: Correctness of high-level transformation systems relative to nested conditions. Math. Struct. Comput. Sci. **19**(2), 245–296 (2009)
7. Poskitt, C.M., Plump, D.: Hoare-style verification of graph programs. Fundam. Inf. **118**(1–2), 135–175 (2012)
8. Liu, S., Nakajima, S.: Combining specification-based testing, correctness proof, and inspection for program verification in practice. In: Liu, S., Duan, Z. (eds.) SOFL + MSVL 2013. LNCS, vol. 8332, pp. 1–18. Springer, Heidelberg (2014)
9. Owre, S., Rajan, S., Rushby, J.M., Shankar, N., Srivas, M.K.: PVS: combining specification, proof checking, and model checking. In: Alur, R., Henzinger, T.A. (eds.) CAV 1996. LNCS, vol. 1102, pp. 411–414. Springer, Heidelberg (1996)
10. Engel, C., Hähnle, R.: Generating unit tests from formal proofs. In: Gurevich, Y., Meyer, B. (eds.) TAP 2007. LNCS, vol. 4454, pp. 169–188. Springer, Heidelberg (2007)
11. Xie, T., Marinov, D., Schulte, W., Notkin, D.: Symstra: a framework for generating object-oriented unit tests using symbolic execution. In: Halbwachs, N., Zuck, L.D. (eds.) TACAS 2005. LNCS, vol. 3440, pp. 365–381. Springer, Heidelberg (2005)
12. Bak, C., Faulkner, G., Plump, D., Runciman, C.: A reference interpreter for the graph programming language GP 2. In: Rensink, A., Zambon E. (eds.) Graphs as Models 2015 (GaM 2015). EPTCS 2015, vol. 181, pp. 48–64 (2015)
13. Darabos, A., Pataricza, A., Varró, D.: Towards testing the implementation of graph transformations. Electron. Notes Theor. Comput. Sci. **211**, 75–85 (2008)
14. Geiger, L., Zündorf, A.: Transforming graph based scenarios into graph transformation based JUnit tests. In: Pfaltz, J.L., Nagl, M., Böhlen, B. (eds.) AGTIVE 2003. LNCS, vol. 3062, pp. 61–74. Springer, Heidelberg (2004)
15. Molloy, M., Reed, B.: A critical point for random graphs with a given degree sequence. Random Struct. Algorithms **6**(2–3), 161–180 (1995). Wiley
16. Molloy, M., Reed, B.: The size of the giant component of a random graph with a given degree sequence. Comb. Prob. Comput. **7**(3), 295–305 (1998). Cambridge University Press
17. Zhai, J., Wang, H., Zhao, J.: Post-condition-directed invariant inference for loops over data structures. In: SERE-C 2014, pp. 204–212. IEEE (2014)

Automatic Predicate Testing
in Formal Certification
You've only Proven What You've Said,
Not What You Meant!

Franck Slama[(✉)]

University of St Andrews, Scotland, UK
fs39@st-andrews.ac.uk

Abstract. The use of formal methods and proof assistants helps to increase the confidence in critical software. However, a formal proof is only a guarantee relative to a formal specification, and not necessary about the real requirements. There is always a jump when going from an informal specification to a formal specification expressed in a logical theory. Thus, proving the correctness of a piece of software always makes the implicit assumption that there is adequacy between the formalised specification –written with logical statements and predicates– and the real requirements –often written in English–. Unfortunately, a huge part of the complexity lies precisely in the specification itself, and it is far from obvious that the formal specification says exactly and completely what it should say. Why should we trust more these predicates than the code that we've first refused to trust blindly, leading to these proofs? We show in this paper that the proving activity has not replaced the testing activity but has only changed the object which requires to be tested. Instead of testing code, we now need to test predicates. We present recent ideas about how to conduct these tests inside the proof assistant on a few examples, and how to automate them as far as possible.

Keywords: Formal certification · Predicate testing · Proof assistant

1 Introduction

One way to increase our confidence in software is to formally prove its correctness using a proof assistant. Proofs assistants enable to write code, logical statements and proofs in the same language, and offer the guarantee that every proof will be automatically checked. Many of them are functional programming languages, like Coq [2], Idris [3] and Agda [9], and others, like the B-Method [1] belong to the imperative paradigm. These different paradigms are internally supported by different logic. Systems like Coq, Idris and Agda are based on various higher order logics (CoC, a variant of ML and LUO respectively) and are realisations of the Curry-Howard correspondence, while the B-Method is based on

© Springer International Publishing Switzerland 2016
B.K. Aichernig and C.A. Furia (Eds.): TAP 2016, LNCS 9762, pp. 191–198, 2016.
DOI: 10.1007/978-3-319-41135-4_12

Hoare logic. These different foundations lead to different philosophies and different ways to implement and verify a software, but all of them greatly increase the confidence on the produced software. However, these guarantees tend to be too often considered as perfect, when they are in fact far from it. Knuth was– certainly ironically– saying "Beware of bugs in the above code; I have only proved it correct, not tried it". The reality is precisely that a proof is not enough. When we prove the correctness of a function, we only gain the guarantee expressed by the proven lemma, and nothing more.

Say we want to implement a formally verified sorting function for list of elements of type T, where T is ordered by a relation $\leq$. We can decide to define the sorting function with a "weak" type, like $sort : List\ T \rightarrow List\ T$, and to use an external lemma to ensure the correctness of the function. Which property does this function has to respect? First, the output has to be sorted, so we need to define this notion of being sorted, here as an inductive predicate:

```
data isSorted : {T:Type} -> (Order T) -> (List T) -> Type where
   NilIsSorted : (Tord : Order T) -> isSorted Tord []
   SingletonIsSorted : (Tord : Order T) -> (x:T)
                       -> isSorted Tord [x]
   ConsSorted : {Tord : Order T} -> (h1:T) -> (h2:T) -> (t:List T)
             -> (isSorted Tord (h2::t)) -> (h1 ≤ h2)
             -> (isSorted Tord (h1::(h2::t)))
```

The first and second constructor of this predicate say that $[\ ]$ and $[x]$ are sorted according to any order, and for any x. The third one says that a list of two or more elements is sorted if $h1 \leq h2$, and if the list deprived from its head is also sorted. In order to express that the result of $sort$ is sorted, we can prove the following lemma: $sort\_correct : \forall\ (T : Type)\ (Tord : Order\ T)\ (l : List\ T),\ isSorted\ Tord\ (sort\ l)$. The problem with this specification is that it does not say anything about the content of the output. The function $sort$ could just return the empty list $[\ ]$ all the time, it would still be possible to prove this correctness lemma. Here, the problem is that the function is underspecified, and it is therefore possible to write a senseless implementation, which is unfortunately provably correct. Only a careful reader could realise that the lemma $sort\_correct$ forgets to mention that the input and output list should be in bijection, meaning that everything which was originally in the input list should still be in the output, and that nothing else should have been added.

Another bug in the specification could have been to simply forget the third constructor $ConsSorted$. But things more nasty can happen. Imagine that this constructor would have been written with a typo, and that the condition $(h1 \leq h2)$ would have been incorrectly written as $(h1 \leq h1)$. Any list would be seen as "sorted", just because of this single typo, and the algorithm could for example return its input unchanged. One could object that when doing the proof of correctness, we should realize that the proof is being done too easily, without having to use the essential property that the output is being built such as any element in the list is always lower or equal than its next element. The reality is quite different because many effort are going in the direction of proof automation, which aims to let the machine automatically generate the proof for some kind of goals. For example, Coq has already a Ring prover [7] and many others automations, and Idris has been recently equipped with a hierarchy of provers for algebraics structures [6]. There are even extensions to languages, such as Ltac [4] and Mtac [10] that aim to help the automation of tactics. The problem is that the machine is never going to find a proof "too easy", and will never report that something seems weird with the specification given by the user.

Thus, if we want to trust the proven software, we're now forced to believe that there is adequacy between the formal specification and the informal requirements. A switch has occurred. We used to have to trust code, but we now have to trust logical statements and predicates. But when the specification is too often as complicated as the code, why should we blindly believe in it, when we've first refused to blindly trust the code? The primary aim of this paper is to raise awareness on the adequacy concern, and to see how heterogeneous approaches, that mixes both proofs and tests, can help to go a step forward in the certification process, in the context of proof assistants based on type theory. More precisely, we:

- Show some basic approaches to the problem of underspecification (Sect. 2)
- Present a new way to test the predicate in the proof assistant, by automatically generating terms, and we completely automate these tests. We also show how we can go a step forward by replacing these tests about the predicate by some proofs (Sect. 3)
- We discuss possible directions for making dependently typed programming languages more adapted to the testing of specifications (Sect. 4).

We use Idris, a dependently typed programming language, but all the ideas that we present here can be applied to any proof assistant based on type theory. The running example that we use in this paper can be found online at https://github.com/FranckS/ProofsAndTests.

2   Naive and Usual Approaches to the Adequacy Problem

When confronted to this problem of adequacy between the intuitive notion and the formalised one, a first possibility is to formalise the notion multiple times, with different predicates, and to prove that they are equivalent. With our example, that means that we need to find another formalisation $isSorted'$ of being sorted, and to prove the following lemma. $pred\_equiv : \forall\ (T : Type)\ (l : List\ T), (isSorted\ l) \leftrightarrow (isSorted'\ l)$. This approach aims at increasing the confidence in our formal definitions by assuming that if we've managed to define multiple times the same notion, then we've surely succeeded to define the notion we wanted. The biggest problem with this approach is to be able to find some alternative formalisations that are sufficiently different from the original one. Obviously, if the new formalisations are too similar to the original one (and in the worst case the new ones are just syntactical variants of the first one), then we won't gain any guarantee. The ideal would be to capture the same notion by using very different points of view, and we will show in Sect. 3 an original approach for doing so.

In order to gain confidence in the formal specifications we write, another traditional approach is to test the predicate on some values. That consists in defining a few terms, usually by hand, for which we know if the predicate should hold or not, and to prove that the predicate effectively holds when it should, and that it does not when it should not. For example, with the predicate *isSorted* defined above, we can prove that it holds on the list [3, 5, 7] that we know sorted.

```
isSorted_test1 : isSorted natIsOrdered [3, 5, 7]
isSorted_test1 =
  let p1 : (3 <= 5) = tryDec (lowerEqDec natIsOrdered 3 5) in
  let p2 : (5 <= 7) = tryDec (lowerEqDec natIsOrdered 5 7) in
    ConsSorted 3 5 [7]
      (ConsSorted 5 7 [] (SingletonIsSorted _ 7) p2) p1
```

This test is a *test done by proof*: we show that the predicate holds on some specific value, here [3, 5, 7], by doing the proof. We can go a step forward by removing the need of doing these specific proofs by hand, because in this case, the predicate isSorted can be decided: there exists an algorithm that produces a proof of (*isSorted l*) if appropriate, or a proof of (*not* (*isSorted l*)) otherwise.

```
decideIsSorted : (Tord : Order T) -> (l:List T)
                   -> Dec(isSorted Tord l)
decideIsSorted Tord [] = Yes (NilIsSorted Tord)
decideIsSorted Tord [x] = Yes (SingletonIsSorted Tord x)
decideIsSorted Tord (h1::(h2::t)) with (lowerEqDec Tord h1 h2)
  | (Yes h1_lower_h2) with (decideIsSorted Tord (h2::t))
     | (Yes h2_tail_sorted) = Yes
                (ConsSorted h1 h2 t h2_tail_sorted h1_lower_h2)
     | (No h2_tail_not_sorted) = No [...]
  | (No h1_not_lower_h2) = No [...]
```

Now, in order to do *tests by proof*, we can simply run the decision procedure.

```
isSorted_test1' : Dec (isSorted natIsOrdered [3,5,7])
isSorted_test1' = decideIsSorted natIsOrdered [3,5,7]
```

And if we evaluate *isSorted_test1'*, the system will answer *Yes* and a proof of *isSorted* [3, 5, 7], which means that the predicate has passed this test. With this technique, we can run semi-automatically a few tests on the predicate *isSorted*. It is semi-automatic in the sense that we still have to define by hand some terms that we know sorted or unsorted but we can let the machine produce the proof that the predicate holds or not on these specific values. This is not too bad –and this is in fact all of what is usually done, when it is actually done– but we would like to have a stronger guarantee, and not only that the predicate will coincide with our intuitive notion on a couple of tested terms.

3   Testing the Predicate by Automatic Generation of Terms

The key idea that this paper wants to convey is that it is often easier to generate examples of a notion than it is to precisely define it. We can operate an interesting change of point of view by generating the set of terms that we precisely wanted to describe with the predicate. With our example of sorted lists, that means that we need to define the same notion of being sorted, but this time with a definition example-based. Writing a function that produces all the sorted lists might be a bit more difficult than just giving a few examples, but this complicated function will have the main advantage of being so different from the predicate that if the two notions agree, then we will have gain a great confidence on the predicate. We decide to use coinduction and the type Stream (a coinductive version of lists, potentially infinite) in order to generate –with what we call a generator– all the sorted lists of size n.

$generateSortedList : (T : Type) \rightarrow (recEnu : RecEnum\ T) \rightarrow (Tord : Order\ T) \rightarrow (n : Nat) \rightarrow Stream\ (List\ T)$.

To do so, the type T needs to be recursively enumerable, which means that there must exist a computational map $Nat \rightarrow Maybe\ c$ with the condition that this map is surjective, which means that any value of type c should be hit at least once by the map : $map\_is\_surjective : (y : c) \rightarrow (x : Nat *$ $* (computableMap\ x = Just\ y))$.

We want to check that this function and the predicate coincide. Since the predicate $isSorted$ is decidable with $decideIsSorted$, we can automatically check whether the generated sorted lists of size n are automatically sorted (according to $isSorted$) by running this decision procedure. But since there can be infinitely many generated sorted lists of size n when $n > 0$, we will only check that the generator and the predicate coincide on a finite observation[1] of the resulting stream. The key point is that this observation can be arbitrary big, and the bigger it is, the better the guarantee is about $isSorted$.

We show how the observation is made on an example. Let T be a type that only contains three constant values A, B and C. Since T is finite, it is therefore obviously recursively enumerable. We define on it the strict order $A < B < C$. Let's automatically generate the first m sorted lists of T, of size n, by unfolding m times the result of $generateSortedList$.

```
testGenerator : (m:Nat) -> (n:Nat) -> Maybe(Vect m (List T))
testGenerator m n =
        let x = generateSortedList T TisRecEnu TisOrdered n
            in unfold_n_times x m
```

We can ask for the first 8 sorted lists of size 4 by evaluating $testGenerator\ 8\ 4$:

```
Just [[A, A, A, A], [A, A, A, B], [A, A, A, C], [A, A, B, B],
     [A, A, B, C], [A, A, C, C], [A, B, B, B], [A, B, B, C]]
    : Maybe (Vect 8 (List T))
```

---

[1] A finite observation of a stream, also called approximation at rank m of a stream, is a vector of size m that has the same m first elements than the stream.

Now, instead of simply generating the first m sorted lists, we run the decision procedure on all of these m tests in order to know if the predicate and the generator agree on this portion. The result will be a vector m booleans.

```
testSorted : (m:Nat) -> (n:Nat) -> Vect m Bool
testSorted m n =
  let x = generateSortedList T TisRecEnu TisOrdered n in
    let y = Smap (\l => let res = decideIsSorted TisOrdered l in
                        case res of
                          Yes _ => True
                          No _  => False) x in
      unfold_n_times_with_padding y m True
```

And we can inspect the result of running the first 8 tests of size 4 by evaluating *testSorted* 8 4.

```
[True, True, True, True, True, True, True, True] : Vect 8 Bool
```

When we want to test *isSorted* on a large number of tests, we might not want to inspect manually the result of each test. We can write a function *testSorted_result* : $(m : Nat) \rightarrow (n : Nat) \rightarrow Bool$ that calls *testSorted m n* and does the boolean *And* on each element of the resulting vector. Now, we can for example test the predicate on the first 50 sorted lists of size 9 by running *testSorted_result* 50 9 and if we do so we get the overall result *True* which means that the predicate agrees with the generator on all these 50 tests.

However, if the predicate *isSorted* has been incorrectly written, then the result of this test might inform us that there's something wrong with the formal specification. For example, if we've forgotten the third constructor *consSorted* in the definition of *isSorted*, then the result of (*testSorted* 8 4) will be *False*, which means that at least one of the produced list is not seen as sorted according to *isSorted*, and we will therefore know that this predicate does not capture our intuitive notion of sortedness.

In order to go a step forward, we can decide to replace the tests on the predicate by proofs. Instead of testing the predicate on a finite subset of all the generated sorted lists as we just did, we can try to prove that any of the automatically generated sorted list is provably sorted according to *isSorted*.

```
generated_implies_pred_holds : {T:Type}
   -> (recEnu:RecEnum T) -> (Tord : Order T) -> (n:Nat)
   -> (All (generateSortedList T recEnu Tord n)
          (\l => isSorted Tord l))
```

Proof. By induction on n. When n is zero, there is only one sorted list generated, which is the empty list, and we know that the empty list is sorted thanks to the constructor *NilIsSorted*. When n is some successor $(S\ pn)$, we know by using recursively the lemma on the smaller value pn that all sorted lists of size pn are sorted according to *isSorted*. Since the *Stream* of all sorted lists of size $(S\ pn)$ has been made from the *Stream* of all sorted lists of size pn by adding to all of them –on the head position– an element lower or equal to their respective current heads, we know that the property has been preserved at the higher rank.   □

This lemma has the advantage of not requiring the predicate to be decidable, whereas this was needed when we automatically tested the predicate on a finite observation. However, one could object that this lemma is itself built by using a predicate, *All*, and that we can't necessary trust blindly such a specification. The answer is that no guarantee is perfect, and all we can do is to add some guarantees, but there is necessarily always something to trust. Moreover, this new kind of specifications and proofs –about the predicate itself– uses more primitive components like streams and the predicate *All*, and these components can be provided once and for all. If they are part of some standard library being used intensively, there is very low risk that they do not capture the desired semantic.

4   Conclusions and Future Work

In this paper we've presented a new way to test a predicate based on an automatic generation of terms that should have the desired property. This adequacy between the predicate and the generator helps to gain confidence in the predicate. The technique presented on Sect. 3 was based on a finite observation of the terms generated in endless amount, processed by the decision procedure. We have also shown on an example how these tests can be automated.

We haven't been able to find much work done in the direction of predicate testing in the environment of proof assistants, but we strongly believe that this aspect is crucial, as there is absolutely no point to prove the "correctness" of a function relatively to a bad specification. One could however question why formal certification is needed at all, if after going through all the effort of interactive theorem proving we still have to test the specification itself, and also need tools to support it. We believe that the process of formalisation helps to uncover things that were missing or weakly specified in the informal requirements. For example, the development of the formally verified compiler CompCert [8] has contributed to brought to light many under-specified behaviours in the specification of the C standard.

The machinery developed for the running example presented in this paper is extremely specific and it is not reasonable to believe that this work should and could be done for every formal specification. What it shows is that we really need to explore how proof assistants themselves could help to gain confidence about predicates and logical formulae. A possible direction could be to build execution engines for formal specifications written in dependent type theories. Such a system would take in input a predicate and would produce some of the terms that make this predicate hold. The ideal would be to have a query system where one could ask the system to try to look if some specific terms are captured by the predicate. Since the problem of finding proof is undecidable in the general case in higher-order logics (that's also the case in first-order logic), such a system can't be complete and entirely automatic, and therefore the user would have to help the system at times.

Another possible direction is to equip proof assistants with many robust and generic concepts (like being sorted) once and for all. That would save the user from the error prone activity of writing many primitive logical properties. Equipping proof assistants with many generic and useful concepts already available, like bricks ready to be assembled, is another current challenge to make proofs assistants really usable.

References

1. Abrial, J., et al.: The B-method. In: Prehn, S., Toetenel, H. (eds.) VDM 1991. LNCS, vol. 552, pp. 398–405. Springer, Heidelberg (1991). http://dx.doi.org/10.1007/BFb0020001
2. Bertot, Y., Castéran, P.: Interactive Theorem Proving and Program Development-Coq'Art. Texts in Theoretical Computer Science. An EATCS Series. Springer, Heidelberg (2004). http://dx.doi.org/10.1007/978-3-662-07964-5
3. Brady, E.: Idris, a general-purpose dependently typed programming language: design and implementation. J. Funct. Program. **23**, 552–593 (2013). http://journals.cambridge.org/article_S095679681300018X
4. Delahaye, D.: A proof dedicated meta-language. Electr. Notes Theor. Comput. Sci. **70**(2), 96–109 (2002). http://dx.doi.org/10.1016/S1571-0661(04)80508-5
5. DeMillo, R.A., Lipton, R.J., Perlis, A.J.: Social processes and proofs of theorems and programs. Commun. ACM **22**(5), 271–280 (1979). http://doi.acm.org/10.1145/359104.359106
6. Slama, F., Brady, E.: Automatically proving equivalence by type-safe reflection (draft under consideration). J. Funct. Program. (2016). https://fs39.host.cs.st-andrews.ac.uk/publications/paper_Slama_Brady_JFP.pdf
7. Grégoire, B., Mahboubi, A.: Proving equalities in a commutative ring done right in Coq. In: Hurd, J., Melham, T. (eds.) TPHOLs 2005. LNCS, vol. 3603, pp. 98–113. Springer, Heidelberg (2005). http://citeseerx.ist.psu.edu/viewdoc/summary?doi=10.1.1.61.3041
8. Krebbers, R., Leroy, X., Wiedijk, F.: Formal C semantics: CompCert and the C standard. In: Klein, G., Gamboa, R. (eds.) ITP 2014. LNCS, vol. 8558, pp. 543–548. Springer, Heidelberg (2014). https://hal.inria.fr/hal-00981212
9. Norell, U.: Dependently typed programming in Agda. In: Koopman, P., Plasmeijer, R., Swierstra, D. (eds.) AFP 2008. LNCS, vol. 5832, pp. 230–266. Springer, Heidelberg (2009). http://dx.doi.org/10.1007/978-3-642-04652-0_5
10. Ziliani, B., Dreyer, D., Krishnaswami, N.R., Nanevski, A., Vafeiadis, V.: Mtac: a monad for typed tactic programming in Coq. In: ACM SIGPLAN International Conference on Functional Programming, ICFP 2013, Boston, pp. 87–100, 25–27 September 2013. http://doi.acm.org/10.1145/2500365.2500579

Author Index

Botella, Bernard 130
Brucker, Achim D. 17

Caballero, Rafael 171
Cheney, James 37

Dubois, Catherine 57

Felbinger, Hermann 76
Fischer, Tomas 3

Gabmeyer, Sebastian 94
Genestier, Richard 57
Giorgetti, Alain 57, 130

Julliand, Jacques 130

Kosmatov, Nikolai 130

Liu, Shaoying 112

Makhlouf, Amani 183
Martin-Martin, Enrique 171
Momigliano, Alberto 37

Percebois, Christian 183
Pessina, Matteo 37
Petiot, Guillaume 130
Pill, Ingo 76
Podelski, Andreas 151

Reichl, Klaus 3
Riesco, Adrián 171

Schäf, Martin 151
Seidl, Martina 94
Slama, Franck 191
Strecker, Martin 183

Tamarit, Salvador 171
Tran, Hanh Nhi 183
Tummeltshammer, Peter 3

Wies, Thomas 151
Wolff, Burkhart 17
Wotawa, Franz 76

Printed in the United States
By Bookmasters